A SUPREMELY BAD IDEA

A Supremely Bad Idea

THREE MAD BIRDERS
AND THEIR QUEST TO SEE IT ALL

Luke Dempsey

BLOOMSBURY

Published by Bloomsbury USA, New York
Distributed to the trade by Macmillan

PHOTO CREDITS
Don and Donna Graffiti: elegant trogon, heron, Kirtland's warbler. Donna Graffiti: eastern meadowlark, Luke and David, osprey, stakeout, employee of the month. Don Graffiti: marbled godwit, Pawnee grasslands. The author: hummingbird, green jay, ptarmigan, caracara.

All papers used by Bloomsbury USA are natural, recyclable products made from wood grown in well-managed forests. The manufacturing processes conform to the environmental regulations of the country of origin.

LIBRARY OF CONGRESS CATALOGING-IN-PUBLICATION DATA
HAS BEEN APPLIED FOR.

ISBN-10 1-59691-355-X
ISBN-13 978-1-59691-355-4

First U.S. Edition 2008

1   3   5   7   9   10   8   6   4   2

Typeset by Westchester Book Group
Printed in the United States of America by Quebecor World Fairfield

IN MEMORIAM

Vincent Dempsey

1935–1990

for Lily

for Amelia

for David

for Deborah

Please note that some names and places and times have been changed. But we saw all the birds we said we did. Honest.

Contents

The Northeast:
Falling in Love at Home

I grew up in England, a small country near Ireland where we all love the queen and the sun don't shine. Because of the lousy weather and the unfair distribution of wealth, the place is filled with sad people with not much going for them. My homeland has a strong tradition, however, of inventing safe pursuits for all the losers. We gave the world trainspotting, of course, in which the numbers stenciled on the sides of rolling stock are fervidly scribbled in dirty little notebooks by overcoated men (trainspotters are mostly men). Arrive at any railroad station in England, and a small army of such be-dandruffed homunculi will be huddled at the end of the platform, gently jostling with each other for position so that they can be the first to write down the train's digits. When you do this only at one station, you're called either a "veg" or a "stoat." When you have a passion for just one kind of train, you're a "crank." And when you ask me to join you in your trainspotting, I shall say no and run away.

If trains don't do it for you, sad little Britisher, there's always Morris dancing, in which grown men (and women this time) affix bells to their knees and wave little white handkerchiefs, all the while performing a square dance mixed with the hokey pokey. My intensive research suggests that you really need to sport a full beard to be an effective Morris dancer—especially if you're female.

But if dancing sounds too much like hard work, you could always turn on the TV and watch sheep dog trialing, an endeavor in which smart border collies run scared little lambs through gates and over fences. *One Man and His Dog*, the prime-time BBC series which featured the "sport," ran for twenty-three years, attracting upwards of eight million viewers in the early 1980s. In a population of around fifty-six million at the time, that's one in every seven Brits who regularly tuned in.

Birdwatching in England is part of that proud heritage—the word *birdwatcher* is a synonym for "completely unshaggable"—and it is generally thought of as an exercise for older folks who aren't physically able to play sports anymore, or else never did. If you set aside the attendant social stigma, "twitching," as birdwatching is also called, has its merits: It's harmless enough (unlike Morris dancing), and it gets you out of the house. It also has a social use for younger people, keeping those nerdy kids who have no chance of ever making a real friend out of already overcrowded bars and the like.

Back when I lived in England, I had plenty of real friends, you understand, but during my teen years I did spend a lot of time alone in the fields that surrounded my village in the north Midlands. It was there, when I was about seventeen or eighteen years old, that I saw a gray heron, the equivalent of the great blue heron here, way off in the misty distance. I understood instantly that it was a beautiful thing; but I was so embarrassed about my feelings that I dared not tell anyone I saw it.

Here in the United States, the pursuit of birds is not considered much sexier, though the use of the word "birder" instead of "birdwatcher" connotes a more active participation, I suppose, a veneer of science and perhaps adventure. Still, I met one once, in Central Park, about a week after I moved here. She was rocking back and forth a little bit, and there was dandruff on her mustache.

And bathing? It wasn't clear to me that she was entirely averse to it. No, I wouldn't say that at all.

The great blue heron comes back into our tale later on; it is, in fact, our MacGuffin, so keep an eye out for it. It's the largest North American heron, sometimes as long as fifty-four inches, with a wingspan of about seventy inches, so you can't miss it. It flew into my life, as have so many other wonderful and perplexing things, via my friends Don and Donna Graffiti.

Don Graffiti's a tall man, over six feet, with a blast of salt-and-pepper hair and spectacles sometimes askew on an honest face.

Being his friend, I'm often asked where he's from—given his imposing manner I find a lot of people are too scared to ask him directly. His accent is not unlike mine, so folks often assume he's British. The truth is a bit more complicated. Don's father is Welsh, his mother Irish; he was born in South Africa, but grew up in San Francisco, where his pops was "in the government," though whose government I'm never entirely clear. I do know Don's house was bombed once or twice growing up on the West Coast (these were the years of apartheid, and of anti-apartheid activism); that he spent a year in Ireland, before studying in Italy for a bit; then, in a perfectly natural first career step for a highly educated man, he decamped to Sweden, where, along with a gang of inebriate northern European hooligans, he moved furniture for a living. After a few years, he worked his way back to America and Boston, and finally to New York, where he now earned his crust as a publicist at a publishing company.

Ah, *le pomme grand*—an apple, and an oyster! Like Don, I had arrived here after a great deal of traveling and had been amazed by the city, its sheer noise and motion and variety. There were so many things to choose from: lives, people, professions.

But holding to the great British tradition of "safe pursuits for all the losers," I eschewed the chance to be a firefighter, or a couture salesman, or a stunt double, and instead took work as a book editor. This is just as unsexy as it sounds, though blowing the cobwebs off my desk every morning has loaned me an erotic husk to my voice, not to mention a hacking cough. And it was at the publishing house, during a meeting about what color book jacket should be placed on a halitosis primer, that I met Don.

Donna, Don's wife, I met later, at a party at their house in Brooklyn. She is thin and blonde, a native New Yorker, a gifted potter. At one point that evening I'd said something funny, and a silent scream of laughter left her mouth like a ghost. This was extremely charming; and in any case, any wife of Don's was a friend of mine. She also proved to be the most photogenic person I'd ever met; this might have something to do with her late father, who had been an accomplished photographer.

Don, on the other hand . . . Well, in photographs, something happens to him. The problem was neatly encapsulated that first evening. Donna asked me to take a photo of them both, and as they posed for it in front of their crackling fireplace, Donna said to Don, "Smile, darling. And try not to look Chinese."

I just thought it was a gag, one of those private jokes that only married folks find funny, until I looked at the photo weeks later and realized that though Donna resembled Donna—pretty, smiling, blonde—Don Graffiti had turned into Don Chan. This odd transformation upsets him greatly—he has nothing against the Chinese; he just wishes he looked more like himself in photos. So please don't mention it to him.

As Don and I got to know each other, I realized we had some less obvious things in common. We shared both a weariness with the modern world and an attendant low-grade misanthropy. Don also loved, and hated (as many do), living in New York. We also shared a love of sports, especially baseball, though I lacked Don's ability to rattle off the exact hitting averages, RBI totals, and home runs of every American League player on any given day of every 162-game season—a rare, if defining, symptom of American Male Sports Autism. One winter, I convinced him to join my indoor soccer team, but shortly thereafter, in a particularly gruesome moment against a team called, I kid you not, the Wolverines, he was tripped from behind by some Neanderthal Brit and, falling forward onto the Astroturf-covered concrete, managed to break both his arms in one go.

Despite the accident, he remained loyal to our burgeoning friendship. I found him amusing and refreshing, like a sorbet, and he seemed to feel the same about me—though I noticed that he turned ashen every time I stooped to a scatological joke. This sort of comedy, he claimed, was evidence of "insufficient toilet training."

Mea culpa.

As it happened, in the first months of my friendship with the Graffitis, my wife and I bought a house on a hill in northeast Pennsylvania. When I told Don about it, he commented that he and Donna liked "the outdoors," which was presumably why they were able to leave their house every day to get to work. I invited them—I would have had to, even if I didn't like them, and I did like them, very much—and to our new place they came, arriving late one spring night.

Next day, bright sunlight woke me early. When I came out onto the landing, Don and Donna's bedroom door was open, and they were gone. I stumbled downstairs and blearily looked out over the garden, and there they were, down the hill by a little bench upon which Suzanne, my wife, had affixed a little metal plate proclaiming this to be "Luke's View."

Their hands were raised to their eyes; they swung around to the pines at the east of the property, then back to the valley, then flung their arms high, like deaf people applauding. The tops of the plane trees mimicked them, wafting their branches from side to side in a silent welcoming of something. I realized abruptly that I didn't know them very well. Were they praying to the sun? Were they Aztecs?

I watched them for a while. I couldn't tell what they were doing, but even at a distance, I could sense that they were happy. The day was glorious, and they seemed to be soaking it in. I felt something close to envy—but what for? Wherever my envy came from I wanted to find out quick, because when *Homo sapiens* envy, the results are seldom good.

And then the two of them turned and walked back up the hill towards the house. I heard the screen door slam, the back door catch. They stepped into the kitchen, and they were smiling; they had brought spring inside with them.

Donna wished me good morning, and handed me a gift. It was a pair of binoculars.

"They're spare," she said, "just in case. You never know, you just might like it."

The house had three bedrooms; a French drain (blocked) in a basement (empty); obscenely wide wood panel floors in an obscenely huge kitchen; a view down a valley and up a ridge called Hickory Hill; two acres, demarked by blue tape on metal poles; and one woodchuck. Best of all, it was painted salmon pink and boasted a red tin roof. It was a kind of paradise.

The day Suzanne and I signed the papers, we had driven north from her parents' home outside Philadelphia in a dark blue Cadillac, with black snow banked high on the shoulders of I-476, Pennsylvania's Northeast Extension. It was March 1998, a few weeks before the visit of Don and Donna Graffiti. The car had belonged to my father-in-law, now deceased. He had been gone a month, and the drive from Philly to the corner of the state was made easier by his cruise control and the distant thrum of a V-8.

But nothing was really easy just then. Our blood felt wrong. One of the last things he had said to Suzanne was that she should go and enjoy her pink house, and so.

After a couple of sad hours, the Northeast Extension had dwindled into back roads past ugly Scranton and uglier Carbondale, until the beauty began—rolling hills, a summer camp, and a home. The Caddy's wheels crackled on the gravel driveway, and we pulled under the car porch as though we'd done it a million times. Once we'd unlocked the place, I went off to procure a mailbox—it seemed important to have one immediately. A local woman stopped me outside the post office across the street and said, with not a little hope in her voice, "Will you be repainting it?"

"Oh yes," said I.

"Oh good," she simpered. "A nice white, maybe? Or beige?"

"No," I said, roused. "Exactly the same color as now."

In the weeks before Don and Donna's visit, the snow had receded, and the winds had shifted to predominately southerly. A spring came, and we two partial orphans owned a house. The weekly treks up to that pretty corner of Pennsylvania seemed to soften the grief of the recent loss a tiny bit. In the yard, color appeared. As we were there only on weekends, the change from season to season was more pronounced for us—what had been ice-bound on Sunday would become, by the following Friday evening, a place where something green was peeking through. I thought of Philip Larkin's poem about lambs that get born in winter, and the "immeasurable surprise" they find when the snow goes. A garden was planted; I bought a rod and took the bass I caught from Ten Mile River into the yard to scale it, covering my shirt in tiny bolts of fish-light. But I didn't spend much time in the garden. When there was absolutely nothing better to do I would walk the hills, but most weekends I hid *inside* my house, enjoying each of the three bedrooms and the two bathrooms and the huge kitchen. I'd lived in New York apartments for so long I barely remembered that one could do something like *wandering upstairs for no discernible reason*, and I was determined to make the most of it. I hardly noticed the yard, barely paused to enjoy "Luke's View."

It was no great loss. I hadn't seriously hiked in years. In college days we'd pack up the car and head to Wales most weekends, where my pal Kit and I would traipse across the Welsh marches, get thoroughly lost, somehow find our way, and finish the night with cheese on toast and a raid on Kit's dad's stash of single malt whiskeys. But that seemed like a lifetime ago. I don't know what happened. I guess I thought I was better than that, more sophisticated. The reality was, life in New York had urbanized me. I owned a house in Pennsylvania because that's one of the things city dwellers do. The view sure was pretty, but I never felt the need to do anything more than look.

About halfway down the hedgerow on the western edge of the yard, over by the rhubarb patch and in sight of the biggest of the gopher holes, a mother bird was flitting back and forth constructing a place suitable for a family.

She had been preceded that spring, like every year, by a small male who had flown thousands of miles north, up along what is called the eastern flyway, an ancient course of breezes and geographic contours that funnels billions of migrating birds northwards each spring. As I return extremely important phone calls and compose unarguable e-mails in my New York City office, up there in Pennsylvania these birds face a crucial week. For the male there's singing to be done, and a territory to stake out, all effected in a touching and often happily borne-out belief that a female will eventually turn up and fancy a bit of the other. When nature takes hold, they could get about reproducing. From about six eggs, maybe two babies; from two babies, maybe one adult. Meanwhile, back in New York, my e-mail gets returned to me—it seems the host couldn't resolve the IP, or something. Unlike my agonizing communication with a set of 0s and 1s, this ancient avian process of migration and reproduction has been going on, in one form or another, for years and years and years; it's the embodiment of the very gears of the planet, locking perfectly. Compare this with the panic I feel if my e-mail is sluggish, or if a Web site is too busy to access, or when I read the worst four words in the English language: *The server is down.* Is it any surprise that in my twenty-nine years alive on the planet, until a couple of houseguests arrived one weekend to see our new place, I had given the subject of birds and migration and nesting and the feeding of the young absolutely no thought whatsoever?

The binoculars Donna Graffiti had handed me were a pair of old Celestron Regals, 10×50, battered and everyday and a friendly weight in my hand.

"They're spare," she said, "just in case. You never know, you just might like it."

Don said, "Let's take a walk."

As we stepped out into the day, Donna explained that there had been a change in the weather overnight—a strong southerly flow had come through—and with it, a probable line of migrating birds through the area. I had no idea what she was talking about—the day looked the same as the one before to me, if brighter perhaps, as though the air had been filtered through the promise of a summer just over the mountain. But before I could ask her what she meant, I realized we'd lost Don. He was intently looking down the valley. Every once in a while he would murmur something to himself, then fall silent. This went on for several minutes, and his fervor intrigued me. Donna had also stopped paying me any heed, so there I stood, a heavy pair of binoculars around my neck in my yard in Pennsylvania, wondering what these people were up to.

They turned their focus to a small bush halfway along the south edge of the plot, the one near the gopher hole, now no more than twenty feet away from where we were standing. Donna seemed to be following the movement of something; Don, sensing this, said, "What have you got?"

"Not sure," Donna said. "Can't see it right now. Wait, there, I got it. I can see the mask. Yes, that's it."

"Common yellowthroat," Don said.

"Yellowthroat for sure. Male. Pretty!" Donna said.

"Just there, pretty low down. See the flitting?" She was talking to me now. "Get the movement with your naked eye, and then bring the binoculars up."

I stared at the bush through the Celestrons, but the focus was all wrong and I could see nothing. Twirling the wheel, a brief flit of color sprang across my field of vision, and a branch of the bush swayed a little. Leaves shook. Still nothing.

Donna said, "Keep looking. You'll see. I promise."

Suddenly, there it was.

"Oh my! Wow! Are you kidding me? Wow!"

I was as eloquent then as I've ever been about the beauty of birds. The sheer joy of its handsomeness rendered me dumb.

"How about that?" said Don.

"It's one of the more regular things you can see in springtime, if you're looking for it," said Donna. "A common yellowthroat," she said. "A warbler."

The bird hopped around a bit, mostly keeping low, and I followed it as best I could around the bushes as it chucked and witchity witchitied—that's the sound it makes, *witchity witchity*. A tiny thing, but with such astounding markings: a shining yellow throat, and most vivid of all, a sweeping black highwayman's mask across its face, bordered on the top by a thin white line of feathers. Tamely it came to us, turning from side to side so we could get perfect views. This way, that; that way, this. *Witchity, witchity.*

There—that's the sound of love as it begins.

But I really didn't want this kind of love; I wished almost instantly that it hadn't dared speak its name.

Here I was, madly falling for a bird, but did this mean I had to be—shhh—a birder? I was in my late twenties; I had a bunch of sophisticated American friends who could count on me not to completely let them down in a social situation; once in a while I was able to conjure up both something "witty" and "urbane" in the same sentence. I had, up to this point, no idea that the common yellowthroat existed, or that it came to my garden in the spring to nest and raise its young. All I knew for sure was that, like Saul and the fish I'd caught, my eyes had been scaled; love swelled in my pancreas; and I madly wanted to see more.

As I pondered all this, Don said, "Up there."

I turned to him. He was looking at the top reaches of a plane tree. Donna was looking too.

"Where?" she said.

"See where the tree forks? Very top. Look naked eye. You'll see the movement."

Then, turning to me, Don said, "Trees don't move, pretty much, especially on a calm day like this. But birds do. That's how you find them."

"What is it?" I asked.

"Look. You'll see it."

I scanned the top of the tree and caught a glimpse of bright orange. Even at this distance it was clearly a bigger bird than the common yellowthroat. Black head; sharp, longish beak; bright orange flashings on its sides, same color on the under parts. Dark wings with white markings. It looked like a gaudy racing car.

"Baltimore oriole. Lovely." Don couldn't keep the smile out of his voice. "Lucky you. The birds love this place."

And then, it flew.

All that day we birded. I can still remember the names of every species we saw and where we saw them. I was like a child on Christmas morning, and almost outlasted Don, though I would come to learn such a thing is impossible when birds are involved.

The following day, Don and Donna left to get back to the city. Months passed. The backyard still sloped away fifty feet into the valley, and half a mile across the dip, to where Hickory Hill rose back a full two thousand feet, shielding us from the summer storms. Such afternoons I'd stand under the small back porch and watch the hail and lightning sweep in from the west, stretching the trees till I thought they might snap. Our second summer we lost two apple trees; another year, a large bough on a sycamore by the kitchen fell away from the house, thank god—if it had fallen this way . . . The house survived, its pink paint job and bright red roof announcing what I like to think was something like joy all over the valley.

Now I was filled with joy at all the new things around me too. American robins nested safely in our eaves; an eastern phoebe came every year to raise a family. I saw my first rose-breasted grosbeak at the top of an elm, my first bobolinks in the field up by the Masons' farm. There was a blue-winged warbler down in the copse. American goldfinches dipped and rose and chowed down at our feeder, though a sharp-shinned hawk watched them with murderous intent. Down at the Delaware River, a family of bald eagles watched a belted kingfisher on a wire as it eagle-eyed the spring run of the shad. In a strand of oaks I found a chestnut-sided warbler; out in a distant pond, a family of wood ducks warily skirted a great blue heron.

I said a silent thanks for that heron. When I had pressed Don and Donna on why they birded, they'd told me about the day they rented a boat in New York's Central Park lake and a great blue had whumped by them; speechless at the majesty of it, they curtailed their day trip so that they could rush off to a bookstore to find out exactly what it was they'd seen. They never looked back. Without that bird, who knew where they'd be, or me?

For I, too, had been bitten deep. Each weekend morning at first light I'd slip out of the house and walk, binoculars around my neck and field guide in my man-pouch. (I now owned a man-pouch.) I saw many regular birds—the tufted titmouse, black-capped chickadees, mallards, a bunch of woodpeckers—and some more rare: a scarlet tanager, my first, high in a pine on a Fourth of July (that same day, I happened upon my first black bear snarling at me from halfways up the same tree; *you don't scare me, you wussbag baby bear,* I thought as I swiftly walked in the opposite direction, squeezing my butt cheeks together). I saw an osprey, high on the blue air of spring, turning in widening gyres, and a golden-winged warbler, at that point about the only bird I'd seen that Don and Donna had not. It was in a flock of black-capped chickadees, down by the lake on Old Church Road (I could show you the curve of the road, the very tree in which the bird fed, its actual branch). One spring later, across the same road, deep in the woods I heard a singing hermit thrush. That morning, a nice local couple out walking their dog stopped to ask me what it was.

"We hear it all the time when we go camping in Virginia," the woman said, "and we never know what we're hearing, though we love it. We think it's the most beautiful sound in nature."

And so it may be.

In the middle of all this, more love: twin girls. Suzanne and I were now in proud possession of two kids, two homes, and four of everything else—four high chairs, four Pack 'n Plays, four cribs, four Scooby-Doo sippy cups. Then, before we noticed it, the girls learned to crawl, then totter, then walk, then run, and suddenly it seemed they were gone all afternoon, running like free horses down to Luke's View. In the winter, we'd sled across an acre of ice; the rumbling storms of summer would make them put their hands over their eyes. They came to know the gray catbird whine, the buzz of chipping sparrows, the *witchity* of the common yellowthroat. They watched with awe as the last of the nesting American robin chicks fell out of the carport eaves and somehow made it across to the evergreen, where an attentive mother brought it worms. Sure, they knew about Elmo and the Wiggles and Dora the Explorer; but they also called out, "Red-tailed hawk," as we drove home on the New York State Thruway, or "It's just a turkey vulture, Daddy," stopping me from swerving to the shoulder as the last light of a Sunday evening gave way to the distant lights of New York City and the demands of a career.

But in my deepest heart, I was now a birder. I carried binoculars everywhere. When I drove, I repeatedly scanned the skies for something, I'm not sure what. In the spring, Don and Donna and I met at dawn in Central Park to see what the migration had brought us; all too soon we'd have to trudge to work, leaving the "Central Park Regulars" to rack up their hundreds of birds a day. I haunted blogs like the New York Birding List and NYC Bird Report, scanning them constantly for rarities or big fallouts, days when migrants seem to drop from the sky in droves. On my cell phone I saved the number for a guy with the great name of Lloyd Spitalnik, an excellent wildlife photographer who serves as one of the unofficial conduits for rare-bird sightings in New York. Sometimes I'd chase a bird that he'd posted on his blog, Metro Birding Briefs (I don't think this means he birds in his underwear). And if I got it, I'd call him to confirm it was still there. One day in late April, I was leaving Central Park at the end of a lunch hour when he and a bunch of other "regulars" came charging towards me, a very uncommon bird for a city park, the yellow-throated warbler, having been spotted on the Great Lawn. When I protested I had to go back to work, Spitalnik said, "Quit your job."

The tone of his voice, not to mention his scowl, made it clear he wasn't joking. He's said the same thing any number of times since too, each time with thinly veiled annoyance that one would let a thing like employment get in the way of a rare-bird sighting.

Don and Donna went to Prospect Park in Brooklyn pretty much every weekend, even in the birdless dead zone of late July—"Hey, you never know what might turn up," Don said. The three of us found ourselves in New Jersey more regularly than the NYPD racketeering squad, be it at Sandy Hook in the north, Brigantine National Wildlife Refuge in the middle, or most regularly, Cape May in the distant south, a place where the number of rare birds is matched only by the number of hard-core birders.

This is what we did now.

NOW WHAT?

One Sunday, Don and Donna and I spent a happy day birding at Jamaica Bay Wildlife Refuge, the jewel in the crown of New York City birding. Nestled a few miles west of JFK airport, the marshes and trails of Jamaica Bay harbor endless varieties of gulls, shorebirds, songbirds, raptors—you name it. I lost track of how many times Don would marvel out loud about the place: "Guys, we're in a city! And look at this!"

We'd scan the ponds and reeds and truly it was hard to believe we were still within the confines of New York, given that common eiders could turn up here—a bird of the icy waters off the Canadian coasts—or one deep winter afternoon, a snowy owl, silent on the marsh, another bird more usually happy thousands of miles north. Jamaica Bay had become one of our favorite places, especially in late summer, when it attracts so many migrating shorebirds and gulls. It was our greatest joy to meet at dawn in Brooklyn and drive to the edge of Queens, where this oasis of birdlife twinkled in the early-morning sun.

Elsewhere in my life, however, all was not well. So it was tough to besmirch Jamaica Bay that day with sad news, but I wanted my friends to know that changes were afoot.

When I was fifteen years old, I heard a song by Paul Simon called "Train in the Distance." I was far too young then to understand why it affected me so—it's no exaggeration to say that I spent the days after hearing it in a kind of stunned and perturbed fugue state. Across the years, the song has stayed with me as a kind of talisman.

Now I knew why: the song had been a foretelling. It was a concussive shock to realize that, barring a few particulars, I'd found my recent life had come to echo the song painfully closely. I couldn't explain any of this to Don and Donna, there at Jamaica Bay Wildlife Refuge, so instead I simply gave them the bare and heartbreaking facts.

Don stopped in his tracks and looked at me blankly. Donna closed her birding guide and looked at Don. Above us, a pair of glossy ibis silently rode a thermal down to land on a pond filled with herring gulls and Canada geese and mallards. In the distance, I could hear the sound of the A train heading to the Far Rockaways.

No one ever really knows what happens inside someone else's marriage. It's one of the great secrets, and I happen to believe it should stay that way. Don and Donna didn't need this to be pointed out to them, fortunately. Without another word, the three of us walked back to the car and drove away.

So then I wasn't married anymore, and Suzanne and I agreed that I'd see the girls twice a week and on every other weekend. Each time I had the kids, I'd drive them up to the pink house in Pennsylvania. But among the many things that ended, I couldn't bird there as I used to. I was parenting alone, and their attention spans didn't run to hours on the hills and long mornings in the forest. I was heartsick. The film was growing back across my eyes.

Something had to give.

It was about this time that Don and Donna brought to my attention a new concept: concentrated birding trips to states far away. The sixty or seventy birds I might routinely see in a corner of Pennsylvania, or more in Central Park and Jamaica Bay, could possibly morph into at least twice that number in hot spots like southeast Arizona, or Florida, or Texas, or Michigan. All we had to do was put ourselves in harm's way, and the birds would come.

Running around the country chasing birds suddenly sounded like the sanest thing we could possibly do. I wanted to see as many birds as the country could proffer, and I wanted to see this amazing continent called America. What I couldn't see as much as I'd like were my daughters, so there were a couple of acres of time to fill each month.

My birding guide describes the babies of the common yellowthroat as "altricial": helpless at birth, or in need of parental care. My girls were still so. Nevertheless, I could leave on the Friday morning of a weekend I wasn't slated to see them, and get back by early Tuesday evening. No one, it pained me to realize, would know I was gone.

To cap it all, the house in Pennsylvania was sold. I couldn't bear to go up to the area after that, couldn't bear to find out what color the pink house had been painted.

The red light blinks; the cabin door is shut; we are preparing for takeoff. Through the crackle of bad reception comes my daughter Amelia's sweet voice; she has left me a message:

"If you're going somewhere," she croons, "have a safe trip."

I turn off my cell phone, stow my carry-on, put my seat back to upright, and close my leaking eyes. In a few hours I'll be in Phoenix, Arizona, in line for a rental car; I've reserved a four-door silver sedan for our trip to the southeast corner of the state. In that car, as in all the cars we'll rent, Don will mostly sit beside me, with Donna in the back; once in a while they switch. But what doesn't change is three mad birders peering up through the tinted glass, living one bird at a time.

TWO

Arizona:
Watching Wezil Walraven Work

Lo! I can hear a bird: "Whu-puh-*Whiwwww!* Whu-puh-*Whiwwww!*
Whu-puh-*Whiwwww!*" it calls. It's the song of *Caprimulgus vociferus*, commonly known as the whip-poor-will, a nocturnal bird
which is found, mostly, in the eastern United States. It also has a
half-brother subspecies, hailing from Mexico, that deigns to spend
time in this corner of southeast Arizona.

The half-brother has just woken me up.

In hearing *Caprimulgus vociferus* I've just technically gotten
myself the easiest "life bird" ever—by the commonly accepted
rules of birding, if you hear it, you can claim it. Life birds are
what it's all about for birders. We love to see all birds, of course,
but once one gets past a certain number of species seen and
re-seen, then it's the apprehension of a first-time sighting that
provides the greatest excitement. In our heads we all have a list of
birds that we'd like to see in other parts of the country (and
world), as well as a list of birds that could be seen "at home" but
have so far eluded us. Too often, this latter group turns into a set
of "nemesis" birds, ones that other birders seem to see on a daily
basis, but which for the poor desperate seeker remain just around
the next bend, or always in a different tree. This explains why
we bird so passionately—you never know what's going to turn
up—and why we travel so much: different geographical zones
harbor different sets of birds.

So the Arizona whip-poor-will was a life bird for me, but it was also incontrovertibly true that according to the clock on the bedside table, it has roused me at four forty-eight in the morning in the living room of a small cottage at the Ramsey Canyon Inn.

I lie on the foldout couch as the whip-poor-will witters on. What an ego this thing has—Whu-puh-*whiwwww!* Whu-puh-*whiwwww!*—hollering its own name over and over. I call to Don and Donna, "Hey, guys, you awake? You hear that?"

There's no reply; maybe they're lucky enough to still be asleep. But when I peer through the gloom into the adjoining bedroom, it's clear that I'm alone. I guess that they too were woken by the bird and have gone off to see it. This is, sadly, probably a fool's errand. The whip-poor-will is a dull and flattish bird the exact color of the bough of a tree; it could be right above you and shit on your head, and if you looked up, you wouldn't even see it.

I slip on my jeans and sneakers, grab my binoculars, and step out into the coolness of the spring morning. All around me, I hear the rustle of birds as they flit from branch to branch, eking out breakfast.

The path from our cottage bends down and around a low building, over a little stream, and into the parking lot. It was there, the previous night, that we deposited our rental car after a drive of two hundred miles south from Phoenix to here, Ramsey Canyon, a secluded cut in the side of the Coronado National Forest. The whole of southeast Arizona is a birding mecca, but Ramsey Canyon is up there (literally) with the best places, thanks to its cool temperatures and secluded elevations. As I stroll I have to pinch myself that yesterday I was sitting at a desk in midtown Manhattan, and now, after a reasonably short flight and a drive, I'm in a position to be brought to consciousness by a whip-poor-will subspecies.

In the parking lot, there they are: Don and Donna Graffiti. This is the official start of the first of our fly-drive birding trips. A bird seen by any of us is better if seen by all, and that is why I came to get the whip-poor-will with them, if they've found it.

But this morning, they look a bit sheepish. Don, especially, can sometimes display a distant relationship to the world's more banal realities—how computers work; the best way to stop a two-thousand-dollar spotting scope from crashing to the ground; remembering to wear pants. So the sheepish thing? Not a good sign.

The trunk of our rental car stands open, and as I walk over to them, they both look away at the same time, as though they've found a dead body in the vehicle.

"What's up?" I ask cautiously.

"Morning. Did you hear the whip-poor-will?" Donna says.

"Fucker woke me up," I snark. Don winces. Any display of anything less than the total adoration of all living things—except humans—upsets him greatly. He's a man who coos at snakes.

"Fabulous, yes?" Don says, adjusting his spectacles for the first of probably six hundred times today. "Candy bar!"

It's always a surprise to remember that this is how Don Graffiti speaks. He makes no apology for his bizarre diction. "Foot Locker," "Coolio and the gang," "funk the monkey," "candy bar"—all these phrases are brief mantras employed as mental placeholders for the great joy he feels in engaging with the natural world.

But being woken by a whip-poor-will in the mountains of southeast Arizona before five in the morning after flying 2,500 miles and driving through the night is "candy bar"? I could shit in Don's eye, I really could. For a start, if I were a whip-poor-will, he'd never see me, though that kinda defines "big if."

Donna breaks the spell.

"Tell him, Don."

"You, sweetie," says Don, ominously.

"Tell me what?"

Here we go. Don searches in his pocket for something, and pulls out the car keys.

"Well, it's confusing, Luke. It is. In our defense, it was only just getting light. And we hadn't really focused yesterday. Too much else to think about."

"Don . . ."

"Yes, Luke."

"What did you do?" I'm trying to look at the car keys now, but he's holding them in such a way as to hide all but the little alarm fob.

It's Donna's turn. She is often the spokesperson for Don's troubled relationship with reality.

"Really, Luke, it *is* confusing. You know what we're like. We came down here to look for the whip-poor-will, but I'd left my binoculars in the trunk last night. You know how late it was when we arrived; you guys really need to learn how to read a map. Anyway, Don went back to the room to find the keys to the car—they were in your pants—"

"That's funny. That's exactly where I left 'em—"

"No need, Luke," says Don. "Donna's just trying to explain."

I shoot Don a look, but Donna presses on.

"Anyway, Don came down here, and it's early—he hasn't had any coffee yet. You know what he's like without coffee. In all fairness to him, he really thought it was *our* car . . ."

At this, the world shifts slightly. Don stares at me like a big whale might, still holding the car keys. Then, the whale speaks: "Don't worry, Luke. We realized in time."

At this, he reveals, finally, the Uri Geller–esque vision that is the main key to the vehicle.

"It's only slightly bent. And you can still open the trunk—we found a button inside the actual car."

"You might want to try to start the car, Luke, too. We were going to, but we're not sure where the key actually goes," adds Donna, cheerily.

I wish I were shocked by this.

"What? We're stuck in Ramsey Canyon with nothing but a rental car and a bent key?"

Behind Don, I see Donna's knee give out ever so slightly. Her knees do this at times of intense stress, or when she sees a particularly beautiful bird but can't quite describe where it is in the tree.

"Which car did you try to break into?" I can't believe I'm saying these words at five ten in the morning, thousands of miles from home.

Don points.

"The red one, right there."

I look at the red car. I look at the silver car. I look back at the red compact car. I look once again at the silver full-size sedan. One last time, at the red compact two door; then, at our car, the silver intermediate four door with go-faster stripes up the side.

Don and Donna Graffiti have tried to break into a car one third the size of the one they'd spent three hours in yesterday.

"We didn't get the whip-poor-will," says Don brightly. "But as you know, they're incredibly hard to see."

This corner of southeast Arizona exists, I would argue, entirely and only for birders. On all the little maps in all the birding field guides, it's amazing how many species have a range that slips over the Mexican border into southeast Arizona and no farther. The list of such immigrants is long; they come from Central America to breed in the cool mountain reaches and drink from the rivers and streams. Of the more than 280 species that breed in Arizona, here there are no less than 35—including two trogons (the elegant and the eared); the flame-colored tanager; the buff-breasted flycatcher; and numerous hummingbirds (the magnificent, the Lucifer, the violet-crowned, and the blue-throated, among them)—that pop *only* into this remote corner of the

United States (some go to New Mexico and Texas, too), have a bunch of kids, then fly back to where they came from.

There are two main reasons why southeast Arizona hosts such an abundant variety of birds. The first is that the area's approximately fifteen thousand square miles contain the meeting points of four major biogeographical regions: the Rocky Mountains, the Chihuahuan Desert, the Sonoran Desert, and the Sierra Madres, the rugged mountain chain that runs on a north-south axis from southern Mexico to the pine-clad peaks of the Chiricahuas straddling the Arizona–New Mexico border. Each of these regions contributes a unique flora and fauna to southeast Arizona. Beyond that, each mountain in the area is in reality the top of an island that was once submerged by a prehistoric sea. As the seas withdrew, they left behind different "countries" on top of each of the many mountains hereabouts, meaning each range supports different species of plants, which in turn attract different species of birds.

The other reason why birds—and birders—come here is the San Pedro River. Running nearly 180 miles long, it starts just south of the border, near the city of Cananea in northern Sonora, and ends where it meets the Gila River near a town called Winkelman in northern Arizona. *Birding* magazine called the San Pedro the best birding area in the world. According to the Center for Biological Diversity, nearly one half of all North American bird species frequent it at some point in their lives, meaning you can see more than four hundred birds—including those trogons and tanagers and rare hummingbirds—in any given year along its length. It's almost too good to be true.

Today's first trip is to enjoy the San Pedro. Once I unbend the key enough to start the car, we head down the mountain towards the Southeastern Arizona Bird Observatory's famed San Pedro House, on Route 92 to Bisbee. We edge the outskirts of Sierra Vista, and then we swerve east, away from town. The morning hides its heat behind the Chiricahua Mountains ahead of us, but once we leave the suburban tract homes behind, we face a dead-straight road across the desert. There, in the coming light, stands the woodland line that marks the San Pedro River. Heat haze has already begun to slip up from the scrubland, but through the shimmer the vision of all those jade-colored cottonwoods and willows in a desert takes our collective breath away. I've never seen anything like it; it is magical.

Well, it's magical until Don decides he needs an egg sandwich. In fairness, we all need food (adrenaline has been pumping ever since the car key incident), so after a brief discussion we pull off Route 92 at a nondescript general store. Outside, a gaggle of 4×4s, each with its engine running, sit at jaunty angles.

Don says, "They couldn't turn their homicidal engines off? Do you know what all those emissions are doing to the air? I'd let the air out of their tires, but I don't know how."

He is angling for a fight, or at the very least a well-timed comment in the store. I am right there with him, even though I am imagining a less confrontational approach i.e., saying absolutely nothing.

As we enter, the bell on the door tinkles prettily and then stops short, as if someone very tough had told it to shut up, and quick. There, in a large empty room, a huge man towers behind an even bigger counter. He's easily six feet six; he has a fivehead, and big, meaty hands that I imagine brush against his upper thighs. I think we may have stumbled across Early Man. Aside from a few items on his counter, however, there are no products. Where are all the shelves, the foodstuffs, the cakes and candies . . . ? Lounging about, instead, are the presumed owners of the trucks, various hard-boiled locals, looking vaguely like Minutemen.

Wait a second—could this really be the Minutemen? On the airplane trip down here, Don and I had discussed what to do if we ran across these characters.

Lest we forget, the Minutemen are a loose organization of anti-immigrant vigilantes who spent much of the spring of 2005 sitting in their trucks, or in beach chairs next to their trucks, binoculars in hand, pretending to be border guards.

Two main charmers are responsible for the Minutemen, though a third, more shadowy figure points to what they are really about. The first is Chris Simcox, who used to run a local paper called the *Tumbleweed*, in Tombstone, Arizona (scene of the OK Corral, and now a theme town from hell). Simcox went public with the Minuteman Project in April 2005 in cahoots with a guy called Jim Gilchrist, who was the money behind the whole thing. Gilchrist, in turn, had been long associated in Arizona with Glenn Spencer, a nut in his late sixties who had once faced a number of felony charges for shooting up a neighbor's garage in 2003—he mistook the garage for Mexicans coming to get him— but ended up simply paying a paltry fine.

The Minutemen (whose ex-girlfriends, you imagine, have a lot of wicked fun with that name) garnered a huge amount of publicity all that spring of our visit—in fact, it was our luck that the day we arrived was the same day they began their "crusade." Now we were faced with what could be a room full of them, and three empty stomachs. Would Don say anything about the running engines?

I'm thinking he might not.

Before I can worry about Don's lip, however, the room develops instant Welsh Post Office Syndrome. If you're ever unlucky enough to be (a) non-Welsh, (b) in need of a stamp, and (c) in Wales, you'll know what this means. The second you step inside a Welsh post office all English conversation instantly ceases, then starts again in Welsh. It is, in fact, the only time anyone in Wales speaks Welsh—they save it for the tourists.

And so it is in this general store on the edge of Sierra Vista. The locals mumble to each other in a language that could well have been some lost offshoot of Celtic. All I can think of is Geoff Huish, the young Welshman who had recently chopped off his own testicles to celebrate his country beating England at rugby, and I realize I have two options: to allude to Mr. Huish in a loud voice, thereby alerting these people that I recognize the essential emasculation of their lives; or else to let it go, and order breakfast.

Don, hearing the Welsh of his father's land, immediately draws himself in like a turtle, and turns to me, ashen. He whispers, "I can't do this."

"Do what?"

"Really, Luke, I mean, what is going on here?"

We're huddled now, the three of us. Under my breath I say, "Don, it's fine. It's just a general store. Filled with what could be anti-Mexican militia, yes, but still, it's just a general store."

Don looks at Donna; she stares back.

"No," Don hisses. "I don't mean that. Where are all the cakes?"

"You want *cakes*?" I whisper. "Not a bottle of white truffle oil? Some sweetbreads?"

"No! I want the *possibility* of cakes. But there's nothing here. No cakes, no shelves, no nothing. It's just a big room, with a counter. A high counter, I'd like to point out. Why is the counter so high? It must be a front."

"A front?"

"Yes. I bet the back room"—he nods meaningfully to where the sound of bacon frying is making my stomach growl—"is filled with guns and bullets, AK-47s and the like."

"Don?"

"Yes."

"What do you want to eat?"

This causes him to pause. He shoots a glance up at the ceiling. Then he looks back at me.

"What are *you* having?"

"I'm having what I always have."

"Well, I want the same, just *without* the meat."

"Good, shall I order?"

"Yes, would you? I think the guy behind the counter may not actually be human. You're good with such people. Donna, what are you having?"

"Same as Luke, but *with* the meat."

"And I want the doughnut," says Don, "but I don't know how to ask for it."

On the top of the counter, just below the stratosphere, lies a solitary jelly doughnut. It looks like something from a different planet. The jelly could pass for fake blood, and the moon-doughnut itself sags under the weight of it. It seems to me on brief perusal that the entire edifice defies utterly even the most basic elements of the theory of gravitational forces. I wouldn't be surprised if Early Man comes to work one morning to find a great, unfathomable hole where once the doughnut lay. Why anyone would want to consume such an object—let alone a vegetarian and careful eater such as Don—completely baffles me, but he's a bear when he's hungry, and I wasn't about to argue.

"You don't know how to ask for it?" I whisper.

"No."

"Which bit of asking for it is troubling you?"

By now Early Man, as well as a few of the locals, have given up speaking Welsh and are silently watching us. Here's the scene from their point of view: A group of strangers have recently entered their establishment, and in all that time this odd threesome have huddled like a small football team, whispering a conversation in which the only words escaping had been "AK-47s," "meat," and "not actually human."

Time for action; I break away and approach the high counter.

"Yes, erm, hello, I wonder if we could order breakfast."

Early Man smiles faintly from under his heavy brows, like I'd just set down my handgun, and he had not.

"Sure. We were beginning to think we needed to prepare a counter-offensive."

At this, Donna's right knee buckles ever so slightly and I

turn to see Don grab her by the elbow for the second time that morning.

"Yes, sorry about that," I say. "Just getting everyone's order straight."

"*Counter*-offensive, geddit?" Early Man says with a chuckle. I may have heard Donna whimper. Then he says, "These two friends of yours mute or something?"

"No, no, I just tend to speak for the group when it comes to breakfast. So, we'd like to order egg and bacon on a roll twice, and also, just egg on a roll—"

"No!" Don speaks out loud for the first time.

"Not mute then," says Early Man.

"Don?" I look around at him again. I can't believe this. What's to get wrong with egg on a roll?

Don looks down at me.

"Not a roll! God no. Can't stand rolls. I am not a roll kind of guy. Too much breadiness. You really want a roll? Donna, you too?" He lets go of her arm, as though offended.

"Yes, Don, we eat rolls all the time."

"Do we *really*?"

"What do you want instead, Don?" By now I'm literally wilting from hunger and ready for everyone in this store to rip us to shreds. I wouldn't blame them at this point.

"On toast, I think. Can that be done?" Don asks.

"Oh, yes, we have a toaster. It's the only one in Sierra Vista, so we're very proud of it."

And with that, he turns and shouts our order to whomever he's chained to the grill in the back room.

But his flash of sarcasm seems to ease Don's mind a bit, because as he turns back to us, Don says, "That jelly doughnut. How does that work?"

"Work?" The word comes out like a prehistoric grunt.

"Yes, does one pick it up, or is there some other way of procuring it?"

"Go ahead, pick it up. And if you like, you can eat it too. If you're not going to eat it, however, I'd appreciate it if you didn't pick it up in the first place."

"Got it!" says Don, triumphantly seizing the doughnut and taking a bite.

Back in the car, we finally get most of the jelly off Don's shirt, but we have not done what he needs us to do the most, which is find him a packet of salt. Because both Donna and I have bacon on our sandwiches, we aren't in as dire need of salt as Don, and the lack of it on his egg on toast is cause for a typically maundering speech all the way to the San Pedro River:

"What kind of caveman doesn't salt an egg? And pepper! All egg sandwiches should default to salt and pepper. An egg isn't anything very much, when you think about it. No flavor at all, really, except a vague egginess, but that's not going to do it for me, I'm afraid. You guys got bacon, so you're not feeling it like I'm feeling it. There has to be a salt packet somewhere. Luke, did you bring any? [I shake my head.] Not one? I usually have salt with me at all times. Do you know how many people don't salt eggs? [Again I shake my head.] Too many. It should be that you crack an egg on a hot plate, and before you've even thought to dispose of the shell, you're reaching for salt. They could even be the same movement—crack, salt, dispose, crack, salt, dispose. Perhaps the pepper can come after, but it's all got to happen pretty much simultaneously otherwise you're going to end up forgetting one of them, or, as is the case right now, forgetting fucking both!"

Here he pauses and rummages once again through every pocket in his jacket, his pants, even, at one point, seemingly reaching into the distant recesses of his underwear. Then, suddenly, he finds something, but it's not salt: A truth attaches itself to his brain stem.

And then he speaks: "And it's my life's mission to never go anywhere without a bottle of hot sauce too."

The last splodge of jelly drops quietly to Don's lap as we turn off the road and into the parking lot of the observatory's San Pedro House. It's not yet seven A.M., but already we know what Don's life mission is—I'd always thought it was to see every bird he possibly could, but now I know better. We open the rental car doors, and a new heat hits us, warming our egg-stained faces. It's going to be a hot day for sure.

For the few years before they'd introduced me to birding, Don and Donna Graffiti had been taking trips on their own—to Central America, and the Caribbean, all over the eastern seaboard, and here, once before, to Arizona. As neither of them has ever learned to drive, before I came along they used a combination of walking, cycling, and the odd taxi; outside the United States they might employ a local guide too, given the fact that Don thought the Spanish for "thank you very much" was *mucho garcias*. In Arizona the previous time, they'd signed up, perhaps foolishly, for an organized birding tour, figuring that the area was large enough that to walk it might be a tad too much; they had presumably forgotten they weren't fans of large groups of people.

Leading that tour had been a guy by the memorable name of Wezil Walraven. On the plane out for our trip, Don and Donna had raved to me about him. He had been an astonishingly good guide, they said—they'd seen a feast of rare and life birds—and he'd been hale and hearty and a fabulous storyteller along the way. Wezil lived with his wife, the wildlife painter Lisa Walraven, down in Bisbee, the artsy town we'd reach our second afternoon. (They have since relocated to North Carolina.) Don and Donna's Wezil tales had me almost sad we wouldn't be seeing him on this trip.

But before I can suggest calling him, a vermilion flycatcher lands on a huge cottonwood by the parking lot. And so, as we dive out of the car for a better view, our first full day of birding resumes with another life bird for me. That bird, plus the painted redstart in the parking lot at dawn, almost overlooked because of the car key incident, means in a few hours I've added three life birds, counting the whip-poor-will.

Our dusty walk down to the river still provides a slight early-morning chill—we're in jackets, but not for long, I imagine. The winding path leads across the desert towards the high stand of cottonwood trees and the San Pedro. Along the way, a few sparrows dart here and there, getting breakfast; we look at them quickly, our hearts surging across the desert to where this magical line of trees stands bright in the coming day. It's an extraordinary sight—a thin forest of cottonwoods and willows stretched out across a barren mesquite desert. Our hope is that this green canopy is dripping with songbirds. It's mid-April, just the right time of year for newly arrived warblers and tanagers and orioles. Any bird flying up from Mexico across all this scrub would see the trees and instinctually dive in, knowing that they hide millions of bugs and stand above much needed water.

As we reach it, however, we're struck by the fact that the river is barely a trickle—one can step across it without worrying about one's footing.

Sure enough: despite its importance to the extraordinary ecosystem it supports, the San Pedro River is dying. In March 1904, the United States Geological Survey established a gauge to measure the river's flow at a place called Charleston Narrows, just east of Fort Huachuca, the area's large military base. In 2005, 101 years later, and the year of our visit, the gauge registered a staggering and heartbreaking zero.

The river is dying for a number of reasons: the regular but heavy irrigation needs of agriculture; excessive groundwater pumping (i.e., wells for homesteaders and the like). But these pressures now pale in comparison with the rise in municipal growth in this sunbelt, not to mention the needs of Fort Huachuca. What's happening is that the sucking of the base and the nearby town of Sierra Vista has created a "cone of depression," taking 4.2 billion gallons from the surrounding bedrock and into the main water fields that help turn the taps on in Huachuca and Vista.

Cone of depression is right—4.2 billion gallons per year is a butt-load of water to be short, so you would think that the local politicians would do something about it. How about the Republican representative Rick Renzi, who added a (ridiculous, reprehensible, risible) rider to the National Security Readiness Act of 2003, an act which already allows the military to do pretty much anything it likes with the land it owns. The rider further exempts the military's gardens, lawns, pools, and golf courses from environmental laws, even though the Department of Defense hadn't actually asked for such a mulligan. The golf course on Fort Huachuca is lush green all year round.

But it's not just the golf course. Fort Huachuca is the largest single water user in the valley, as well as the region's biggest employer, and Sierra Vista grows apace to keep up with its needs. In the old days, 80 percent of the San Pedro's water went to agriculture; but now, municipal consumption accounts for the majority, and the trend shows no signs of slowing. Sierra Vista, a place that didn't exist before the 1950s, is now home to nearly forty-three thousand people. More generally, the state of Arizona has also experienced an unprecedented boom in population: it has doubled since 1980, and is projected to double again, to about eleven million, by 2050. So it's not just the resurgence of Fort Huachuca we have to thank for the problems with the San Pedro—arthritis isn't helping either. Given its perfect weather, a whole lot of old folks have fled here, making Arizona the new Florida—only without any water, like a giant cruise ship run hideously aground.

Barbara Kingsolver, writing about the San Pedro River in

National Geographic magazine, describes the loss of water, but notes that "the San Pedro somehow perseveres." She is right—the cottonwoods and willows at least are blooming, suggesting a fairly plentiful water table below, but still, the aboveground river isn't going anywhere fast.

So instead of birds, what we find there that morning are signs of other migrants—the illegal, human kind who use this river's dense trees as a shelter against detection on their dangerous treks north towards work. It's terrifically depressing: empty water bottles, emptied cans of tuna fish, discarded clothes, even diapers—diapers, in this deadly desert? This is the detritus of migration, of rank poverty, and of hope against hope. Many of these poor folk spend upwards of five thousand dollars for some scumbag to drop them over the border and leave them to their fate: in 2005 alone, 282 migrants died crossing the border around here.

All along the edge of the river we find signs of passage, and we can't know if we're seeing the last possessions of a now-dead person, or the discardings of one who made it to a new life. What we do know is that just two miles south of us, at the border, the Minutemen are aiming rifles at those too poor or desperate to care that now is not the time to try to sneak into the United States. It gives me only slight comfort when Donna reminds me that many Arizonans leave food and water out on their properties for the migrants—a genuine act of love in a desert otherwise seemingly starved of it.

It's as if our discovery of these small camps, and the thought of the lives and deaths behind them, takes away our luck with the birds, for that morning pretty much all we see are a couple of Wilson's warblers standing in witness, their black "yarmulkes" perched on their shining yellow heads. Pretty birds, but fairly common even in New York's Central Park in spring. For a full hour we walk up and down the edge of the scant river, but we don't get the rushing flow of migrating birds we'd hoped for. Still, we scope a distant orchard oriole and a canyon towhee, another life bird for me. Back at the parking lot, there are a number of vermilion flycatchers, active, bright crimson birds who perch, then figure-eight out to catch some passing bugs, which they then swallow whole back on their branch. In season, the males will bring a particularly juicy insect to the female in hopes that she'll put out. (It's never worked for me.)

I'm ready for something else. For the vermilion flycatcher to become a ho-hum bird by nine A.M. on the first day I've ever seen one suggests something's not quite right. Don, ever sensitive to the mood of the party, picks up on our frustration.

"At this point, I'd take a MacGillivray's warbler, something like that. I'm not asking for much."

I can't tell if he's joking. So I check: "Are you joking?" The MacGillivray's would be an excellent find—a skulking under-story warbler of the West who is shyer than a teenager with acne.

"Not at all. Aspirational birding, my friend. It's been a slow start, but that's because we're not feeling it. Donna, am I right? You're not feeling it, are you? You don't have the Thing. I know I'm right. We're in Arizona, we have four days of this. Cheer up, people! This is Foot Locker!"

Don peers from behind his glasses. He's right. I could be in an office in New York; instead, I'm wandering along the San Pedro beneath cottonwoods. This I will concede, and do, as we sit in the car and plot our next move.

Ever since our first dedicated birding trip to New Jersey in spring 2004, we have guarded against not having the Thing by creating a count for each day, and each part of the day: before lunch; after lunch; grand total. We call it, amazingly enough, the Number. Within each Number there is also the "life bird" count, should we be so lucky, as well as two of our favorite topics at dinner, namely, "Bird of the Day" and "Birding Moment of the Day," which can be the same thing, but most often are not. As the self-appointed scribe of the group, it's my job to keep an exact list of everything we see so that there's no argument about the Number.

This is as close as we get to being listers. Most birders are listers, at least a little bit. I can, for example, tell you how many species of bird I've seen in the United States but only if I'm near a computer—mine's on an Excel spreadsheet. Don and Donna never know how many species they've seen, but that's because they've seen so many, not only here in the United States, but also across Central America and Europe. Not knowing the number says a lot—we'd much rather waste an hour enjoying a particularly beautiful bird than simply "getting" it and moving on. Some hard-core listers go after birds in the way trainspotters list engine numbers. The numbers such birders "acquire" can reach astronomical heights, but one wonders if they're in love with the birds or just the list.

As an example, in Central Park one winter, a group of regular birders happened upon a long-eared owl, an uncommon bird and one always worth discovering. But almost before they'd finished identifying it they'd hurried off away from it, down the path from the Shakespeare Garden, towards the chance of further birds on the day. I was quietly taken aback, given that owls are mostly nocturnal, not to mention exquisitely attractive. When you find one, it's worth spending extra time appreciating it. I was put in mind of the guy in Scott Weidensaul's book *Of a Feather*, who, on a trip to Central America, complained about seeing a violaceous trogon, a rare and iridescent wonder, by saying, "Why are we messing around with a bird we've already seen?"

That winter day in Central Park, I called Don to tell him that we had a long-eared; he fled his office, jumped in a cab, and joined me there with the owl. Just after he'd arrived, a group of elderly lady birders happened by, and asked us what we were so keenly enjoying.

"Long-eared, you say?" one of them yelled, clearly a bit short-eared herself.

We then spent a happy fifteen minutes helping the ladies up the muddy slope to a safe distance from the owl and showing them how to pick the bird out of the dense evergreens in which it was expertly camouflaged. For me this moment had everything that made birding so special: discovery, appreciation, community; not to mention that it was terrifically moving to watch the elderly ladies, who had presumably birded for many years, still gush girlishly at the beauty of a bird.

Nothing there about a list—this was not a life bird, didn't add to anything other than the dissemination of joy. But sometimes pure listing can get you back on track, so Don orders us to speak out loud how many birds we think we're going to get in Arizona before lunch.

"I say thirty-five," says Don, "fifteen of which will be life birds for Luke. Donna, what do you think?"

Donna likes this game, though she gets flustered when Don throws out a number before she has a chance to. Now, in her mind, there's a benchmark where previously there was only possibility; so she has to fight with herself about whether to go out on a limb with her guess or to stick close to Don's—he's often preternaturally spot-on.

"Don! Come on! You know that makes it harder for me." Donna stamps her foot in the dust. "Now I don't know. What did you say again?"

"Thirty-five."

Donna thinks for a second.

"I say . . . thirty-four."

I see my chance.

"Donna?"

"Yes, Luke?"

"You know what this means, right?"

"Do I?" She looks at me.

"If I say thirty-three, then thirty-five or above Don wins, thirty-three or below I win. You've just made it so that only thirty-four will deliver you the victory you so richly desire."

"Yes, Luke, but you're so bad at the Number that you won't say thirty-three. You'll say something ridiculous."

"Bite me."

Don, who can't stand an upset, even a joking one, intervenes. "Come on, Luke, the Number?"

"One hundred and four," I say, swinging the car out of the parking lot and back onto the main road.

It was time for a reading from the "Book of Green." Richard Cachor Taylor's magnificent and endlessly useful *A Birder's Guide to Southeast Arizona*, with its green cover, was our bible on this trip, and as Don intoned aloud from it as we drove, we realized that we were almost spoiled for choice. But there was a place not too far away that promised a host of birds we'd kill to see: Carr Canyon, in the Huachuca Mountains south of Sierra Vista. Taylor notes two in particular that set our hearts afire: a pair of warblers, the red-faced and the olive.

What Don neglected to make clear from his reading, however, was the bowel-loosening drive up the canyon. We climbed nearly two thousand feet via nine long zigzags, most of the upper parts of which were on an unpaved, single-track road that clings to the edge of a cliff. There was no guardrail. Don was whistling (merrily) and leaning out to take pictures of the view (spectacular). Donna, when her eyes were open, would yell at him not to fall out the window. I was simply working out how to change my underwear and still steer the car. Every once in a while we'd stop and look out across the Upper San Pedro River Valley towards Tucson, and the Santa Catalina mountains beyond. Then on we'd go, ever upwards, my transverse colon somewhere up near my larynx.

The lunchtime heat cooled as we reached the Ponderosa Pines of the Ramsey Vista Campground. We were 7,500 feet up, and pretty much the only people there, and as we wandered around the deserted campground, with its burned-out barbecue pits and leaky restrooms, I thought about how as a kid in such places, I couldn't wait to break free of cars and parents and simply run, run all over. On this dense carpet of pine needles you could fall and not care; you could hide and never be found; you could shout and laugh and think that childhood might be endless, and perfect, rather than too short, and all too compromised when looked back on from age.

And with that, I was broadsided by a mental image of my children's faces. It was often at such times they came to mind—somewhere spectacular, somewhere I'd want them to see. Here I could imagine *them* running free, from tree to tree, playing tag and pretending to be wild horses, their little dog, Princess, yapping at them and tearing around in glee.

I started to tell Donna what I was thinking about when suddenly the image of my girls was overwritten by what birders refer to as a traveling mixed flock, one of those mysterious moments when ten to twenty different species of bird appear all around you, and you have trouble keeping up with what is passing. Don and Donna started to hyperventilate, and not because of the altitude. We'd come this high in the canyon primarily in hopes of finding the startlingly beautiful red-faced warbler, a small gray bird with a scarlet and black head, and a close cousin of the Wilson's warbler we'd already seen that morning. Though it never showed that day, we were delivered of something equally amazing: many other warblers and songbirds, surging through the pines above our heads. Here, now, were the black-throated gray, Grace's, and Lucy's warblers, all flitting around, feeding and chirping, a feast of beauty, dripping from the trees. Don was giddy; Donna kept exclaiming, "There, there!" We'd see a bird, and it wouldn't be immediately clear what it was—this was, after all, a new set of birds in a new place. It was hell, then, to have to take our eyes off the birds and repair to a field guide to work them out, as Don called out the particulars: "Yellow face, but with a big black eye patch. Actually extends behind the eye. Two white wing bars. Black streaking on yellow breast. What is it, what it is? Can it be a Townsend's?"

I flipped the pages and there it was: Townsend's warbler. Then back to the binoculars, and another new bird would flit past the lens. And we'd look at it, call out details, consult the book, and look once more.

But with one bird, we didn't need the field guide at all. We had been taking a quick breath from all this tiny, flitting color when a zone-tailed hawk—a fine contrast to the warblers, being one of the darkest of all the hawks—passed to our west. But as the hawk disappeared, Don exclaimed, "Guys, guys! Quick!" And there perched the very best of all that day, right above us: the olive warbler, the name of which does not do justice to the vivid urgency of its olive-orange head and throat, the surety of its black face patch, the brightness of its white wing bars, and the comedy of its titmouse-like *pita pita pita* song. This last bird is happy only above seven thousand feet, so those last few hundred feet of terror were worth every inch. We turned this way and that, giddy with it; in my mind I saw a movie camera tracking around us, our smiles crazy, our laughter uncontrolled, carousel music playing. I said, "My girls would love this," but not loud enough for anyone but me to hear. Instead, I'd call out a bird and be almost disappointed it wasn't a lifer, but there were so many dancing above us that day amidst the ponderosa pines of Carr Canyon that I knew I was lost to it. This was the rest of my life, in a moment, given to me as a gift.

We would happily get such delights for the rest of the trip, but all would be for naught if we didn't find a particular and solitary bird, and a distant cousin of the violaceous trogon, the bird that the guy in Central America didn't want to see more than once.

The elegant trogon is a real rarity, one of those neotropical species whose northernmost range extends only to southeast Arizona, and then only at elevations above four thousand feet. It joins others like the aplomado falcon, flame-colored tanager, and boreal owl, to name just three, as the most coveted birds to see in all of North America. It has been claimed that up to twenty-five thousand people a year travel to Cave Creek Canyon, near Portal, to chase the elegant trogon (and other birds, of course). So popular is the trogon that according to the Cornell Lab of Ornithology, by the mid-1970s it was viewed as an "important socioeconomic factor in the state."

It's also damn beautiful. Cuckoo-sized, these magnificent birds boast a bright red lower breast, a gleaming white chest band, and a green head and back; they have long tails and a strong yellow beak. Best of all, according to Don, who once saw one in Costa Rica, they turn their heads so slowly as to make the movement almost imperceptible. It gives the bird an air of almost unanswerable superiority, like a nun in a classroom.

Probably because of its hard-won moral certitude, the elegant trogon is a skittish bird, and any look at it would be a fortunate one indeed. Studies show that it spends no more than 4 percent of its daylight hours perching—the rest of the time it spends flying or foraging or making out, meaning that it doesn't stay still much at all. Plus, the territory for each nesting pair is thought to be at least a mile long, meaning that even in a place known for its trogon sightings, there ain't many of them around. But Don was determined to see it in North America; his enthusiasm was infectious; and much of our trip was now predicated on its discovery.

With the bird in mind, the next morning we drive across southeast Arizona heading for Cave Creek on the far side of the Chiricahuas, through a boggling expanse of table-flat deserts and high mountains. At a half-a-horse town called Apache, Arizona, a few miles shy of a two-horse town called Rodeo, New Mexico, we stop and scope the desert from Geronimo's surrender monument, a phallic stone that proclaims the surrender to have "forever ended Indian warfare in the United States." In the distance, we watch a flouncing golden eagle hunt the plains, dark and huge in the heat haze.

Up above four thousand feet, South Fork Cave Creek's clear and bubbling stream is edged by Arizona sycamores and bigtooth maples. We are here because a recent blog posting had indicated the return of an elegant trogon to this very spot—good news indeed. We park at the Stewart Campground at the base of the creek and start our walk, trying to step lightly, and talking only in whispers.

Deep in the canopy, probably half a mile upstream, we hear the deep croaking sound of a bird. Could it be? Don and Donna have brought with them their iPod, and we quickly circle around it as Don spins the dial to the call of the elegant trogon. The iPod is now an invaluable tool for identifications; we hear a bird, find the song on the machine, huddle around the buds, listen, then go back to the bird in nature. So is the sound we just heard really that of an elegant trogon? The trick of distance, and even the minute it takes to find the sound on the machine, leaves us unsure.

"Shh! Listen!" we hiss at each other, as the bird calls again. It's closer, but the canopy is dense. "There!" Don squeaks out the word as a flash of something flies past us high in the thick brush, heading farther up the canyon. Is that the elegant trogon? If so, we need to head up the trail to relocate it.

Donna whispers, "Let's split up, leave a hundred feet between us, signal if we see anything."

It's a good idea. We'll need six eyes at different parts of the forest if we're ever to find this bird. In a way, we're mimicking what birds do when they flock—one theory for the avian phenomenon is that when a predator is around, a thousand eyes are better than two. I go up ahead; Donna comes with me but stops after a while, whereas Don and his iPod stay down where we'd first heard it. Have we seen it? I so want to think we have, but it was not a good look, and now I sense a desperation in us as we signal up and down the trail: palms to the sky, over and over, a shrug, nothing seen.

We spend an hour this way, but the thumbs-up never comes. We don't even hear the call anymore. The canyon climbs another two thousand feet or so, and we could scale it, but as I look down the trail, I see Don sitting on a rock, his feet near the water, and I know we're done.

We cluster together and discuss our options.

"I think we saw it," says Donna.

"Oh, we definitely saw it," says Don, "but we saw it fly up the mountain."

"Are you sure we saw it?" I say. "It was a flash, and it could have been a crow, or a raven, or even a small raptor." Size is impossible to judge at that speed, in this heavy stand of trees.

"I think we did," says Donna.

"I think we *want* to," I say. "It could have been any bird of the trogon's size. We saw no color; we saw no real shape. We want to see it, so we now think we did. I don't think we can claim it."

"You make a valid point," Don says glumly, looking at his shoes.

"I think we could claim an elegant trogon. Don is usually pretty good with his guesses," says Donna.

I'm truly surprised at her.

"But you're so careful, Donna. You never give in to birding desire."

"I know," she says, looking at Don.

Don looks up at Donna, and I look away. We're all sitting now on a log by the river. The day is clear. The light catches the top of the highest pines, and behind them, shines hard on the mountains. The river stalls at our feet, then babbles away.

Eventually, Don speaks: "There is a difference between merely *getting* a bird, and *seeing* it. I could almost say for sure that we just *got* an elegant trogon, but we didn't have anything like a satisfying look. We can count it for a damn list, but it's not nearly enough."

He lets the day settle a little more. Then he stands up and says, "A photo."

Don walks away, places his digital camera on a rock, sets the timer, and comes and sits down. We don't smile; the shutter shuts.

Slouching under the eastern slopes of the Chiricahua Mountains, a few miles from Cave Creek, the tiny town of Portal is settled against the rock like a chick in a nest. It's a quaint little place, with a café and a post office and around 4.2 million birders. If you're visiting Portal, you're either one of us or you're lost.

For many years, a couple called the Spoffords had a house in Portal that welcomed birders to watch its many feeders. They died recently, alas, but despite the loss of access to the Spoffords' property, birders can still see plenty of birds in town. We got three separate oriole species in five minutes—Scott's, Bullock's, and hooded—and they were all life birds, if briefly apperceived.

Sadly, it wasn't all perfect: Donna was eating the last of a much-needed Reese's peanut butter cup and missed a brief visit to a feeder of a lazuli bunting, a Western bird that Easterners such as us rarely see. Now, one of us had "seen" the elegant trogon, and two of us had seen the lazuli bunting, but both experiences didn't add up to three entirely happy people. *A bird seen by any is better seen by all.* We did everything we could to summon the bunting back, but to no avail.

Was the trogon a vision, the bunting a waking dream? We might never know. All that was left was to load up the car once again and head back to Ramsey Canyon.

By now our birding trips had become fairly major logistical operations. We carried binoculars, spotting scopes, iPods, birding guides, maps, snacks, various clothing options including any number of hats, travel guides, itineraries, suntan lotion, bug spray by the gallon, and one each of pretty much everything else you can imagine. All this stuff made us look like a small private army.

Once again, however, Don had lost his baseball cap.

"Sweetie! Sweetie!" he trilled at Donna in the back seat. "I've lost my favorite hat again, sweetie! The one from Costa Rica, the one with the coati stitched onto it . . ." His voice trailed off as if a combination of self-reproach and a sense of cosmic injustice had rendered him powerless against the fates.

From the back of the car, Donna very sweetly pointed out that he was, in fact, wearing it.

The drive back from Portal was a long one, and as there was still some light, another reading from the Book of Green convinced us to break up the ride with a stop at an inn by the trickling San Pedro.

Standing at the fence was the Englishman who runs the place. When we arrived, he was avidly birding, and barely noticed us pull up; it looked to us like he'd been there all day—there were deep dents in the grass under his feet.

As we got out of the car, he greeted us, and instantly displayed one of the strongest upper-class British accents I've ever heard. So strong was it that I was momentarily convinced that he was, like the guys in the deli before him, speaking Welsh:

"You're welcome to bird the pwoperty. We have a ban*al*. In the barn."

"A ban*al*?"

"Ears, a ban*al*."

"Really?"

"Ears, scope's all set up at-side."

"That's lovely. A ban*al*, you say?"

"Ears, a furmail ban*al*. Fail free to take a look-see."

"A ban*al*. Nice."

"Ears, it *is* rather! People enjoy it."

"I'm sure they do."

"You can't beat a laffly look at a ban*al*."

"That's what I always say. Thank god for a ban*al*."

"Of course, it's fanny that it's trerrly in a barn."

"I was going to say the same thing."

"A ban*al* in a barn. Laffly!"

[Pause]

Then his accent momentarily cleared and he said, "You don't know what I'm saying, do you?"

"Not a clue," I replied.

Later, after we'd finally seen the laffly ban*al* and taken a walk across darkening fields to watch a loggerhead shrike aggressively dusk-hunting off some barbed wire, we headed back to the lodge and found Mr. Ban*al* still standing where we'd left him, the dents in the grass even deeper. As the light was fading and birding becoming almost impossible, we were able to engage him in semi-understandable conversation, but we were as bemused as ever when he described his life before Arizona. Texas ("Ticks-iss") we understood, even New Mexico ("N-maxica"), but one phrase left us bereft of comprehension.

"It's all a long way from being the come trawler off the Caveman's Lands."

Was everyone in this part of Arizona Cro-Magnon? Whatever it was he claimed he'd been, it sounded pretty serious, not to mention disgusting. Though he had proved to be charmingly odd, there wasn't much left of our day, and with attempts at cheery, though careful, waves, we left Mr. Ban*al* to his birds.

The barn owl in his barn really was lovely, though. Ears, trerrly laffly.

Back at Ramsey Canyon, we walk down the hill after dinner into the most beautiful light of the day, a hazy ending. But just as we're enjoying the stroll, up the hill towards us speeds a Ford Explorer. Don says, "Uh-oh, Minutemen."

We stop, ready to abuse them roundly. As the car passes us, it screeches to a halt (causing Donna's knee to buckle again and her eyes to slam shut), and the driver's-side window slowly winds down.

"How ya doin'? Anyone got time to go see some owls?"

"Wezil!" says Don, as Donna opens her eyes. It is, against all odds, Mr. Walraven himself, unexpectedly delivered to us like a rare and unexpected migrant.

"Come on, you losers, jump in."

A man with a name like Wezil Walraven should resemble something out of a J. R. R. Tolkien novel, and I am a bit surprised to find he's a perfectly handsome middle-aged man with a ready smile and the look of someone for whom human beings are sort of beside the point. As Don and Donna remake his acquaintance and introduce me, it is clear that all he wants to do is go scan the trees and the skies and find birds. There's a warm vacancy to him, and we jump into the back of the car quickly, as the light fades a little more.

Sitting next to Wezil in the passenger seat is a man who has presumably paid him well to show him around for the day, but no matter—Wezil seems too fond of sharing his knowledge to worry about the little issue of an exclusive financial arrangement.

Once we reach the trailhead, word has clearly spread. A small gang, maybe ten people, are standing fifty feet from the foot of a bigtooth maple, next to where a bubbling stream crosses the road. Wezil sets up his spotting scope, points to the tree, and says, "That hole, halfway up, is where he's nesting. He comes out just before dusk, and often bathes in the ford. A whiskered screech owl. It's really a Mexican bird."

(I read later that like other screech owls, this bird will actually defend any number of possible nest sites. Most birds find a single site to nest, defend it vigorously, then build. This guy, however, is basically a rich Manhattanite with the equivalent of an apartment here, a house in the Hamptons, and another place down in Florida.)

Wezil continues: "He's hard to tell apart from a *western* screech owl. The whiskered likes to nest a bit higher, about five thousand feet, which helps tell 'em apart. Sounds different too.

"Anyway, folks, look! It's showtime."

At "look," all eyes go to the tree, and then something unforgettable happens: As Wezil reaches the "w" in "showtime," the bird's head slips up and out of the hole in the tree. There it is, right on cue, yet another life bird (I wish the short-eared ladies from Central Park were here). I am amazed by Wezil's ability to read light so perfectly. He had noticed what to the rest of us was an imperceptible shift in the tenor of the evening, just enough that he knew the exact conditions by which the owl would appear and begin preparations to take its bath in the ford and then go out on its nighttime hunt. I understand then I will only ever be a keen amateur.

Wezil's gifts to us this night continue. Later, farther down the hill, he brings us to a family of elf owls, which, at just over five inches each, are the smallest owls in the world (they're a tiny bit smaller than a European starling). Hilariously squawking on a telegraph pole, they resemble misbehaving puppies; their little yelps even make them sound like tiny dogs.

The last gift is a less concrete one, and is not only of perception, but also of affection. To him we aren't strangers, we are part of a set of people for whom the natural world means more than being hired to do a job. Commerce can't compete with an owl who needs a bath, nor does it seem to mean all that much to a man who can show you where, on this entire planet, you can laugh at the antics of the smallest owls of all.

Before he left for the evening, Wezil told us that there was an accessible spot for us to see an elegant trogon in Garden Canyon. This meant nothing to me until later when Don explained that Garden Canyon is slap bang in the middle of Fort Huachuca, the massive military base on the edge of Sierra Vista. First thing next morning, before daylight fully arrived, we found ourselves driving back down Ramsey Canyon and towards the fort.

In early 1877, a camp was established in the Huachuca Mountains, mainly because of its strategic importance (you could see the entire valley below) and because Apaches were going nuts all over the area, given that the U.S. government had done away with the Chiricahua Apache Reservation the previous year. The camp also helped block traditional Apache escape routes to Mexico, sixty-five miles to the south. Later, it became the base for the war against Geronimo, but once he had surrendered for the last time (on his fourth attempt at giving up) in 1886, the place lost a bit of its prestige, except for just before the First World War when it was the home to the Buffalo Soldiers, the legendary guys who went after Pancho Villa. Through the rest of the twentieth century it was at a bit of a loss, whistling to itself so as not to be noticed, hidden as it was in the peaceful Southwest. Then, in the late 1950s and early 1960s, it got new life when it became one of the country's main electronic and communications testing centers. It is now the spy and gadget center of the U.S. military, and as such, it's maintained with a level of security that would shock a Scientologist.

Fort Huachuca, and especially Garden Canyon, is also a place of extreme natural beauty, as well as an excellent habitat for rare birds. We arrived at seven A.M. to find a long line of cars with locals entering to work at the base, and amongst them, a few vehicles that were clearly filled with birders. We knew they were birders because even their cars smelled bad.

We had time to kill, and what happens at such moments is that Don feels the need to get my dietary preferences straight.

"So, I have a question to ask you," said Don, as the line into Fort Huachuca crept along. This was an old game.

"Tomatoes, right?"

"No. I was wondering if you had given any more thought to what Mr. Banal actually said to us."

"It was a barn owl, Don."

"Not that. The Caveman's Lands thing. Very intriguing, yes?"

"I suppose so," I said. A quiet moment.

Phew. I'd gotten away with it.

Then Don said, "You don't like anything with tomatoes, yes?"

"No, Don, he likes pizza. Right, Luke?" Donna was, as ever, the picture of serenity.

"Donna's right—I officially like pizza."

"What about tomato-based sauces on pasta? A nice Bolognese, for example. How about it?"

"Fine," I said, my teeth beginning to clench.

"Very interesting," said Don, warming to the task. "Let me ask you this: Do you like tomato sliced thinly on a sandwich?"

"You know he doesn't," said Donna, sagely.

"Well, I *think* I know it, but I need to check. So, Luke, tomato on a sandwich. What's your final position?"

"As I told you last week in New Jersey, and a few weeks ago in Central Park: No, I would not choose sliced tomato on a sandwich."

"Fascinating!" Don always rates this as a revelation. "What is it that you don't like? It can't be the flavor. You like other tomatoey things."

"I have no idea, Don. Why do *you* like or dislike the things you like or dislike?"

"We're not talking about me. I love all tomatoes. I am consistent. But you do not display the same array of reliable reactions to foodstuffs as me. Your position on bananas, for example, is utterly confusing."

By now, we'd reached the checkpoint, and I told the soldier we were here to bird. He, in turn, told us to go park and apply at a little office across the way, though as he pointed, he used his other hand to pick up the receiver of a large red telephone. This may have been because next to me Don was muttering, "I got it," over and over.

We parked, and all agreed it would be best if Donna and I handled the paperwork. Access to the base required form filling, passport/green card showing (you needed at least one U.S. citizen with you in order to be allowed on, though even that has subsequently been changed now and then to bar all noncitizens), not to mention obsequiousness towards the military, all things at which Don probably wouldn't excel.

As we walked to the office to show our papers, from the car we heard Don's voice through an open window, "I got it! Tomato soup! What's your take on it?"

By now, the unspoken thing between us was the fear that we would not see the elegant trogon at all. We had only one more full day—today—and it wasn't looking good. Though we'd made it through the checkpoint and onto the base despite our suspicious behavior, we didn't feel any better about our chances. Surely all this ordnance would drive away great big hawks and eagles, let alone already-skittish trogons. That said, there was no real need for us to be glum—it had been one of our greatest ever birding experiences. Arizona was eye-delightful, and we'd seen already nearly 120 birds on the trip, which was perfectly good given how little time we'd had. Most significantly, 60-some of them had been life birds for me, making the trip outstanding. But Don, I knew, felt that the success of the trip now depended on the elegant trogon. As we drove past a bunch of soldiers shooting guns at a distant target, he said as much—but with the windows firmly up: "Good for you, boys, learning how to kill. Very nice. Lovely way to spend a morning."

He waved sarcastically, and one of the grunts gave a friendly wave back. Chagrined, Don put his hands in his lap and continued.

"I'm not saying that the trip will be for naught if we don't see the trogon," he said. "It will just make it so much more . . . you know?"

"Don't! Don't say it, Don! Donald, don't say it! No!' Donna was barking like an elf owl. We held to the superstitious belief that if you want it too much, or actually say it out loud, the bird surely won't come. Don stopped talking and went back to watching the soldiers.

We were heading up Garden Canyon. Wezil had told us that the first picnic area boasted an easily found elegant trogon. It was Monday; Walraven had warned us against weekends there. The picnic areas on Saturdays and Sundays were said to be usually filled with folks from the base letting off steam, and were therefore pretty much useless for birding—too many cookouts, too much Wiffle ball. But at least early that Monday morning we figured we'd have the place pretty much to ourselves.

Oh, how wrong we were.

Down by the creek, massed like an army of Saracens, a group of about forty elderly birders and their guide marched back and forth under the willows. As we got out of the car and started to get our spotting scope set up, we could hear their guide calling out birds as though it were a game of avian bingo: "PAINTED REDSTART! PAINTED REDSTART! OVER HERE! CLICKETY CLICK, SIXTY-SIX—PAINTED REDSTART! TWO FAT LADIES, EIGHTY-EIGHT! RED-START, REDSTART!"

In my mind, the last two elegant trogons in North America heard this shrieking voice and fled for Mexico, never to return. Oh, good sweet Jesus, strike this woman dumb.

Donna said, "Luke, don't say anything. They're old. They probably can't hear."

"Donna, you already know my views on the elderly. I do *not* understand why they get to behave badly just because they're old. It's not a good enough excuse. Plus, old-man smell? Can we have a moment about old-man smell? What is that?"

At this, Don, who had momentarily wandered away, said, "Flycatcher."

"What do you think it is?" Donna asked of no one in particular.

"What do I think it is? I think it's pee," I said.

"What?" said Donna.

"Old-man smell." What is she, an idiot?

"No, Luke, our *flycatcher*. What do you think it is?"

"Oh! I have no idea. I haven't seen it properly yet."

Squeamish Don, perhaps fearing he'd have to hear more on the old-man smell question, marched purposefully towards a small tree, in which the difficult *Empidonax* flycatcher plied its trade, and we followed him. After testing a number of hypotheses, we came to the conclusion that the busy bird was probably a buff-breasted flycatcher—a life bird, naturally, its range being so limited in the United States—but without hearing it vocalize, it was difficult to know for sure. *Empidonax* flycatchers are all similar in appearance; their songs are what give them away, though the buff-breasted is the smallest, and the most easily identified when silent.

Not that if the flycatcher *did* sing we'd have heard it. By now, the group and their guide had come walking back from the creek towards where we stood in the glade. The guide, a woman in her middle age, continued to call out the names of birds as though her clients were not merely old but also actually deaf from birth. She had found a song sparrow, and apparently it was the first one ever discovered in southeast Arizona—the first ever, in fact, given her screaming, in the contiguous United States.

"SONG SPARROW! LEGS ELEVEN!"

I had had enough, and gently called across to her to quiet down. She ignored me; I am used to this, being both balding and short. After a few more foghorn calls to her clients, I again asked her to please keep her peace. This time, she broke away from the group and strode towards us. Don and Donna took this as their cue to walk away, leaving me to face her alone.

The woman's handshake was lettuce-like. I liked her already.

"Jane Doe. You seem to have a problem with my group."

"No, actually, I don't," I said. "But I *do* have a problem with *your* behavior. You're shouting. It's unacceptable."

The woman looked as though I'd called her a bitch, which, trust me, had never crossed my mind.

"No, you're the ones with the problem. We've been here for half an hour, and we've been having a great time until you arrived. I'm working with elderly people here, and it's their first time birding, so I'm making sure that no one misses anything."

"You're kidding me, right?" My eloquence, when faced with intransigent stupidity, knows no bounds. Nor is there any limit to my ability to get self-righteous. The American Birding Association has a section in its ethics principles specifically for group birding, and the woman had broken any number of rules already. Rule 4(c), for example, insists that "[group leaders] be an exemplary ethical role model for the group. Teach through word and example." If only I could have quoted this at her verbatim then, with the "(c)" and everything. I'd like to claim this would have not just been so that I could prove myself to be the world's most ridiculous prig. On the contrary, he lied, I was trying to help her: her behavior was almost hilariously self-defeating—making this racket was the very best way to *not* deliver birds to her clients.

Instead, I said this: "This is their first time, and you're teaching them the ethics of birding by screaming out loud every time you see a bird? How long have you been a guide?"

"More than twenty years."

"And you never learned the code? That you should do nothing—including making way too much noise—to disturb nesting birds?"

"These people are old, and many of them are hard of hearing."

"You make a living being a guide, and you seem unable to modify your behavior when other birders are present. We've been trying to see an elegant trogon for days, and you've probably blown our last chance."

"Well, you clearly don't know the first thing about birds," she said, in an almost overwhelmingly conciliatory manner. "If you did, you'd know my talking loudly will not affect whether or not the elegant trogon comes to the canyon. It's either here, or it isn't. You're just going to have to get over yourself." And with that, she turned and rejoined her group.

By this point, I was ready to maim. I indeed knew less than some about birds, but I was pretty sure that screaming under their nests was one of the best ways to scare them off, and much worse, cause distress, even failure, in their attempts to reproduce. The three of us had run into unprofessional birding guides in New York City, for sure—a certain young guy in Prospect Park was a one-man wrecking crew from whom we steered well clear whenever possible—but for some reason, I thought we'd find better here in Garden Canyon. Wezil Walraven had been impeccable in his behavior with the owls the previous night, only gradually shining his flashlight on them for the briefest of seconds; but this woman clearly saw herself as just another tourist guide. She could have been pointing out landmarks in the middle of Manhattan—"Look, that's where Carrie throws up in *Sex and the City!*"—and it was clear she was making a fabulous living off it too, if her ostentatiously non-eco-friendly vehicles were anything to go by. After a few more minutes belting out the names of the birds, she and her group piled into two huge SUVs—if I remember correctly, they strapped a couple of the old folks onto the roof rack—and away they screeched, through a low ford and up the canyon. But not before I'd gotten her name off the side of her car and written it down in the back of my birding guide. If she had indeed done what we feared she'd done—taken away our last chance of a trogon—I was going to shame her ass, and the rest of her, in the birding community. She had clearly forgotten the old adage: Never mess with a short, balding Brit looking for an elegant trogon at a picnic area in a military base in southeast Arizona.

Don and Donna were now beyond the ford, pacing and looking solemnly into the trees. When I rejoined them, Don's blood was up, though his voice was down.

"Sorry, Luke, but if I'd spoken to her, I'm not sure what I'd-a said."

"That's OK. She didn't get it at all. Felt she did nothing wrong."

"What a bitch," Donna said, speaking for us all.

Now, though, we were at an utter loss. Not only had the search for the trogon turned ugly, but we had heard nothing in the canyon to suggest it was around, noisy guide or no. Worst of all, its absence probably wasn't even her fault, which made us feel doubly cheated.

I had been vaguely aware, out of the corner of my anger, that another couple had been birding the glade for the last fifteen minutes and had probably seen my confrontation. After a while they joined us, and the man spoke, though notably softly:

"She's notorious. Never mind it. I saw her last year with a huge group. She was just as bad. You don't need a license, sadly, to be a guide."

"We're just worried that she's blown our chances of the elegant trogon," I said, as plaintively as I felt.

"No, she hasn't," the man said. "Look over there."

Sometimes, that's what love is: after searching so hard, you finally find what you so desired, and then you run away. When a male elegant trogon appeared that Monday morning on an Emory oak fifty feet from us, Don instantly turned tail and ran to the rental car, parked a good half mile away by this point, to get the spotting scope and the camera. I was scared to death he'd miss his "satisfying looks," but I needn't have worried. The bird stayed for nearly half an hour, enough time, in fact, for Don to make his trademark lapping sounds, which he saves for only the most pretty birds—*slurp, slurp, slurp,* he goes, signaling just how much he loves what he's looking at. Long enough, too, for him to realize how ridiculous he sounded and say, "I'm just drinking the bird in," so that our new friends didn't think he was having trouble breathing; for them to take turns with our scope to get the best looks possible; for Don and Donna to argue over the correct setting on their digital camera as they took as many pictures as they liked; for us to forget all about Jane Doe; and oh yes, enough time, too, for Wezil Walraven to arrive with a birding group, and for *us* to be able to show *him* something.

Enough time, too, for Walraven to give his group, and us, yet another lesson in birding etiquette. My favorite photograph from that morning is not, in fact, the wonderful ones Don and Donna took of the elegant trogon; rather, it's a picture of Walraven gazing through his binoculars in awe at the bird, as though it weren't the hundredth time he'd seen one. And around him, a group of birders learn from him all about what's most important in the world.

Having ironically avoided the Patagonia rest stop, now famous for lending its name to a birding theory that the more birders bird a particular spot, the more rare birds are found, we went instead to the nearby Patagonia–Sonoita Creek Preserve. The most notable thing we discovered there was that Don and Donna were dressed like twins; we hadn't noticed all morning, but once we realized, it was actually quite upsetting. It seemed to put us off our stride, and something about finally getting the elegant trogon had reduced our birding fervor a bit in any case.

We'd finished birding the preserve by two, had lunch in the quaint town of Patagonia, and as it was now mid-afternoon hot, we went back to the Book of Green to see if it could revivify us. Sure enough, it took no prompting to get Don and Donna to accompany me to the Patons' home on Pennsylvania Avenue. As Richard Cachor Taylor coyly notes, even when the fun dries up in the major heat of the afternoon, "There are more hummers at the Patons' . . . than at any other place in . . . Arizona."

Don was entirely nonplussed by my giggling at this. Double entendres being a generally closed book to him, how was I to explain that "hummers" are not only big SUVs, but are also the peculiarly vocal sexual favors that drivers of said vehicles hope owning one will get them? No matter. He was as desperate as I was to spend time at the famous Patons' property, even if he had no idea how many hummers he'd be happy with.

"We could get a lot, honestly," Don said, ignoring my smile. "People sometimes lose count."

The place owned by Marion Paton and her late husband, Wally, is unprepossessing, but for many birders it's the best place in Arizona. She keeps many feeders hanging from the eaves of the low-slung house, and birders are invited to stop in and see what's there at any time of the day. She and her husband had not only established all these feeders across the years, but also provided some chairs to sit on, a bunch of birding guides, and eventually even a canopy to save birders from the hot Arizona sun. I read somewhere that because of the storms that come through here, she's on her seventh tent, which seems almost biblical.

We'd been there a few minutes when the great lady appeared. Mrs. Paton hurried about, filling up all the feeders with sugar water and giving a running commentary. At one point, as she reached up to a feeder, I swear she seemed to hang on to it a bit too long, as though she were suspended from it; then, she sort of Tarzaned to the next one, clung on for dear life, swinging in the breeze until the feeder was filled, and so on until she finished. It was a bit like watching Ed Viesturs summit Mount Everest; I imagine the IMAX movie of Marion Paton replenishing her feeders would be something to see.

I could barely look at it straight on, so afraid was I that she'd fall. I needn't have worried; she was entirely in control of the proceedings. In any case, there was a sign inviting visitors to contribute to the sugar fund—it takes pounds and pounds and pounds of sugar every week to keep the feeders running—so to take my mind off her fantastic acrobatics I walked over to the little bucket and filled it with nickels. By the time I came back, Mrs. Paton was gone. I guessed she was in a bariatric chamber, replenishing herself after her arduous climb.

It was wonderfully restful, there under the awning. For a while I closed my eyes and listened to the day. When I opened my eyes, in the space of half an hour I was delivered of four wonderful hummers, as birders unironically call them—Anna's hummingbird, a broad-billed hummingbird, the rufous hummingbird, and the best of all, the violet-crowned hummingbird, yet another rarity, with its shining white belly, violet head, and strong red bill. It hovered for a moment at a feeder by the corner of the house and was gone. We could probably be nowhere else in America and so reliably see this bird as at Marion Paton's.

And let's be clear what such hovering consists of: in that one second we saw it, the violet-crowned hummingbird beat its wings around thirty-four times. It's a number to boggle the mind; I can't even conceive of doing anything thirty-four times every second. This felt like the most salient fact about the world that I could muster, right then. And many times since. When I squeeze onto a train in Manhattan, or when I'm stuck in traffic getting out of Manhattan, or when someone is screaming at me on the phone about a tiny, tiny thing, more often than not what comes to mind is this fact: somewhere in southeast Arizona, a bird is beating its wings thirty-four times a second. It does so to enable itself to extract much-needed sustenance from Mrs. Paton's feeders, or from flowers, whichever it can find. As we pave over the flowers, the commitment of citizen birders like Mrs. Paton, just like that of her husband before her, will become even more critical. There on Pennsylvania Avenue—the irony of the address was not lost on me—Marion Paton's actions were so selfless as to be a manifestation of the good, and seemed a fitting punctuation to the magic that was this corner of America. We'd come expecting rare birds, but we'd found rare people too.

That night, our last in Arizona, we decided to celebrate the elegant trogon, the ban*al*, the olive warbler, and my getting four hummers. And so, inevitably, after four days of birding—days which pointedly did not include the lazuli bunting for Donna in Portal, or the red-faced warbler in Carr Canyon for any of us—we found ourselves at dusk back at the general store where four days earlier Don's egg had not been salted. Early Man was nowhere to be seen—he was probably holed up in a cave in Ramsey Canyon somewhere, lighting fires to keep marauding mammoths at bay. By night, the place had bizarrely transformed itself into a liquor store. We weren't sure how they'd managed it, but what a few hours earlier had been an egg-and-bacon joint was now selling cases of Budweiser and bottles of Jack Daniel's. Who were we to argue? All we wanted was a few Coronas and a good night's sleep. Back out in the parking lot, as the evening was still warm, I wondered aloud about how to keep the beers ice-cold.

As we contemplated what to do, Don suddenly ejaculated: "I've got it!"

With a sigh I said, "I've already told you a million times since Huachuca, I *love* tomato soup. Can we please change the—"

"No, not that," said Don. "I know what he said."

"Who?" said Donna.

"Mr. Ban*al*. He wasn't some 'come trawler off the Caveman's Lands.' He was the comptroller of the Cayman Islands."

"Oh thank god," said Donna.

The light shifted once more, and I imagined owls preparing for their showtimes all over these mountains.

Then Donna said, "We have earned the coldest beer known to mankind."

Don said, "We have a cooler. It's in the trunk."

"Perfect!" I exclaimed.

I flipped the trunk from the inside—it being impossible to do from the outside, what with the broken lock—and hopped out to get the cooler. What I found, however, as the trunk slowly yawned, was the stench of unmitigated death.

"Holy mother of Jesus!" I yelled. "Something crawled in the trunk and died!"

And for the second time that short week, Don and Donna Graffiti appear at the trunk of our car, and sheepishly try to explain.

"We just thought it would be nice," Donna says.

"Nice?"

Don says, "We packed the cooler before we left—before we

left *Brooklyn*, that is—with some cheeses: Emmental, Gouda, a nice brie. We kept meaning to have a picnic, we really did, but we seem to have forgotten we brought it. You know how it is—why waste time eating when there's all these wonderful birds to see?"

"You're telling me that cooler is filled with cheese?"

"Yes," admits Donna.

"And it's been in the hot trunk of our car since we arrived in Phoenix, four days ago?"

"Bingo," say Don and Donna, in perfect unison.

"You brought cheese to the desert."

I can't believe I'm saying these words at seven o'clock in the evening, thousands of miles from home.

"Candy bar," says Don, as he and Donna head back into the general store to buy god knows what.

NOW WHAT?

Princess, the dog, is barking; it's four ten in the morning. She is, like the singer Michael Jackson before her (allegedly), a *frotteur*; if you fail to constantly massage her poodle pudenda, and other scraggy bits of dog, she moans and whines and won't leave you be. The payoff is that she's not much of a barker, and never at night. I'm grateful for this: getting kids to stay asleep, especially when a marriage ends, can be tough.

I'm back in Astoria, where I lived for ten years. Tonight I'm baby- and house-sitting. Suzanne is away on business in Florida, the state Don told me yesterday he's chosen for our next spring trip. He's regaled me with tales of mangrove cuckoos, and limpkins, and La Sagra's flycatchers. "If you think Arizona was something, wait till you get to Florida," he said. He's already researching the best places to go and compiling a list of great birds to see. For the next few months, every conversation will at some point come around to Florida. This is especially true in the dead of winter, the snow piled up on city streets, birds as far from us as possible. But for now, it's four ten in the morning in the fall, and Don's probably asleep in his house in Brooklyn. I'm wide awake in Queens, and the Jacko of dogs is going whacko downstairs.

My kids and my ex-wife obtained the pooch the week I moved out. We all drove in the rain to an animal shelter in some godforsaken town in industrial New Jersey. An hour passed as a military macaw gnawed at its bars, now and then trying to blaspheme, though it clearly didn't know how. I noted to myself, as I would *not* have a couple of years before, that there are fewer than ten thousand of these birds left in the world; the pet trade has decimated them. This is not the only thing from that year I sometimes wish I could forget.

Eventually, a sad black poodle shuffled out from the back rooms where it had, that very day, been fixed for life. Two five-year-old girls cooed and fell in love; their mother too. The dog was woozy with its recent physiological loss, and lay around our feet as we looked over the paperwork. We swallowed whole the story about a new landlord and how he wouldn't allow pets; put a blanket over the car upholstery; watched as the lights of approaching New York City died as we disappeared into the Lincoln Tunnel.

I wasn't being replaced.

One thing the shelter woman had said before we left was that Princess barks but only at strangers, and this makes Suzanne feel a bit safer in her now-emptier house. I see my kids on Tuesdays and Thursdays, every other weekend, and when needed, such as now. The poodle yowls and squalls every time I ring the doorbell, but when the kids let me in, I often reach down to pet her until she calms. She seems a bit afraid of me, but then I've never much cared for dogs.

Now, nearly two years later, she's going batshit downstairs.

I swing my legs off the old marriage bed and stand. The blue sheets are tangled up from the dream I'd been having, one in which I was being shot at with small magnetic objects. I pull on a T-shirt from my old drawer and head down. When I get there, Princess is frantic at the front door. For some reason, I leave her be and step into the living room. Instantly, I know something is wrong, though I don't know what exactly.

Then I see that the TV's cable box is rebooting itself, but not in its usual way. Instead, it too is going batshit, the LED

readout spewing random letters and numbers and general gob-
bledygook. Out in the hallway, the dog continues to hurl herself
at the front door. I sit on the couch and wait.

He's passing over. I don't think that then—I'm too busy trying not to soil myself—but in the cold light of morning I know it.
I don't even believe in such balderdash. But in this case it's clear:
he's passing over again.

It's fifteen years to the day since my father died. Back then,
in 1990, in his last hours he told my mother that he was "waiting
for a sunny day." Francis Kilvert, the nineteenth-century preacher
whose diary I reread every year, describes one Welsh morning as
breaking "cloudless, after a sharp frost," and I suppose that's the
sort of thing my father had in mind.

Bright September Tuesdays. That Tuesday, in 1990, the day
did indeed break cloudless, after a sharp frost. Dad's oxygen tank
was little use at the end; he drowned in his own congested heart,
like a fisherman. My mother said his death was beautiful, but as
Lou Reed puts it, "You can't always trust your mother." In the
funeral home, they dressed him in a stole, as though he were a
priest. He was a dead civilian wearing the Sacred Heart of Jesus.
My brother took me and made me see him, in case I didn't believe that it was true.

It's not possible to look at some things straight on. There in
the chapel, I brought to mind a *Life* magazine photograph of
children in India, looking at an eclipse. They were using mirrors
and shades and corners of their eyes. It was as if they believed
they'd not only burn their retinas if they saw the sun directly, but
actually turn to stone.

Fifteen years later, the TV finally stopped rebooting, and
the dog stilled. She came to nestle by my feet, scared. I heard
someone in the park outside yelling.

"Heard" was the word Dad always pronounced incorrectly:
"hear-d," rather than "herd." No one knew why, and he never explained it. A few hours earlier, right before I put them to bed, my

girls had found one last piece of homework they had forgotten to do. They were charged with learning a set of sight words for the next day's test.

Beautiful. Laugh. Borrow.

Heard.

My father believed in coincidence more than he believed in the Sacred Heart of Jesus. I corrected my girls: "No," I said, "it's not 'herd,' it's 'hear-d.'"

In their confusion they looked down at the safety of their dog, who in turn rolled over and exposed her privates. It was September 18, 2005. Late that night, he would pass over.

By the time the TV rebooted he was gone again, for another year.

THREE

Florida:
"This Is Indian Territory!
This Is Not the USA!
Go Back to England!"

O Florida! Home of the endangered manatee, the endangered mangrove cuckoo, and the endangered car-kicking man-baby, only two of which are actually endangered, and only one of which we actually encountered. Where the land that is the United States of America ends not with a fence or a cliff or an army, but with a soft wasting at a place called Flamingo.

It seems everyone I encountered in the months leading up to the trip had a theory about Florida. One friend told me I'd loathe the state, no questions asked. Another said, "If it's weird—and not in a good way—it happens there." Don Graffiti also had theories. His centered on "drug-addled gas pump attendants," "deli counter clerks whose relationship to reality was generally affected by low IQs and methamphetamines," and a tad more high-mindedly, "the devastation of development." But I had no real opinion; I knew very little about Florida. To me it was merely a gun-shaped slice of Africa that some time before I was born floated across the Atlantic and snuggled below Georgia like a cat under a bed. A place to which one might buy a plane ticket, in hopes of seeing birds.

Donna and I JetBlued there in April. The flight attendant had intoned a very special good morning to each and every one of us, but antisocial Donna just sighed and went back to her iPod. She had been intent on learning birdsong but nothing had seemed to stick, so she said. My attempts in the weeks leading up to Florida had been spectacularly unsuccessful too, so much so that we would spend the next few days misapprehending any number of the simplest of birdsongs, but especially that of the prairie warbler.

With her batteries dead, Donna slept some on the plane, dreaming, perhaps, of finding Don rested and ready to bird. He was already in Florida on business, and we were going to save him from it. Sometime after, I fell asleep too, and woke on the runway, where we'd touched down like a skein of geese on a stormy lake.

From the airport, Donna and I drove west, passing vast developments on either side, mile after mile of construction sites keeping scant water in little channels by the side of the road, dribbles and drabs where common moorhens and cattle egrets kept one eye out for PANTHERS CROSSING. A pickup truck parked beyond an intersection offered FILET MIGNON OF JERKY. We passed a sign for EYELID SURGERY.

We didn't stop; we had a date with Don.

We found him standing outside his corporate hotel in a business suit, but I'm guessing he was the only person at the convention wearing Swarovski binoculars. I didn't want to ask him what he thought he'd see from a conference room, and something about binoculars and work shoes in the same getup always makes me laugh, so I laughed. Don was not amused. His desperate need to go birding was being hampered by one last meeting that had been thoughtlessly scheduled for *after* lunch. The three of us walked a wooden causeway behind the hotel, but our hearts weren't entirely in it; I couldn't take my eyes off his loafers either. Eventually, the blessed afternoon came and we finally sprung him from Fort Myers, and we drove across the causeway to our first destination, Sanibel Island. Even here, on the road to the conservationist miracle that is J. N. "Ding" Darling National Wildlife Refuge, perhaps the most famous wildlife sanctuary in America, the push of development was inexorable—the causeway over to the island was under construction. It looked like they were widening it from four lanes to a couple of hundred. On the scanty beaches by the side of the road, Wilson's plovers scurried to and from the shoreline, unawares that their ecological time, at least on Sanibel, was pretty much up.

Don, as usual, had labored over our lodgings. He takes such plans extremely seriously. Here he claimed to have a found an extra-special place for us, thick with the local charm for which Fort Myers, Florida, is roundly unfamous. So keeping our eyes to the skies, we drove until we found Captain Dennis Hendrix's Kona Kai motel, where a sign above a white telephone outside a locked door instructed us to call if no one was about. Don did so, left a brief message, and got an instant callback, making us wonder if we were being watched.

"Yes . . . yes . . . OK, many thanks. Yes? OK. Great, that's really great, Dennis. What's that? Yes, OK. Got it. Can't wait. Uh-huh. OK. Great. Yes.

"Pardon me?

[Pause]

"Erm, no, actually . . .

[Pause]

"Baby pineapples . . .

[Pause]

"OK, got it, I'll be sure to . . . OK, great, thanks. Got it."

Don hung up and stared at me.

"Baby pineapples. Outside the office door, apparently. We are to look."

The voice on the other end had offered no help in a checking-in kind of way; instead, we were to appreciate the captain's efforts of forced germination and go find our room on our own. The three of us stood on the path and looked: no key, no fruit basket, certainly no thoughtful little soaps. Just three sad, pulpy little cacti in plastic pots.

"Well, there they are," said Don, referring, we inferred, to the pineapples. Captain Dennis and his crew were nowhere to be found.

"What an impressive rattoon!" I said, perhaps a bit cheekily. Donna asked, "Luke, are you being dirty?"

"When is he not?" Don asked, still upset, I guessed, that I laughed at his shoes. Not to mention he clearly didn't know what a rattoon is.

One of the greatest environmentalists America has ever known, and this is how his awareness began: with a beating. Idyllic late-nineteenth-century summers spent at his uncle John's farm in Albion, Michigan, had given Jay Norwood Darling a deep appreciation of nature. He was also sometimes sent out to get "a mess of ducks for dinner." One day the boy shot a wood duck in mating season, and Uncle John had thrashed him for it; you only killed ducks when they were done for the year making more ducks. Later, as a young man, he had watched with other Iowans as Covington, Nebraska, separated from his hometown of Sioux City by the muddy Missouri River, slipped into the roiling waters, and was gone. This was the power of nature: an entire town fell into the mud because the Missouri had wandered under the town and sucked it away. Later still, when Uncle John died and Darling went back to the farm to pay his respects, he found that his uncle's soil had long since degraded to the point where nothing grew, and no birds or other wildlife remained. He was horrified.

Darling's father, a clergyman, was determined the young outdoorsman get a schooling, and enrolled him at Beloit College in Wisconsin. But the budding artist was thrown out of school for a year because he drew one of the professors wearing a tutu; he also sketched the principal, a devout teetotaler, singing "Give Us a Drink, Bartender." In that important year off he picked corn in Castana, Iowa, and went to Florida for the first time.

When he was mature and modest he claimed that his annus mirabilis came about because he didn't work hard enough at his grades. Let's not allow his modesty be the last word: in Wisconsin in 1899, you didn't draw the entire faculty of your college as chorus girls and escape unpunished.

After Beloit, the web of work trapped the young Darling; he became a reporter-cartoonist, gently lampooning local issues in Sioux City, Iowa, and national agenda items out of Washington. But on days off, he still wandered around eastern South Dakota, shooting and hooking. Over time, his work in Sioux City and in Des Moines—not to mention his nickname, Ding, which came from the signed shortening of his surname on his cartoons—drew national attention, and at the start of the second decade of the new century he found himself heading east, towards the *New York Globe*. But he hated New York and fled back to Des Moines, where he stayed.

Back in the Midwest, he became the country's leading political cartoonist at a time when cartoonists were very much in the public eye. In addition, he was the perfect storm of conservation: a friend of politicians (the Roosevelts, both Teddy and Franklin Delano, and also Herbert Hoover), a hunter, and an avid lover of nature. In July 1934, FDR appointed him to take charge of the Bureau of Biological Survey (what would eventually become the U.S. Fish and Wildlife Service). It was there that Ding faced the ultimate question: How, given the seeming conflicting priorities of appreciating and eating, to keep both sides happy? It took him less than two years to come up with a brilliant solution: a license that looks like a postage stamp. If you were over sixteen years of age and you wanted to hunt, you now had to buy a Duck Stamp. The proceeds would go towards conservation, including land purchases, so that there would be more ducks to shoot, and therefore more ducks to appreciate. Put simply, the hunters would pay for the birders to have something to look at. In the first year, 1935, the Duck Stamp program raised more than half a million dollars; in the nearly seventy-five years since then, the Migratory Bird Hunting and Conservation Stamp, to give it its rightful name, has raised more than seven hundred million dollars—seven hundred million!—and has bought 5.2 million acres of land for the country.

Ding! Jackpot.

Now, we found ourselves in the wildlife refuge named for the great man. From the moment we left the car, we were rapt. The place was incredibly, ecstatically packed with avifauna, and it gave me the same thrill as if I were lucky enough to be at a Paul Simon concert in which Joni Mitchell perched on Van Morrison's shoulders and sang a Bob Dylan song. Everywhere I spun my glasses a new bird popped up. In just one hour I bagged nine life birds.

In fact, the joy I felt was not unlike hearing a new album by Simon or Mitchell or Morrison or Dylan. Picture this: After five years of waiting, the musician you love has finally come out with a new release, and you're first in line on a Tuesday morning at the record store. You rush home, struggle with the packaging until about noon, then sit back and listen. And what do you get? Well, it's obviously by the great one, but do you like it? Yes, yes, of course—all those clever chord changes that seem so obvious once you've heard them but which you never saw coming ahead of time; the dazzling new rhymes, leading to that infectious refrain in the second track, a refrain that you sing out loud like you've always known it; even the workaday track, two songs from the end, has about it a kind of interest, but perhaps only because it's not as good as all the rest. But the fact remains that the newness is something to overcome too. You have all the other CDs by your number-one musician, and they're like beloved old friends. Now, you're faced with forty-five minutes of fresh stuff, familiar but strange, uncanny. Is it more beautiful than the last record, or is it something to admire but not love? One will only know with repeated listens. It could take weeks.

And that's how it feels in a new birding zone. The birds are still birds, but they're not ones you instantly recognize; there's work to be done in appreciating them, and it can't happen instantly. You're gorged, and your senses are too full of new colors and shapes to fully enjoy the birds. You don't have weeks. They are fascinating because they're new, but one also has their newness to conquer—the first few times seeing a bird, one is simply identifying it, rather than soaking in its jiz.

Let me explain. The jiz—the word is derived from GISS (for "general impression of size and shape")—is, to birders, an account of the essence of a species. It is intuited through combining impressions of how a bird moves and flies and sits on a branch or other perch—something like the way you can identify a friend from afar by recognizing her walk and her beautiful hair and her winter coat, even if you can't see her face. When I walked the fields of Pennsylvania and enjoyed the regular inhabitants of any particular season, my awareness of the jiz around me (oh god) made me more able to pick out something that shouldn't be there. One early morning in late spring, I was groggily birding when all of a sudden I felt strongly that the jiz of what I'd assumed was a black-capped chickadee was not chickadee jiz at all. I looked again, and saw a bird that associates with chickadees, which are common, but that is itself much rarer in this part of the state and really worth seeing, a bird in migration with the wonderful name of the golden-winged warbler. Without an innate awareness of chickadee jiz, I probably wouldn't have refocused myself and looked again.

Birders of a certain ability are very big on jiz, especially in Europe. On one British blog, someone arguing for or against a red kite/black kite sighting wrote, TO ME WHEN THE JIZ IS NOT QUITE RIGHT, ALARM BELLS START TO RING!

I couldn't agree more.

Privileging jiz has become one of the most fashionable movements in birding in recent years. Pete Dunne, an eminent birder and one of the most popular bird writers, has focused heavily on using jiz as a tool. His book (with Clay Sutton and David Sibley), *Hawks in Flight*, remains a kind of bible for raptor watchers and jiz aficionados both. Though it details all the requisite plumage variations, etc., what it really asks the observer to focus on is the essence of the specks of bird as they fly up there in the distant sky. I've seen Dunne on the hawk watch platform in Cape May, New Jersey; he can certainly tell a hawk from a handsaw, and often at extraordinary distances, so he must be doing something right.

But here in Florida, I was all out of jiz. So many of the birds were new to my understanding that I could go only on book memory, built by hours of poring over *The Sibley Guide to Birds* or the *National Geographic Field Guide to the Birds of North America*. It had been a year since my trip to Arizona, and though I'd worked hard on getting a jizzic sense of the birds I'd regularly see in New York and New Jersey, here I was able only to use my book learning and, erm, wing it. In all those months waiting to come to Florida, I'd wondered over and over if I'd ever get to see a magnificent frigatebird or a roseate spoonbill. I got a half-glimpse of the latter, and wonderful looks at high-flying numbers of the former, on that first morning. It was almost too good to be true. The roseate spoonbill, for example, I saw in the very corner of my eye—had I been alone, I wouldn't have claimed it, but Don got it straight on. As he called it out, I was actually busy making sure a nearby American alligator didn't come any closer. Before I could truly worry, a warbler flew by, and we went running after it. Once we'd found that bird (a prairie), we turned back to the water and scoped some distant anhingas eating fish—they flip them up and swallow them whole down their snakelike throats. Behind the anhingas, a little blue heron was coming into its color, splotched cerulean on white. In the end my head was spinning, and I was almost relieved when we all agreed we were hungry and ready to call it a day.

On the way back to the motel we figured we'd get some predinner beers and snacks, and pulled off the main Sanibel drag, Periwinkle Way, into a small mall featuring a bunch of small stores, as well as one big one called Jerry's Grocery. To our considerable horror, in the mall courtyard we came upon a number of caged parrots. We were three miles from Ding Darling, but here in this shopping mall we found a bunch of birds entombed and crowds of vacationers taking flash photos and barking laughs. Children ran back and forth on this warm evening, posing for pictures and putting their fingers into the cages. The birds hopped around in obvious distress, squawking and snapping. Don looked stricken; Donna could barely speak. Eventually, we beat an unhappy retreat to the car and Don muttered, "I need to take an irritation pill."

Next day, the morning air at Ding Darling was riddled with no-see-ums, so bad that Donna and I quickly retreated to the car and left Don on his own to photograph a comical male reddish egret. This particular member of the egret family is a hilarious predator: He looks like the Sugar Plum Fairy but is, in fact, a natural-born killer. Almost wiped out by nineteenth-century plume hunters, its numbers have mostly recovered, though it is still pretty much limited in North America to coastal waters here in Florida and in some other Gulf States.

There he went, prancing across shallow water (the bird, not Don), his wings outstretched, creating both a disturbance and a shadow that the fish can't resist. Once in a while he ran, then maybe he hopped, sometimes flying across the water for a bit, all in order to scare the fish into being a meal. Don spun his spotting scope and focused his digital camera. In best Don fashion he'd set up where the view was most felicitous: trouble was, that happened to also be in the middle of the road. Donna and I watched from the safety of the car as he was interrupted by traffic once, twice, a half-dozen times to move the scope; we didn't dare tell him to set up on the grass to the side, as we knew he'd mumble and mutter about the annoyance of other human beings daring to drive where he wants to stand.

And so it goes: drive, stop, photos, drive, stop, photos. A morning spent; hours gone before you know it. There were so many birds at Ding Darling—everywhere anhingas and egrets and more high-passing frigatebirds. It didn't feel like anywhere else in the world.

The one thing we weren't seeing much of, though, was migrants. While we were delighted to be getting all these resident birds, one of the reasons we'd come to Florida in April was to get the first wave of eastern-seaboard migrating songbirds. The winter had been a long one, and by March we'd become desperate to see a warbler or a tanager or an oriole. Such jewels start to pass through Florida by mid- to late April, yet here we were, in the right place at the right time, and there was no sign of them.

No reason to worry yet. The temperatures were high, which might account for the lack of action. Were the birds avoiding the heat and using the hot, southerly flows to help their migration farther north? In any case, as in Arizona, my life list was growing with or without migrants, but that late morning so were our appetites, and reluctantly we escaped to a restaurant in Sanibel called the Hungry Heron for some lunch.

Inside, the walls of the café were painted a sea blue, but were otherwise covered in neon fish. The waitress looked uncannily like Dick Cheney. Donna asked her, "Do you have any local beers?"

"We have Yuengling," the vice president said. "It's from Pennsylvania."

A TV in the corner was showing baseball highlights from

the night before—Ronny Paulino, then-Pirates' catcher, stoically swung through a pitch.

Don said, "It drives me crazy when fat people can't hit home runs." He extrapolated an explanation, something to do with "tender wrists" and "chicken hands."

I couldn't really follow him; I was too busy counting up how many birds we'd seen. I announced the Number—it was ridiculously high for just one morning—but then the conversation turned back to baseball, and this time which Yankees resemble which birds. Joe Torre we likened to a black-crowned night heron—deliberate, glum, but effective. Gary Sheffield is a peregrine falcon, attacking the baseball the way the raptor falls on an oblivious passing duck. Randy "Big Unit" Johnson is a great blue heron, though that's a bit unfair to the bird, it being fairly attractive.

Don said, "And branching out a bit, Tom Wolfe is a snowy egret"—an all-white egret with yellow "spats" for feet.

Donna nodded; I nodded; Dick Cheney brought the check. I think we were starting to get the hang of Florida.

As we left, two young girls about my daughters' age were using a metal claw to fish for small useless toys in the quarter arcade game by the door of the restaurant. For a moment, all the beautiful egrets and warblers in the world were just a bunch of birds.

Don, being a nondriver, doesn't fully understand traffic, or traffic laws, and as a consequence I know he finds me unduly conservative when it comes to the following: illegal U-turns; leaving a car in nonlegitimate parking spaces; the speed limit; locking a vehicle; looking at a map at least fifty feet before any possible turn. On the newly expanded bridge from Sanibel to the mainland he insisted we park in a clearly off-limits construction area so that we could chase the Wilson's plover. It would be a life bird after all, and what's a traffic law compared with such a thing? It was an insane proposition—have you ever parallel parked next to an earth mover?—but we got the bird: a small shorebird with a ring around its neck and a black beak. I only wished it was mating season—Wilson's plover pairs sometimes fall over backwards when their copulation is complete. What a lovely image: spent, they collapse on the sand, presumably with a postcoital giggle playing on their big, black beaks.

And with that, we were on our way to Key Biscayne. After a night in a Lake Worth motel adjacent to a toll booth on I-95, assiduously researched and reserved by Don, we awoke as refreshed and perky as one can be after a night next to a sixteen-lane turnpike exit. With the sound of toll money tumbling into baskets, we headed for some breakfast. A hard, high sun baked us, and it was early still; pleasantly sated by salted eggs and coffee, we wandered back to the car. In the almost-empty parking lot, our car now found itself next to yet another sun-blocking SUV—a nonevent in car-mad Florida. And then it happened: as Don opened the passenger-side door of our car, he lightly tapped the monster's side. The blow barely registered—a fly on a freeway might do more damage. Instantly, though, the driver of the car jumped out red-faced and hissing at Don to "wake up." Now, Don can be a sleepyhead; for a start he suffers from terrible "carolepsy," which on long trips makes him fall asleep in mid-sentence, even mid-word. But this morning, in the glare of the sun, he's fully awake, and what's more he's utterly baffled. The other driver was a big, meaty guy, with a dandruffy 'stache and pants held too high by a thin belt. He had on the freshly starched shirt that bespeaks "registered child abuser," and I can't let it stand.

"Aw, come on, buddy. He barely touched your car," I said, cheerily enough.

At this—and as I write the following words I can still barely believe what I saw—the guy, who had started to walk away, stopped, ran ten yards, left his feet, and launched a huge and vicious kick to the back fender of our rental car.

"There," he said triumphantly, coming down to land. "I'm barely touching it."

I have no real idea why I became Small Injustice Man, but at least I know when: His birth arrived one sunny spring morning in Manhattan, when I remonstrated with a stunningly rude traffic cop who was giving a lecture to the Afghani guy from whose breakfast cart I bought my coffee every morning. She could have waited, honestly, until the line had dissipated; or she could have simply written him a ticket. Instead, she chose eight fifty-five A.M. to lecture the poor fellow on some kind of obscure parking infraction. As I remember it, his truck was parked twenty-four feet from the corner of Sixth Avenue, thereby violating Section 4-08, subsection (n), part 4, of the New York City Highway Rules, which states quite clearly that he must be at least twenty-five feet from said corner. When I politely asked her to wait a second until the coffee guy had dealt with the customer ahead of me, she turned on me with all fury and accused me of picking on her. In hindsight, I only wish I *had* been picking on her, but I couldn't have cared less. She was simply a rude human being, and as a fellow human being, I felt it was my place to point this out to her in the politest way possible.

I therefore looked at her badge, and loudly spoke her name back to her, in an effort to show her that I could indeed report her to some kind of supervisor should she continue to screech at me like a caged parrot. She seemed to get my meaning, because with that she quickly covered said badge with her bulging ticket book, and ran off along Sixth Avenue. By now, my incredulity served only to hold up the line; the coffee was in the cup, the doughnut in the bag. It wasn't free, either: I may have been sticking up for a guy from Kabul, but he wasn't about to lose out on a buck fifty.

That night, on our way to New Jersey for—what else?—a birding trip, I told Don and Donna of my incident with the traffic cop, and Don christened me "Small Injustice Man," a man whose job it is to bring punctiliousness to the streets of New York...

... and elsewhere, like here and now in Florida. For a moment, I was dumbfounded, aghast, maybe even a little frightened. If such an innocuous bump of one car door against another could elicit such violence, what else might this psychopath be capable of? But then that moment passed, and I felt Small Injustice Man's cape rustle down my back as it unfurled. As soon as the car-kicking man-baby turned his back to walk away, I saw a red the color of dried blood. Not to say that I lost my composure. I may be Small Injustice Man, righter of tiny wrongs, but I am also a graduate of Oxford University, that hallowed repository of a six-hundred-year-tradition of rhetoric and argumentation. I had spent three delightful years there being taught by the great, now-late Avril Bruten, a wisp of an English professor who knew classical rhetoric like some people know their own names. I understood how to settle this, tactfully and with the dignified calm for which my countrymen are famed. I would use *ars rhetorica*.

I thought my best shot was to begin with the trope of anaphora, given the power that a feigned halting can bring:

"Fuck you . . . motherfucker . . . you fucking fuck . . ." I therefore began. "Come on, motherfucker, come back!" I elaborated, knowing surely how the repetition—*conduplicatio*—would amplify my argument. "I'll fucking kill your fucking fat ass!" And, drawing to an irresistible, even *epizeuxistic* summation: "Fuck fuck fuck!" With that vehement repetition, I was off, chasing him up the hill back towards the restaurant where just five minutes earlier we'd been having a peaceful breakfast. In the background, I faintly heard Donna calling, "Luke, no, come back," but in the words of that other great rhetorician, Van Morrison, it was too late to stop.

"Fuck fuck *fuck!*" Here, I'm sure you'll agree, the emphasis on that ultimate "fuck" slipped us into the suburbs of *asyndeton*; I think we can all hear the echo of "I came, I saw, I conquered." The guy, his starched white back like a mainsail before me, started to slow up a bit and turned to look at me. Beneath his mustache, his face held a complicated look: dumbfounded, aghast, and maybe even a little frightened. Either that, or he had studied with Avril too, and warily admired the power of my rhetorical stance, not to mention the coincidence that here we both had ended up in Florida.

Physically, too, I was gaining on him. Some kind of confrontation was inevitable. I was still screaming like a sports fan after a bad call. And at that moment, as we hove towards each other, an altogether cheesy deus ex machina occurred: A cop car turned the corner and came down the hill. Valor quickly turned to discretion, which even more quickly turned me back down the hill and away from the Florida po-po, back, indeed, to where Don and Donna waited by our mercifully undented rented car.

I was still shaking, and not just from my efforts of poesy; Don and Donna displayed their usual mixture of bemusement and relief that my behavior had not gotten us killed. We stood for a long while in the heat and roaring silence.

Then, Don said, "That ass put himself into the state of raw nature by kicking the car. He broke the bounds of what is normal human behavior. But here's the thing: if this was truly wild nature, we would chase him, beat him with sticks, and eat him. Fortunately, the police car came—the ultimate symbol of a restricted society—and suddenly both he and us are back in it."

Donna said, "Back in what?"

And then, to the blushing rhetorician,

"Didn't you hear me calling?"

"So, I have a question to ask you," says Don, to calm us all down after our nasty upset.

"Tomatoes, right?"

"You don't like anything with tomatoes, yes?"

"No, Don, he likes pizza. Right, Luke?"

"I officially like pizza."

"But we never talked about tomato soup. How about it?"

"Fine," I say.

"Very interesting," says Don, warming to the task. "Let me ask you this: Do you like tomato sliced thinly on a sandwich?"

"You know he doesn't," says Donna, sagely. "We discussed it in Arizona. And some other times."

"Well, I *think* I know it, but I need to check."

"I would not choose sliced tomato on a sandwich."

"Fascinating! You like other tomatoey things. What gives?"

"No idea. In fact, I'm still a bit shaken by that twat who kicked our car. May we change the subject?"

"I just find you confusing."

"I know."

"OK."

There is a pause.

"It's the texture, I know. I understand, you see, that you're weird about bananas. But avocados? I don't know *what* to say about your views on those." Don nods to himself, and watches Florida slide by.

I believe that birders are quietly heroic folk. Given all the choices one faces in the modern world, it's admirable, to my eye at least, that some people give up the chance to stand on line to buy iPhones, or DVR *CSI Scranton*, and instead go out into a field to appreciate nature. It bespeaks something about their souls that animals and birds are worth their time. I don't say this of myself—I'm only in it for the money, and the girls—but most others garner my abiding affection.

It's not like it's always a picnic: one is often out in foul weather; the birds don't give a shit, at least not *for* you; and it's not the sexiest pursuit in the world—no one's going to mistake a birder for a supermodel. I can't log how many times I've seen a blank stare, even a twitch of an eyeball, when I admit that, yes, I love to look at birds. With strangers I can go from mildly interesting to completely written off in about a second and a half. Birder. It's like saying "registered sex offender," or "Pleased to meet you, I'm Andy Dick."

So to me, birders are generally wonderful people. We'd meet one such hero on the southern tip of Key Biscayne. For weeks up to the trip we'd monitored the blogs to see what kind of birds were passing through the Keys, and one name kept coming up as a fount of knowledge: Robin Diaz.

(Ms. Diaz's name—her *first* name—brings up an odd tendency in the birding world: a suspiciously large number of birders have bird-related names. Apart from Robin, there's Wezil Walraven, and his son Merlin. There's John Flicker, president of the National Audubon Society. And let's not forget the former editor of *Winging It*, the American Bird Association's newsletter, Matt Pelikan. For sixty years, Chandler "Chan" S. Robbins worked at the famed Patuxent Wildlife Research Center in Maryland—he was a senior author of the *Field Guide to Birds of North America*, as well as organizer of the North American Breeding Bird Survey, along with many other credits. Then there's the former executive director, and now incoming president, of the New York chapter of the Audubon Society, Marcia T. Fowle. And how about the bird and wildlife author, and professor of wildlife biology at McGill University, who goes by the name of David Bird? He swears that's his given name too.)

As for Ms. Diaz, her reports were always detailed and enthusiastic, and I had come to look forward to the posts of her latest sightings when I was entrapped in my New York office. One such report had caught my eye in the week leading up to our trip: Bill Baggs Cape Florida State Park, a place Robin birded seemingly every day, was boasting a La Sagra's flycatcher, a rare vagrant from the Caribbean—specifically, a Cuban/Grand Cayman/ Bahaman resident. (Vagrants are birds that by rights shouldn't be seen in any given geographical area, but do indeed show up from time to time.) Robin had carefully noted each time and place she'd seen it, so when we arrived at the park, we were able to go straight to the actual tree where the bird intermittently showed. She'd also pointed out that it doesn't move much, and when it perches, it does so at a forty-five degree angle. Just like a tree branch if it's at forty-five degrees.

For an hour we stood there, in the parking lot, watching a grove of sea grapes and green buttonwoods in case the bird showed. Birding can be like this sometimes: a whole lot of standing for nothing, then a brief something, then a whole lot more of nothing. There's any number of strategies to break up the monotony though. You can stand on your right foot, your left hand on your binoculars. Other times, it's left foot and right hand. I have been known to use both hands at the same time, and both feet, though I'm in a minority. I'll twiddle the focus ring (you bet I will!) and then I'll stop. Then, I'll twiddle some more, back and forth, like I'm trying to crack a combination. I'll break the binoculars wide apart, as though my eyes are on the sides of my head, then I'll bring the two sides close together, like I'm cross-eyed. When my back starts to ache from standing, I will haunch, and while haunching will explain to anyone who's listening that *haunch* is now a verb. But haunching makes my legs ache, so more often than not I will pop back up, refreshed in the lower back, and I start the focus ring twizzling all over again.

Wait a second, I'll think. What if, given my mad twizzling, I'm now set up for a long-distance look, not close by as required? Here I'll raise the binoculars to the tree wherein one hopes the elusive bird dwells, focus the bins perfectly, and set them back upon my breastplate in eager readiness.

But how high should the binoculars really hang? I was once

yelled at by an elderly birder because my binoculars were slung down by my belt, à la Bill Gibbons and Dusty Hill, the bearded geniuses from ZZ Top. "No," the old fart said, "you need 'em up high. It'll take you too long to raise 'em if you keep 'em that low. Like this." Here he hoisted my glasses up where to a Gypsy King keeps his *guitarra*, right below the chin. I wore them up there for a while too, as he seemed to know what he was talking about, but after a particularly gruesome chin injury caused by trying to get a look at a flitting hummingbird, I settled on a compromise position: nestling my binoculars where my chest hair would be if I could grow some.

Such are the things we think about when the birding gets quiet—we talk about this shit too, trust me. After half an hour of such chitchat Don and Donna, amazingly enough, got bored and took a walk, while I remained to loiter like someone hankering after some illicit action.

The action came in the form of a middle-aged woman dressed like a birder similarly loitering, and to my great joy the person turned out to be Robin Diaz. When Don and Donna returned, the four of us took a brief walk around the grounds. Ms. Diaz, a sort of semiofficial birder for the park, was able to tell us where some of the best spots were. She agreed with us when we expressed frustration that we seemed to be missing migrants. By now we realized that the weather had truly been against us. These hot, southerly flows did indeed mean that the birds probably just keep going farther north until they ran into a front in the Carolinas or some such. In addition, the flora of the park had been much affected by two successive hurricanes: the strong remnants of Katrina, post its New Orleans destruction; and Wilma, which had done even more damage here in Florida. Ms. Diaz explained, to our amazement, that the trees had gone into what she called "defensive mode" after Katrina, meaning they had hunkered down and focused on surviving rather than thriving. And when Wilma followed, the damage only deepened, to the point where the boughs of many of the trees sprung leaves directly out of the bark, rather than from branches. The effect on both tree and birdlife had been notable, and Ms. Diaz had seen far fewer migrants this particular spring.

It was chilling stuff. But Ms. Diaz maintained a calm and enthusiastic face, and gave us a couple of great tips, along with a hand-drawn map for where to see mangrove cuckoos and other target birds of the trip. The map would be an enormous advantage—too often we'd get vague descriptions from otherwise well-meaning birders, descriptions which would leave us driving round in circles trying to find a single bush or a long-since chopped-down tree. We enjoyed her company immensely, and were disappointed to have to leave her, but we had the Everglades ahead of us, as well as a long trip across the state back towards Fort Myers and the dreaded flight home. We thanked her for everything, including the map, and away Ms. Diaz walked, into a lowering sun, pausing as she went to scan the trees for whatever it was she wished was there to be seen.

On the way south to the Everglades we birded, as we so often did, from the comfort of our car. I have a secret mantra that "birding by car should never be rewarded"; and yet, on that road south we came upon a crested caracara in the far distance—a life bird for all of us!—and Donna also managed to whisper that we might want to slow up a bit as she may have seen something a mile back. God bless her, what she'd seen was in fact a field filled with sandhill cranes, birds I'd only ever happened upon once before as they came to roost one night outside of the town of Modesto, California.

The Everglades sort of snuck up on us, until suddenly we were surrounded by grass and mangrove, not to mention an overwhelming sense that we could barely do the place justice. This was not simply an aesthetic failing on our part; it also had to do with the conflicting and confusing claims and counter-claims as to the state of the area come the start of the twenty-first century. It would be foolish of me to attempt to synthesize all the competing opinions on the status of it—for a start, the place positively shone that day, the grasses swaying in a proto-summer breeze. But it pretty much came down to this: when we drained it, we really screwed it over, and now we're trying to fix it. One thing we knew for sure: at two thirty in the afternoon, the Ever-glades are hot and the bugs just about chew yer face off. I must also admit that it was the site of the second of our four Florida fights; so, seconds out, round two.

The tip of the state, at a wide place in the road called Fla-mingo, boasts one of the few known spots to see the Cape Sable sparrow, a pretty little bird whose status is extremely shaky, given that we've screwed the place over, etc. We spent an hour trying to identify a bird we thought might be it, but it was too far away and the heat haze off the road made a positive nod either way impossible. It had been tremendously exciting to try to work it out, given the chance that we might have seen a very rare bird; it in some ways didn't matter that we couldn't say for sure in the end. The effort had been exhilarating, and it gave us hope for the rest of the day.

After a while we wandered into a little campsite by the wa-ter's edge, where unused raised barbecue grills shone in the af-ternoon sun. There were a few people about, but nothing much to see. Out at sea, an osprey circled and suddenly plunged, pluck-ing from the surf a good-sized fish, and we watched as it heavily flew back to land. Just when we thought the bird would disappear, it suddenly curved back and landed on one of the metal grills not a hundred feet from us. The fish still squirmed in the grip of the bird's talons, until the fish slowed its thrashing enough to start being eaten. By this point, we had our scope trained on the spec-tacle and marveled at the amazing scenes the lens offered up. Donna took lots of photographs as the fish's mass decreased and the bird's increased. One of these would subsequently win first prize in a photo competition in *WildBird* magazine—not to be confused with the less reputable British publication of the same name.

It was too good to be true. If you're having a *National Geographic* moment in a public park in the United States, it's a (pardon me) cardinal rule that a dunce family is probably going to show up and ruin it. And so it was.

For a while the dunce mother, dunce daughter, and dunce son kept a fairly respectful distance, but we guessed it was only a matter of time, and we were right. As the bird devoured the fish, first the dunce boy, a young man who'd evidently enjoyed the manifold fruits of America's fast-food industry, then the dunce mother approached; fifty feet, then thirty, then twenty-five. I was incensed. The osprey as a species has been much stressed in the past thirty years, and largely by our actions; our use of DDT made their eggs too brittle to successfully carry babies, and it's only in the last few years that they've made a comeback. Plunging into a roiling sea, scooping up a fish, and with great effort flying back to land . . . well, it ain't much of a life. Such a moment is not something to own, or even disturb; it's something to witness at a respectful distance, especially if your belches smell like an unwashed ventilation fan at Kentucky Fried Chicken, which was surely the case here.

"Hey, move back please!" I shouted across the campground.

The son made a gesture.

"Excuse me?" I felt a vein in my neck quiver.

"Oh dear, not a good idea on his part," said Don.

"Luke," said Donna.

"Really, I can't let it lie." The family edged closer still.

"*Now!*" hissed Don to Donna, obsessing on the perfect moment for her to release the shutter.

"Don, he's going to start again."

"Don't blame him," said Don.

"He's not happy," continued Donna.

"We can't blame him, Donna. They're getting too close. *Now!* Can I, can I?" Don wanted a shot at shooting, and in his futile attempts to wrestle the camera from Donna's talon grip, I sensed my chance.

"I'm just going to ask them politely to keep back."

"Oh no," said Donna.

And so, with my invisible Small Injustice Man cape once again flapping in the breeze, I set off to confront the family Dunce, who by now were less than twenty feet from the stressed osprey.

"Hey! Hey! Come on, move away from the bird!" I shouted, adjusting all the way my underwear, over my pants as it metaphorically was.

Blank faces.

"Come on! Do you know how close you are?"

"No," hissed the boy, "I don't have a measuring tape."

Oh, a smart mouth. I was clearly going to have to quote Tony Soprano.

"Move out of the way," I yelled. "And while you're at it, have you considered salads?"

Now, as a piece of abuse I'll admit it's a bit obscure, but it worked. Obviously confused (and perhaps rattled by the thought of vengeful vegetables), the young man moved back from the bird.

"What's your problem?" shouted the mother, not unreasonably.

"Move back! It's against the law to harass a wild bird." Here, in a staggeringly ineffectual gesture, I whipped out my cell phone—ineffectual because (a) I had no service in this part of America, and (b) no cop anywhere in the world would turn up to move people away from an osprey having lunch. (What would you have to do to get busted down to the osprey beat?) Nonetheless, I bluffed: "Move, or I'm calling the cops."

"Jesus, what a loser!" said the girl, rolling her eyes. I pretended to dial the phone anyway; it saved me from fully assessing her "loser" claim. When I looked up, the harassers were off in the distance, walking away and muttering, one can safely presume, about mad dogs and Englishmen.

Back at the photo shoot, Don and Donna pressed on.

"Now!" Don shouted, gently pointing out the perfect photographic moment.

"Don!" Donna replied angrily. "I'm not an idiot."

"No," said Don, "*you*, my love, are *not* an idiot."

I was about to reply, but something caught the corner of my eye. Turning, I saw a bald eagle roaring in from the north, heading straight for the osprey. The osprey, smarter than all of us put together, abandoned the half-eaten fish and hightailed it out to sea. The eagle whumped down, snatched the fish, and headed west to a grove of trees by the water. The three of us picked up the scope and ran after it, hoping we'd get great looks at such a supreme beast. But the eagle was smarter than us too—it huddled pretty much out of sight, way up in the canopy, where it presumably snacked on the osprey's leavings.

All thoughts of the Dunces were gone. Instead, sublime nature had reasserted itself. Who cared about Small Injustice Man and KFC, about cell phone coverage and federal laws? Out in the Atlantic, in the hazy distance, we saw the osprey resume hunting. It would circle a while, fall out of the sky, miss, relaunch; then circle again, dive, splash a fish out of the salt, fly, struggle, and fly, over us this time, away into the interior, away from eagles and humans and barbecue pits, away into the safety of nothing at all.

Away, as birds always will.

Despite the drama of the osprey and the eagle, I wasn't entirely unhappy to leave the Everglades behind, especially given the opportunity to go to Big Cypress National Preserve, yet another premier Florida birding spot. But first, we needed a bunch of disappointments, and got them easily on Key Largo.

Our lodgings were fabulous it should be said—a series of cabins by the water, and the most ridiculously pretty sunsets possible as standard features. And yet, it's no real surprise that I ruined it. As we checked in, I joked with the spectacularly old woman who ran the place that we were much looking forward to enjoying her motel, and once we'd enjoyed it, we planned to thoroughly trash it. I have no idea why I thought this was funny; she avowedly didn't, and neither did Don. I had proved yet again that I was no better than Shawmut, Saul Bellow's character who will be known for eternity as "him with his foot in his mouth."

Once the sun was down and back up again, and our rooms untrashed, we piled back into our car to head out for another bird chase: this time, the mangrove cuckoo. One thing we knew for sure was that there would be limited opportunities in our lives to come here and see a bird that is restricted to coastal southern Florida—it can be found nowhere else in the United States. It would be worse if we'd come for this and for this only, but still, it would be a special thing to see such a bird. Cuckoos are wonderfully interesting and handsome animals, some of Don's favorites of all. The mangrove, however, is said to be one of the least understood birds in all North America, and that has a lot to do with its behavior: the bird is basically silent when it's not breeding, and in addition is a real skulker. But we had a map!

And so it was with great excitement that overcast Florida morning that we turned to the directions Robin Diaz had kindly drawn for us. Oh dear. Apparently, it's old-fashioned to think that there's just north, south, east, or west. According to this map, once we'd nearly reached the place we were going, we should turn around and head back the way we came, but not exactly, as that wouldn't take us northsouth west, or eastwest south, or something. In addition, there are roads on that drawing that haven't yet been planned by the state's engineers; I'm pretty sure the Atlantic doesn't touch the west of the Panhandle; and as far as I can recall, Georgia is, in fact, north of Florida. In all, it's a map that Don and I still haven't made head nor tail of years later. We were so grateful to Robin, yet Don's comment—"maybe no map is better than a misleading one"—was unarguable. A frustrating half hour of driving back and forth on a surprisingly busy road found us, eventually, next to a small electricity substation (this doesn't appear on the map, let it be stated). The bird was supposedly nesting somewhere hereabouts, but if it was there, we were unable to either see it or hear it.

It was a big miss on the trip. We try hard, when we're traveling, not to get hung up on what we haven't seen, and enjoy what we have. Don's aspirational approach to birding—the second we get a great bird, he starts to list the others he now considers crucial to the happy fulfillment of the trip—was not much helped by missing this resident, albeit one that even professional ornithologists have a hard time studying due to its reticence. (I saw a mangrove cuckoo months later in Puerto Rico, way out in the open in a grove. It seemed almost tame, and spent many minutes turning this way and that so I could get amazing looks at it.)

With frustrated hearts we instead repaired to the mainland, where reports of common mynas had been posted online. Bizarre, Southeast Asian birds, these are members of the starling family, and in Florida, mynas are probably escapees that established a native population and are thereby considered "exotics"; as such, they can't be counted for a United States bird list. But as I've said, we're not really listers. And more to the point, a common myna, like the mangrove cuckoo, is not a bird you're going to find in Brooklyn or northeast Pennsylvania.

Down a deserted back road we drove, to a dead end, and sure enough, there they were, common mynas, harassing a pileated woodpecker nest three quarters the way up a disused telephone pole. What odd birds they are! One might even be uncharitable and say they're ugly, though Don was adamant that they are "quite, quite attractive." They sport large yellowish skin patches behind their eyes and have a strong yellow beak; otherwise, they are dark brown birds with a blackish head and white under-tail feathers. Somehow the whole thing comes together to make them look kinda pissed off. And boy do they make a racket—imagine an old tractor engine trying to fire in a classroom filled with children scratching their nails on the chalkboard. George Laycock, in his book *Alien Animals*, says that in Hawaii, where they are common, the birds are considered by some to be "a threat to the mental health of the human race." Here, though, they were just a threat to the pileated, who kept popping its bright red crest out of the hole, only for the mynas to go, well, bat-crazy at it all over again. I half expected the mynas to pull mallets out of their wings and bash the poor woodpecker each time it appeared, like a carnival game.

Finally, we got back on the main road, heading west on the Tamiami Trail, the road that links Miami with chichi Naples and then heads north to Tampa, hence the name. The Trail seemed put there to confirm my most snobbish opinions of Florida: mile after mile of places selling authentic "Indian" schlock and airboat rides by the dozen, alongside bad restaurants and tram tours and churches. A litany of megachurches had been raised there, one after another, all built over God's green land and sided with parking lots the size of football fields. Between them was an endless row of nonreligious developments, mostly named after what had once been there naturally: Photogenic Copse Apartments, Pretty Little Glade Condominiums, Unspoiled Fields Shopping Mall.

By now we were ready to see a snail kite. The guidebook said they were easy enough to find. They were not. We parked on the edge of the road by a tourist café, thinking we'd seen the possibility of the bird across the fields, but all we got was the odor of french fries. After ten fruitless minutes, we bought lunch and headed back on the Trail toward Big Cypress.

Out of the blue, Don said, "I have green pepper and chickpea."

I liked the sound of the words, and supposing he was referring to the sandwich he'd just acquired, I let him in peace for once. He was in the back, and his carcolepsy would soon set in and he'd be gone. Now and then we'd pull over and scope the water on either side of the road, but my mood was summed up by the sign that only I saw as we sped along:

THIS IS INDIAN TERRITORY!
THIS IS NOT THE USA!
GO BACK TO ENGLAND!

For an Englishman this was both funny and disturbing. My recurring nightmare had recently become the revocation of my green card and a forced repatriation to the land of overboiled vegetables. I may well have even dreamed the sign.

Florida had been too many roads, too many car journeys, too much modern, too many fights. I yearned for something to admire. We reached Big Cypress National Preserve late in the afternoon, the heat bearable, a lovely wash of light coming off a high sky. One more hero, that's all I asked.

He was dressed in long white shorts. Well, they would have been long if he weren't quite so plump. As it was, his paunch pulled them up a half measure until what could have been culottes were now short-shorts with an inbuilt atomic wedgie (I'm assuming). Thank god for the socks! Nice long white ones, the kind that fifteen-year-old schoolgirls wear in the minds of perverts. Only, his weren't exactly white: Midnight gray, they might be described. Or more succinctly, grimy.

Don and I were sitting on a bench. We had taken a slow stroll around the swamp, and tired as we were after our full day of birding, the fifth in a row, we had paused at a water hole, where a bunch more egrets and a wary red-shouldered hawk stood on their perches like museum pieces, watched by a day-tripping family or two. Mr. Paunch was idling near us, and by his continual entreaties—"Where are you from?" "Ooh, is that an Australian accent?" "I like birds, don't you?"—it was clear that he wanted to be our friend. Donna was over by the railing, setting up the spotting scope. Don and I were trying our best to ignore the guy. To that end I was pretending to watch Donna fiddle with the scope, but out of the corner of my other eye I saw Mr. Paunch stride forward towards Don . . . and then I heard it: the kind of sound I knew from childhood years of watching Batman and Robin. *Pow!* The noise of the blow echoed around the watering hole, scaring away a couple of grackles and causing the red-shouldered hawk to briefly cock its head to one side. Like an elegant trogon, in slow motion I fully turned my head and saw the look on Don's face—*surprise* doesn't have nearly enough syllables—and I don't think even he knew exactly what had happened until Mr. Paunch raised his palm to Don's eyes and said, "Got it!"

There, in the middle of his palm, a formerly alive-on-Don's-cheek mosquito lay like a bloody exclamation point.

Don had just been full-force smacked by a birder wearing dirty kneesocks. Donna looked at the guy and took a step forward. I imagined that she was going to hit him right back. But before she could punch him, he'd stepped away and proceeded to go from person to person—women and children first—hitting them on their backs and exposed arms and once, with a frail old lady, right across the left ear. "Got it!" he chimed with each dead insect he claimed.

By this point the red-shouldered hawk was squawking at him, but it made no difference. He seemed determined to solve the West Nile virus crisis single-handedly.

I looked at Don; Don looked at Donna; Donna looked at the man.

"Shall we?" said Don.

And so we did.

It's hard to fathom, as we approached Marco Island from the east on Route 92 that spring afternoon, that just thirty years ago there wasn't much here at all. Now, Marco Island is one of the most developed spots in all Florida. In early 2007, the U.S. Census Bureau calculated that Naples–Marco Island was, percentage wise, the seventh fastest-growing metro area in America in the years 2000 to 2006—the population up by a staggering 25.2 percent. From a distance the construction cranes swung everywhere; beachfront hotels and condominiums seemed to outnumber whirling seagulls. It looked like every one of those people who accounted for the 25 percent increase was getting his or her own apartment. I thought I was kidding, but it turns out to be true—the 2000 census listed the population as 14,879, and 14,871 "housing units," meaning no more than 8 people need to share at any one time. And here are their names . . .

We were on Marco Island to chase an owl, the same kind that is the subject of a recent book and movie. Carl Hiaasen's story *Hoot* is a pleasingly comic tale of some kids who push back against "Mother Paula's All-American Pancake House" as they build their 469th family-style restaurant right on top of a nesting site for burrowing owls. Here on Marco Island, however, it would take more than three pesky kids to halt the inevitable end to the birds' habitat. It's such a shame; it's a singularly charming bird. I have read that during mating, the male sings, and the female sometimes gives a "smack call and a copulation warble." Sounds like something from a rare German movie I once saw.

Currently on Marco there are still a few empty plots of land,

and it's there that the bird continues to nest and smack and warble. These lots where the birds nest are so obviously valuable it's not even funny, and you can imagine how the local developers view the bird's presence. Let's hear from Brenda Talbert of the Collier County Building Industry Association: "The rules are very strict. At what point do you also need to serve the habitat of human beings as well?"

The "rules" to which she refers are, in fact, laughably slack: because the bird is only a "species of concern," and not officially "endangered," a developer has only to get a state permit to destroy an owl's burrow. Currently, there are about 113 burrowing owls on Marco, but who knows how many will survive the continuing rush to development. Recent incidents of harassment include one burrow being filled with sand and another being filled with—wait for it—mangoes.

We'd spent the afternoon on the beach, watching as a Louisiana heron palled up with a couple of net fishermen and ate their leavings. Later, a pair of blonde girls not much older than mine had run past me in the sand. Don and Donna were busy taking photographs of the milky moon, high as it was above this corner of Florida. I looked up at the moon and tried to appear interested in Don's pictures, but my heart wasn't in it, so we left the beach and headed to Spinnaker Drive, a likely spot, to see if we could indeed find a burrowing owl.

I didn't notice the guy at first. We were casing a substantial lot adjoining the beach, as it seemed prime habitat for the owl. The pickup truck was parked about a hundred yards away, up by a bend in the road. The man was standing by the truck, and he watched us warily as we approached him. He said nothing; we felt no need to say anything either.

As we turned to walk away, he opened the driver's-side door and said, "There you go. You got him. Good boy."

We watched in amazement as an attack dog careened into the lot and directly to one of the burrows. The dog sniffled around a bit, then gave up, trotting back to the truck. The guy patted him effusively and let him back into the cab.

I know we should have said something, but what? He didn't look like the kind of person one would want to challenge, and frankly I was done with fighting for one trip. Donna, though, had the wherewithal to get the name of his company off the side of his truck. But when we subsequently tried to report the guy, we knew we didn't have enough evidence to have him fined, and by now who knows how many houses have been built on the land? It was clear his effort was to get rid of the owls so that his boss, or his boss's boss, could green-light some condo building. We watched his brake lights disappear around the bend, and we knew that this spot on that afternoon wasn't going to yield any owls. With heavy hearts we got back into our car to head to Naples, where we'd spend our last night in Florida.

The light had changed. It had gone from bright to crepuscular in a heartbeat. Don and Donna were volubly fuming at the guy with the dog; I, on the other hand, hadn't given up yet. I scanned every vacant patch for action. As we turned onto a side road, there, there it was: a small bird on a perch in the center of a lot.

"Guys! Guys! Owl!"

"Oh my, your eyes!" said Don.

"He's twenty-twenty," said Donna.

"Better, surely," countered Don.

"What's better than twenty-twenty?" she said.

"Guys!" I bellowed, pulling the car to the curb and turning it off. "Can we please go look at the owl before we lose the light?"

And that's how three people stood on the side of a road on Marco Island, Florida, and watched a burrowing owl turn its tiny head this way and that, looking for a predator, or a bulldozer, or an attack dog. And that's how, too, three people watched as four police cars, three ambulances, a howling fire truck, a stream of SUVs, thirty-seven Harley-Davidsons, a car carrier filled with all the latest models, and a low loader with a double-wide passed that particular intersection that twilit evening.

The bird, on the other hand, stayed perfectly still. When we could barely make it out through the gloom, it flew up above us to the slanted roof of the house outside which we stood; then it returned to its perch. And then, Florida went dark.

NOW WHAT?

It's the middle of May, eight thirty in the morning. I'm due in the office in half an hour. But instead of thinking about work, I'm looking at the top of a huge plane tree right in the middle of Central Park's Ramble. A woman on a cell phone, her dog off its leash, wanders by with her binoculars at her chest, asks her cell phone pal to hang on, and barks the archetypal birding question at me: "What have you got?"

I want to answer, "A woman on a cell phone, her dog off its leash." But instead I say, "A kinglet," because it's true, and because I know this common and tiny bird will not entice her to stay. I am right. Her phone call eventually over, I watch as she walks off, stuffing a *Peterson's Field Guide to the Birds of Eastern and Central North America* down the back of her pants. I suddenly feel enormously sorry for a paperback birding guide.

Work is beckoning, so I leave. But on and off, all day, as the phone rings and the e-mail pings, I see in my mind's eye the rose-breasted grosbeaks hanging out at the top of a plane tree; the magnolia warblers turning this way and that, displaying the tip of the tail "dipped in black paint," as Don always puts it; the indigo buntings buzzing on stalks by Azalea Pond.

That evening, I give the park another shot. As I walk east from Columbus Circle, I meet a guy standing by the Hallett Nature Sanctuary. The sanctuary, a four-acre plot of land at the southern tip of the park set aside for wildlife, has been closed to the public for more than seventy years, but along the edges one can sometimes find intriguing things. Like this guy, for example, who introduces himself as Ben. He is clearly a birder, though he seems to be scanning the distant heavens, rather than the nearby trees. He reminds me of the guys in Cape May, New Jersey, who each spring listen for flight calls at dawn way above them, and shout out the names of invisible migrating birds. I know it's science, but where's the fun in that? But then, I'm not into fantasy football either.

Ben, I discover, is not, in fact, doing migration research. He's watching a pair of nesting peregrine falcons on the G.M. Building. Every so often, one of the birds swoops away from the nest, and Ben writes down the details: exact time, direction of flight, everything. He's very concerned that the new twenty-four-hour Apple store, situated as it is at the foot of the G.M. Building, will disturb the birds—Apple has installed huge lights up near the nests. As we talk about his citizen research, he drops his bombshell: He does this same thing, lunchtimes and evenings, pretty much every day. He's been doing it since 1996. Ten full years.

I still say I did very well not to exclaim out loud at this news. Instead, I think, "ten full years," over and over. I have to change the subject, so I mention Fort Myers, as we've just gotten back from our Florida trip. Ben reports that he used to date a woman there, but things didn't work out. You don't say.

Don arrives and is unimpressed by the speck of bird way up on the G.M. Building. When I fill him in on Ben's ten-year effort, Don first looks at me , then begins to quietly back away. The light is fading as we bid Ben farewell and we walk back towards midtown, exclaiming at the range of nuts one can find at any time in this park. One guy removes his shirt to show someone a torso entirely covered in tattoos, while another stands by the pond and honks and skirls on a set of bagpipes.

Unperturbed, Don says, "Florida was something, but we are quite mad to be going to Michigan."

He is right. On the back of the joy that was Florida, we've now taken the birding madness to a new level. Gone is the birding vacation, where we enjoy both the fauna and the fact that we're in a new state, learning its ways, enjoying its people. No, now we're going off the deep end. We've decided that on Memorial Day weekend we are heading to northern Michigan for a few days, all in order to chase a single bird. We know that we're probably nuts. But it's one of the rarest birds in the world, and we would be actual nuts not to go have a peek at it. Who am I to say that Ben's obsession with the falcons is unhealthy? At least he cares about birds, and I find that attribute to be the one I care about most in people. Do you care about animals?

No? Good-bye.

FOUR

Michigan:
What Charles Pease Shot

Veering right, she turns off the freeway, driving briskly ahead of us in a beat-up government truck. She's twirling her long, wavy hair in one hand and steering with the other. We follow. It is seven thirty A.M.; the day has broken somewhere behind the clouds, but for now, a low mist aches around us like a hangover. The woman in the pickup had been on the freeway for an exit or two until darting back into the forest; our caravan of six or seven cars just about keeps up.

This is not what I expected. For years I'd dreamed of this place and the bird it harbored. I'd studied its habitat, its life cycle, the color of its feathers, the sound of its song; one of the rarest birds in America, one of the rarest birds in the world, and one could only see it here. In my imagination, the bird lived in a place so remote that a rental car couldn't even reach it. Instead, we'd stalk the bird for days on foot, setting down such soft soles that small animals wouldn't notice us. This is what we'd have to do: pause, listen; pause, *pray*, listen. And then, perhaps, we'd get a brief glimpse of it, our hearts would soar, and it would be gone. We'd trudge back to our vehicle, our feet heavier now, and follow our government guide carefully back to the world.

Instead, this: A place in Grayling, Michigan, that might as well be on the way to my old house in Pennsylvania. The road is red clay, and a bit unkempt, but it's well-traveled, and there are single-wides and more salubrious houses all along; plenty of people live here. Small government signs are dotted about, forbidding intrusion into the forest, but otherwise it's a regular American rural area. Dogs are attached to washing lines so they don't run off.

After a few miles the woman pulls her truck to the side of the road across from a couple of spacious homes, and we all park behind her. From the six or seven cars, probably twice that many people pile out. In some ways it's a fairly typical birding group. We've seen crowds like this everywhere we go. In most, the men outnumber the women, though the sight of mainly older people is changing as some of us young 'uns cotton on to it. Birding is, according to Scott Weidensaul in *Of a Feather*, becoming "(well almost) cool." He goes on, "A birder today is more likely to have body piercings than a tweed coat."

Not here though, Scott. Today's gang is dominated by middle-aged men with spotting scopes, crew cuts, and impressive bellies ("the Pregnants," as I secretly call them). But there are some oddities too: A couple of the men look like farmers who've signed up for the wrong outing; not even carrying binoculars, they both wear camo baseball caps and might be happier tinkering with tractor parts, frankly.

There's also a Japanese woman. Don, under his breath, puts on his best Robin Leach voice and hisses as we wait, "Dressed for our pleasure today, she disports in a gray and white striped shirt under a tunic that is sky blue and punctuated with white fluffy clouds. Her hat, a floppy velour creation with an upturned brim—in mauve—is so tightly bound to her head by the toggle strap that it wouldn't blow off in a typhoon, though it may yet strangle her. The rest of this starlet's 'look' consists of a backpack of red, yellow, and green.

"She has accessorized with a neat little husband, who is for some reason wearing lace gloves, the color of which match the sky blue of his darling wife's jacket.

"Truly they are today's couple for today's times."

Giggling, we notice that the Japanese couple have brought with them their own personal guide, a handsome young man with a Canadian accent who seems not at all fazed to be accompanying two color-blind clients who don't speak a single word of English, and who may yet scare off the bird with the loudness of their attire.

Rounding out the group is one other smallish woman who holds her pale lime green coat together at the belly in the classic pose of the self-consciously ill-at-ease. She clearly wants nothing to do with looking at birds, and seems faintly nervous about something (the imminent threat of conversation, probably). We guess that she's with one of the Pregnants, but then again, it could be that she's recently escaped from somewhere.

The real surprise in this morning's group, however, is the young woman leading it. Back at the motel, our group had met at seven in the quaintly named Maple Room and had been shown an obligatory government video in which we learn about how great the government has been in saving the bird and then thinking to make an obligatory video about it. This meeting, and the subsequent official trip, is the only legal way to see the bird in this part of Michigan, so the video must be endured. Though I appreciate the sentiment and the strictures, I am left with a question: Why, when humans put together a visual montage with wild nature as the theme, do we reflexively back it with spooky, synth-based music, as though all animals are from Pluto? We don't fully understand nature, I get it; but the more we make them sound like a visitation from a distant planet, the more, surely, humans will view nature not as an organic part of the world's existence, but as something to fear, and thereby pay scant respect to. The narrator's basso profundo sounds like God, or his current agent on earth, NPR's Corey Flintoff. His portentous speech ends with a quizzical, "If the bird survives, is there then hope for all mankind?" kind of thing. Then the lights come up, and we're not, after all, on Pluto. We're still in the Maple Room, in Michigan.

And I'm sorry to say this, but the world is still going to hell in a handbasket.

Imagine, then, my surprise that the person who turned off the TV at the merciful end of the video and invited us to drive behind her into the forest is not the standard-issue government guide, the one who has all sorts of keys hanging from all sorts of belt hooks, and believes the hokum we've just sat through. Instead, it's a perfectly attractive young woman who clearly misread the job description.

Now, standing around on the road waiting for one last birder to assemble his Hubble Space Telescope, we find out that Jenny— for this is her name—is seemingly quite well adjusted. It's everything I can do to stop myself from saying, "Hey, you're actually normal!" Something is horribly wrong, so I check my thesis by muttering something about the scope guy, who, given the massive pieces of equipment he continues to assemble, seems to think the bird is actually *on* Pluto.

Jenny briefly smiles at me as though I've said something that someone, somewhere—perhaps in a parallel universe—might one day think almost witty. We continue to mill about, birding the trees around the houses, chatting a bit, but there's just one agenda item today, and finally we're all ready to set out down the dirt track.

Once we're walking, it comes to this: Don and Donna and I traveled a thousand miles to see a single bird, we've given ourselves a couple of hours to do so, and there's no promise we'll see anything at all. (Jenny made it clear at the end of the movie that there are no guarantees.)

It wasn't as if we hadn't earned some sort of guarantee though.

The previous evening we'd nearly missed a flight to Detroit, thanks to Don's inability to leave the shackles of his all-consuming job. Donna and I had sat in the lobby of Don's office building, and a full half an hour after he was due to meet us he arrived, puffing and huffing and generally trying to pretend he didn't know the time. In the cab on the way to the airport, I'd felt a faint urge to discuss the philosophical reasoning behind getting to the door of an aircraft as it's closing. I presume that arriving with time to spare would be, to Don, an example of giving in to the TSA's post-9/11, shoes-off, breast-milk-drunk-to-prove-it's-not-Semtex lunacy. Homeland Security be damned—Don was having none of it.

"I know we'll talk about this later," he said. "*On* our flight. I'm still confident. Plenty of time."

When neither Donna nor I gave him the succor he desired, he looked out the cab window and said, "The traffic's bad, granted."

Traffic on the freeway to La Guardia was, in fact, not traffic at all—it was parking. Donna sighed and looked out the window; I mentally paced up and down; Don furtively looked at his watch, then forced us to discuss what target birds we'd most like to find in Michigan. This distracted us for a few minutes, but our hearts weren't in it. Then, just as I was preparing a plaintive speech about the pressures of work, and how his company would not, in fact, actually go out of business if he'd left a few minutes earlier, a pocket of New York tarmac finally opened up, and despite Don's and the city's best efforts, we made our flight with two minutes to spare.

This was a complete disaster, especially as once aboard, we sat on the tarmac for two hours waiting out a spectacular late-spring storm. The exciting weather notwithstanding, Donna and I realized that next time, Don would only be happy if we cut those two minutes down to mere seconds.

But who knows, maybe even seconds would be too long. As we finally lifted off from La Guardia into a clearing sky, I imagined Don sprinting down the runway, almost supersonically keeping up with the plane, until he throws some kind of heavy wire at the vertical stabilizer and the wire catches, swinging him up into the sky. There, he spends the ninety-minute flight trailing like a piece of fishing line off the foot of a Canada goose. And with him dangling, his smile as wide as a passenger plane, and us leveling off at our cruising altitude, I fell blissfully asleep.

And then I'm waking up in Detroit, picking up the car and driving north, sleeping for what Don described as "four blissful hours," and now it's seven thirty A.M. and we're walking off into a pale morning.

Not used to being guided by an expert, before we arrived in Grayling we imagined knowing the birdsong would be an important part of the morning's endeavor. Don and Donna and I had tried to memorize it the previous night, but out in the field it's always a shock to realize that something about the aspect of a sound in the real habitat (rather than through the pods of an iPod) tricks us. In Florida, we'd heard the prairie warbler many times, but it never sounded quite the same way twice. But then, we hadn't really thought about the fact that we would have someone helping us in Michigan. Still intrigued as to why a perfectly normal person is working the fields with a bunch of birders, I resolve to ask Jenny what she's doing in a gin joint like this.

Turns out she didn't misread any job descriptions. Jenny has a B.S. in environmental studies and since graduating has been doing all sorts of cool wildlife research, including studying wolves in the Canadian Rockies, and endangered parrotbills on Maui, where she's helicoptered out to the wilderness to spend ten days at a time counting birds. I find myself instantly green with envy for her life, but the envy is quickly replaced with gratitude that we lucked out that this summer she's in Michigan. As we walk, her modest brilliance as a birder is much in evidence. The gray light is hardly conducive to seeing birds easily, and yet she calls out, "Upland sandpiper," and there it is; "field sparrow," "thrasher," "goldfinch," most of it by sound before she even sees the bird. Her generosity is infectious, and I find myself enjoying her palpable pleasure—she seems to be getting a kick out of the group, even though we're weird, and she's not.

This is not our usual way of birding, and we're surprised to find ourselves having fun. But if our target bird doesn't show . . .

Don has already chastened us in the car drive from the motel: "I'm not saying the trip will be for naught if we don't get it, but if we don't, just imagine! It's very early in the morning to contemplate not seeing the thing."

"Then why are we contemplating it?" I muttered. "Wasn't the sign at the Holiday Inn a *good* sign?"

"I didn't see it," said Don, a tad disingenuously.

"Well, I did."

"So did I," said Donna.

"You guys have amazing eyesight," said Don, sadly.

"The letters were a foot high, Don. WELCOME, WARBLER TOURS, it said, and I think that's good news."

"Why didn't you tell me?" asked Don. "I feel much better."

In all these hours in cars and fields and airports, I'm getting to see one of Don's most salient birding patterns: he deals with his overarching desire to see something rare by willing a sort of disaster, namely, the very real possibility that the bird doesn't care that we've come all this way and won't show up. That way, the *actual* not seeing of the bird will be somehow more bearable if he's already faced the possibility of a bad day.

And then I dismantle my psychoanalyst's couch and instead bring to my mind my late father. It was 1976. Our beloved Manchester United soccer team had just lost in the English F.A. Cup final to the lowly and heavily unfancied Southampton. It was a huge upset, and I was hugely upset. I threw myself down on the couch as big, seven-year-old's tears rolled down my cherubic face.

Dad said, "Don't be a big girl's blouse."

Don's face, as we walk farther away from the cars and closer to the possibility of not seeing the bird, is not hard to read: this bird better show. Otherwise, Donna and I are going to be spending the entire long weekend in Michigan with a big girl's blouse.

And then, it shows.

The warbler is named after one Dr. Jared Potter Kirtland, a mid-nineteenth century physician and naturalist. The first specimen was taken on Kirtland's property near Cleveland, Ohio, on May 13, 1851, by his son-in-law, Charles Pease, who, despite his pacifist-sounding name, acquired the bird for science by shooting it. Back then, killing birds was the accepted way of studying them—the life of John Audubon, for example, is littered with scenes of bird slaughter. Subsequently, Professor S. F. Baird (there we go with the "baird" names again) of the Smithsonian Institution dedicated the new discovery to Kirtland, a man described as knowing more about the natural history of the Mississippi Valley than "anyone living."

The first nest wasn't found until just over fifty years later, and then only by some fishermen on the Au Sable River who heard an unfamiliar song. Since then, the story of the Kirtland's warbler has been, until recently, one long downer: a steady decline in population punctuated by its being listed as an endangered species in the early 1970s.

Now, I'm all for conservation and for berating humans for their mismanagement of the world they lease from the future. But in the case of the Kirtland's warbler, its rarity is due in no small part to the bird's own damned finicky behavior. Yes, we've screwed up our land management across the years and strained their nesting habitat; and then there's the matter of overdevelopment bringing in the invasive and destructive brown-headed cowbird (we'll come to those little bastards in a minute).

All that said, the Kirtland's warbler still behaves like a pampered superstar. It only nests at the foot of young jack pines. That's kinda specific, don't you think? Especially when the only way to get a young jack pine is to keep either replanting jack pines, or else burn stands of perfectly healthy grown-up jack pines. Now that we manage forest fires so effectively, such burnings seldom happen randomly, but even so, you'd wonder why, given the state of the world—all greenhouse gasses and holes in the ozone layer—the Kirtland's warbler wouldn't take one for the team and nest, oh, I don't know, how about *halfway up* a freakin' jack pine? But no, it refuses to breed in a stand of pines less than eighty acres in size; each bird apparently feels cramped if it has less than six to ten acres of its own. (For comparison's sake, my New York apartment is seven hundred square feet.) And once an individual tree reaches sixteen to twenty feet high, the Kirtland's abandons the nest and freaks out yet another generation of ornithologists.

Oh, and the sand at the base of the tree? Grayling sand only, please.

The news for the Kirtland's warbler used to be very bad indeed, but amazing efforts to ensure a secure habitat by birders, conservationists, and the U.S. Fish and Wildlife Service has led to this happy fact: by the late 1980s there were still only a few hundred left, but in 2004, some twenty-seven years after the "endangered" listing, the annual census counted a wondrous 1,341 singing males.

Still, if you want to see a Kirtland's warbler, you really have to want to see it. The young jack pines are cut down and replanted (and once in a blue moon, burned) in a few small national forests in northern Michigan, and at breeding time, in May, access to said public lands is strictly controlled. And so it was that we were with another group of unwashed birders and Jenny one chilly spring morning in the merry month, more than eight hundred miles from home.

Beyond the jack pine issue, one of the biggest threats to the Kirtland's warbler is the aforementioned brown-headed cowbird. Now that we've subdivided so many forests in order to develop them, there are more woodland edges than ever before, and brown-headed cowbirds are naturally attracted by these edges, just as songbirds are. Unfortunately, cowbirds are nest parasites. They don't make homes of their own, preferring instead to lay eggs in the nests of warblers and other birds.

They're also smart little bastards. Female cowbirds arrive earlier to the nesting grounds than female Kirtland's, and in an amazing display of adaptation, time their egg release to coincide with the Kirtland's nest completion. For each cowbird egg laid, a warbler egg is jettisoned by the cowbird. And that's when it gets really nasty. Even though the Kirtland's boasts the biggest of all the warbler eggs, the cowbird egg is still bigger, and the warbler doesn't realize it's incubating the wrong bird, along with its own, until it's too late. (The cowbird egg gets more heat too, meaning the warblers often fail to thrive and hatch.) Cowbird babies are hatched a couple of days before the warblers in any case, so they get more food, meaning the warbler babies starve.

Every way you look at this it's not a good thing.

One of the main thrusts of the recovery program for the bird, therefore, is the elimination of cowbirds in the Kirtland's warbler habitat. To that end, dotted around the fields where we stand are a number of cowbird traps, mesh death boxes about twenty feet by ten. They are filled this and every morning with a small assortment of birds but mainly flapping cowbirds, not even dimly aware, I guess, of what's coming their way. Every few days, folks like Jenny come by and, metaphorical sickle in hand, let the other birds go but bring the cowbirds' days to an end.

So her job is one part tourist guide to three parts murderer.

"The most common way is squeezing them to death," Jenny says, looking off across the field. "They lose the air out of their lungs in about ten seconds. You put your forefinger on their backbone, behind their chest, and your thumb on their breastbone or keel, and then you squeeze. First time I did it, it was brutal, but you do get used to it, mostly. I do buckets of 'em."

"Jesus." I can't believe she has to do this.

"Oh, there's another way too. You can also take a Leatherman, or needle-nosed pliers, pinch their vertebrate right below the base of the skull, and it will sever the spinal cord. That way is quick and painless if you do it correctly."

Jenny winces ever so slightly. It is, after all, killing a living thing, and though cowbirds are devastating to native species and all that, they are also undeniably pretty: deep black with a chocolate-hued head. Jenny and her colleagues kill around four thousand per spring—unless a sharp-shinned hawk gets into a trap, as has happened, and their job is done for them.

"Just a lot of headless birds, that day," Jenny says, smiling a bit. "We tagged the raptor, let him go, and then we swept up the bodies."

Musing on bird murder I barely notice as a Kirtland's perches on a short bush not five feet from me. It's an extremely attractive bird—a bright yellow throat and underbody; a slate gray/blue head and back, with some faint streaking on the sides; and a broken white eye ring and a darker band of blue connecting the eyes. At nearly six inches, the bird is a little bigger than the usual tiny warbler, though when they're fledglings, they often hide out low in the pine thickets and are, according to the Cornell Lab of Ornithology, "easily mistaken for [a] pine cone." Best of all, when the adult bird sings, it throws its head back and whistles a perky tune that speeds up a bit at the end, as though it has not a care in the world. It seems to have a lot to say, though at this time of the year, with its womenfolk back from wintering in Bermuda, its message is right out of the Marvin Gaye songbook: "Let's get it on."

As we marvel at this bird—a survivor of both human excesses and of what George Meredith might have called its own "damn punctilio"—one of the Pregnants starts madly pishing at the bird. The onomatopoeic technique of pishing, a human approximation of a noise that may or may not freak out a bird enough for it to come see what's up, is most often used when a bird is being recalcitrant or skulking. I still don't know how I feel about it as a technique—we should probably leave birds well alone. But in this case, it's simply irrelevant: the bird is five feet away on the top of a jack pine. I want to say, "How much closer do you want it—up your nose?" Instead, I hiss, "No pishing!"

The Pregnant stops pishing and looks a bit ashamed. Jenny smiles behind his back. I briefly wish upon him the same fate as a trapped cowbird.

But it's not difficult to go back to marveling at this tame little thing, the object of our interest. It's completely unaware of its situation as one of the rarest birds on earth. So, it looks at us without emotion, pauses, flies. In its flying it almost fixed up our spirits. I felt a bit giddy, that morning, as though in seeing the Kirtland's warbler all over these fields (there were a good number of them about), we were cheating something, or watching as something so vulnerable cheated forces that usually win. Don and Donna took hundreds of pictures and videos, and the three of us found ourselves beaming at Jenny, who was beaming right back.

We'd had no breakfast, so Jenny suggests that the group head back to civilization and food. But the Mad Pisher has other ideas, and insists on walking off ahead, almost out of sight, to search for another upland sandpiper. Jenny told him he can't go on his own—this is federally protected land, after all—but he pretended deafness, and Jenny, because it's her job, agreed to accompany him. We watched as she and Mr. Potato Head receded over the hill, then turned tail and headed away from the Kirtland's warbler, and back to Planet Earth.

For now, we had seen one of the rarest birds in the world; Don and Donna had celebrated by touching fingers and quietly saying, "Ch-ching, candy bar": the Japanese couple had driven away with the Canadian; and the cow had jumped over the moon. Our day was still young, however, so after breakfast in Grayling town, we set out southeast for a place called "the mecca" for birders in Michigan, Tawas Point.

We never get far without pulling off a road and seeing what we can find, though, and this morning was no exception. Not thirty miles down the road, we found an adult bald eagle perched on a downed tree in the middle of the Au Sable River, and we spent a wonderful couple of hours at a place called Loon Lake, where we all saw ourselves a life bird, and a significant one: the trumpeter swan. By the mid-1930s this bird, so prized in previous centuries for its skin and feathers, had been reduced to the startling number of just sixty-nine recorded individuals. Thanks to concerted conservation efforts it has come way back now, to the point where it's doing fine, but that prewar number served to remind us again just how fragile is the health of the avian world. The birds we saw that day were clearly in need of an appointment at a hair salon though—their heads were stained rusty pink from iron oxides in the pond foliage.

Nevertheless, Tawas was calling to us, and not even a "Recovery Station for Unserviceable American Flags" in Hale, Michigan, could keep us from it.

The drive was serene and beautiful, the road winding through some lovely Michigan farmland. But as ever, Don, invigorated by the miles, couldn't leave well alone.

"So, I have a question to ask you," said Don.

"Tomatoes, right?"

"You don't like anything with tomatoes, yes?"

"Don, do we have to?" Donna wailed.

"I like pizza."

"Very interesting," said Don, once again amazed at what's he's relearning.

With that, we pulled off the road and bought snacks from Bub's Country Market. They were advertising a three-pound pizza (whatever that is) for only $9.99. Don looked at me meaningfully, but I ignored him.

Nestled on the eastern edge of Michigan in a corner of Lake Huron, Tawas Point juts out like an upside-down fishhook into the inland ocean of Saginaw Bay and thereby serves as an extraordinary migrant trap. Each year, the list of birds seen at "the Point" is second to none in the state. We'd been reading and talking about it for weeks, and now we found ourselves seeing signs for Tawas City as we drove east on Route 55, and our blood raced. I'd already booked us a night in the Bambi Motel in Tawas, and we were delighted to find the place as kooky as we'd hoped. The sign out front read,

EXTRA * NEAT * CLEAN
FULL, QUEEN & KING BEDS * AIR
NO SMOKING AVAILABLE
PRAY FOR PEACE!

Once we'd checked in, we jumped back in the car and drove the two miles to the Point, only to find a late-afternoon horror-movie mist rolling in off Lake Huron. Donna kept referring to the lake as a "sea," and one could see why—we were indeed standing on a "beach," scoping scurrying shorebirds in the hazy distance. Unable to pick anything out, we headed inland to walk the park paths. We soon realized that the place was birdy—extremely so.

Birdiness is what we three birders dream of. To us, it means that even though we may not have identified all the birds in the trees, we sense there are lots there, and they're not just everyday ones like northern cardinals and blue jays and American robins. Birdiness is an intuitive thing; its presence sharpens the senses

 elegant trogon is one of the most sought-after sightings in the United States. Here, one such bird,
gnizant of the fleeting spring, checks train timetables back to Mexico.

You try doing this for a living: a female **ruby-throated hummingbird**, one of the first birds I saw after I started birding, hovers before an all-you-can-eat buffet.

As we drove along a back road in Florida, I noticed an **eastern meadowlark** in, well, a meadow. Don Graffi one of my traveling companions, was asleep at the time, and nearly missed the moment—an occupation hazard in a hobby that requires a level of sustained attention similar to that of antiaircraft gunnery.

on Graffiti and his wife, Donna, seemed unable to stop their camera from creating "red-eye" when
ey took this close-up of a **black-crowned night heron.**

The author and Don Graffiti, shown here trying to find Don's
wife, Donna, a woman who spent a number of years in a
paper bag, unable to find her way out thereof.

Donna won first prize in a *WildBird* magazine competition for this snap of a feasting osprey. The mome was subsequently ruined by a family of roaming nature-haters (another occupational hazard), and then redeemed by a bald eagle.

One of the rarest birds in the world, the Kirtland's warbler has some of the most particular nesting needs of all. Think pampered rock star, crossed with an archetypal Romanian head of state. Here shown deciding between ecru and taupe for the blinds.

ally equipped with Mercury Grand Marquis, holsters, and coffee and donuts, Don Graffiti and the author go undercover to stake out a **cerulean warbler** in Michigan.

The **marbled godwit.** The godwits get their name from the noise they are said to make, but how you can hear "god-wit" from a bird that basically says "kwek" is beyond me. "Marbled kwek" isn't as attractive, of course.

Mix a blue jay with a yellow warbler and this is what you get: the astonishingly attractive green jay of southern Texas.

The author is photographically chastened by his companions after yet another enthusiastic but inaccurate rare-bird sighting.

irding can entail lots of aimless driving back and forth, trying to spot small, distant creatures who on't care a whit whether you see them or not. Occasionally the driving is as lovely and soul-satisfying s this, the Pawnee Grasslands in Colorado.

y the time the snows come, this bird's plumage will be whiter than a polar bear, but for now, captured here midsummer Colorado, the white-tailed ptarmigan handily turns the color of the Rocky Mountains.

The **crested caracara** (or, as it should be known, the red-faced greater mullet bird). This fearless scavenger will eat pretty much anything: young alligators, skunks, birds, insects, fish, eggs, and, by one report, a nine-banded armadillo.

too, brings a quiet excitement to the day, and makes the neck aches and back aches recede a bit.

Don said, "This place has already kicked ass," and he was right. There were Baltimore orioles everywhere, and bunches of warblers flitting around. We came upon a den of foxes; above them, a least flycatcher called to us, ka-*bick*, ka-*bick*. We were happy. What a miracle to be able to say those three words. I didn't think of my daughters too much that day—just enough to know the difference between joy and unadulterated joy. I hoped one day they'd feel the same way, and understand.

Once we'd slept extra neat and clean, and prayed for peace, we headed back to Tawas at dawn. What followed was another blur of birds and foxes. Above the den and cubs, peacefully lazing in the spring morning, yellow warblers seemed to grow out of the leaves, scarlet tanagers, eastern kingbirds, and more orioles, Baltimore and orchard, fell from branch to branch in a snaggle of orange and ochre. One Baltimore in particular skewed almost red rather than the bird's usual color, but we figured it was just the light. Later we discovered that a couple of widely distributed ornamental bushes—Morrow's and Tartarian honeysuckles—are causing a number of Baltimore orioles, as well as some other species across the eastern seaboard, to exhibit a reddish discoloration. Seems the birds love the red berries, and the rhodoxanthin in the fruit stains some of their feathers. This probably wasn't true of our bird; he still vibrated at a wavelength of about 600 nanometers (orange), rather than 630 to 700 (red). But it was yet more evidence that we humans were affecting the very essence of birds' lives. We were changing their colors goddamnit.

Out in the bay, the morning glare gave way to a softer afternoon, and we walked and looked, and Donna and Don took about thirty-five thousand photographs, and it was then that I wanted to kill them.

I don't remember when they started to take so many photographs; one day we were birders, next Annie Liebovitz had shown up, bringing David LaChapelle with her. I appreciate the results later, but the actual process can come close to being maddening. Partly that's because of the way they take pictures, which is to place their digital camera against the lens of their scope and click. It's a bit Rube Goldberg, but it works superbly. Not only did Donna win the *WildBird* prize for her osprey photo in Florida, but before that the two of them won first prize in the international category in the same magazine for their snap of a purple honeycreeper in Trinidad. Unfortunately, it needs such a skillful hand that more often than not it goes wrong, making it more labor-intensive than if they simply took a picture with a telephoto lens.

The other problem is that the camera they use hates them. The thing is two parts human to one part camera, though I think Don would argue it's four parts evil to five parts useless. The most annoying thing it does, among many, is to flash even when you explicitly tell it not to. I lost track of how many times that day in Tawas I heard Don yell, "Did it fucking flash, Donna?" and Donna say, "Yes, the fucker!" Then there'd be a few minutes of rumbling about the iniquities of modern science; exasperation at the dumbing down of America ("Why does it have to default to flash every single time? Aren't we adult enough to decide on our own?"); a refocus on the bird at hand (if it's still in the bush); and the whole thing would start over. But now the camera's not focused right; or else Donna, who's often the shutter person, doesn't click it at exactly the right moment for Don's aesthetic needs, or else she does but the machine has a slight delay in actually shuttering, at which point they both go nuts all over again.

The existence of movie-shooting capabilities in the evil camera is what has ratcheted up an ongoing annoyance to a seering agony though. At Tawas, Don got a very bright Baltimore oriole in a tree, scoped it, made Donna put the camera against the lens, and started to shoot a movie. It was going to be a classic, but the bird had other ideas.

"Did he fly, the fucker?" yelled Don, looking up into the tree as the bird seemed to leave.

"No, it's still there—and no swearing; I'm taking this for little kids," Donna said, as the bird continued to bounce around, perfectly in frame.

"Little kids?" Don said.

"Yes, for my nephew's class."

"Sorry, sweetie," said Don, "but I had it perfectly in focus, and the fucker moved."

The previous day at Grayling, Mr. Potato Head had come over to Donna as she was filming a Kirtland's warbler. He'd spent a few minutes perorating on how a distant bird "can't be a thrasher—must be an osprey." (For the record, a brown thrasher is a bird not much bigger than an American robin, and an osprey is a great huge raptor, sometimes seen with an entire fish in its talons.) He'd spotted Donna lining up a shot and crept over, then suddenly exploded, with startling volume, "All it takes is a steady hand, huh?"

He couldn't know that the making of movies and the taking of photographs had, by this point in Don and Donna's lives, become as much an obsession as the actual birding. I was going to have to find a way of telling them that it was beginning to get in the way of what I thought we all loved the most, the finding and seeing of the birds. Sometimes I felt we hung around places an extra half hour so that they could get the perfect photo, when what we used to do was walk farther, see more, and revel in the teeming wonder of it all. It's different from listing, of course, but it had the same feeling once in a while; there was an acquisitive nature to the photography that, to my eye at least, curtailed the purity of walking and finding. Plus, I knew from the times I'd taken pictures that it can get in the way of simply looking at the bird. I had once had a barstool conversation in a pub in Ireland about this urge to snap instead of look. The man I was talking to summed up the impulse perfectly: "That ashtray! Let's film it!"

But the tough conversation with Don and Donna would have to wait. As always, however, there was much more to discover, and the southern part of Michigan was calling to us.

We headed south along the coast of Lake Huron towards Nayanquing Point Wildlife Area, which although described in *A Birder's Guide to Michigan* as "[stirring] the imagination of every Michigan birder," failed utterly to stir much of anything in us, so devoid of birds did it seem to be. We did get a look at the wonderful yellow-headed blackbird, but it was one bird, and it was far away. Don tried to argue that his imagination was stirred, but we didn't entirely believe him, even though he took seventeen or eighteen photos of it.

Farther south, we stopped in at Chippewa Nature Center in Midland, a few miles west of Bay City. As we entered, Don suddenly grabbed Donna, thrust his arms around her neck, and yelled, "What am I doing?"

Donna quietly said, "You're snapping the neck of a starling."

"Ha!" Don said. "And to think some people would say it looks like a hug."

Then he said, "Lisa Walraven kills starlings."

It had looked something like a hug, and the mention of Arizona raised our spirits. We spent the next part of the day remembering all the wonderful birds we'd seen on our first trip, and in bringing that to mind, we seemed to reinvigorate ourselves. As ever, our greatest joy was to pull off the main road in the woods and simply bird—nothing more, nothing less. So we did, there in the middle of Michigan, and leaving the scope and the camera in the car, Don and Donna walked with me for a mile down a deserted country lane.

We paid no real heed to the first part of the sign we found at the side of the road:

NO TRESPASSING . . .

(that's pretty standard; so far so good). But we were given pause when we read on:

**PRISON PROPERTY
ENTRY INTO THIS AREA WITHOUT
A PERMIT IS A FELONY.**

Because both Don and I are green card holders, a serious crime is probably not in our best interests. Plus, we were in no real need of coming across an acrobatic convict who's just jumped the razor wire.

We needn't have worried. All we found were a mixed flock of warblers, including something we'd never seen before. It took us many minutes of looking and studying to nail down its particulars. As it flitted, Donna shouted out, "Golden-winged warbler?" I said, "Surely a blue-winged?" The bird was indeed an odd combination—a thick black eye stripe (blue-winged) instead of a fatter area of darkness (golden-winged), but no white above and below the patch, which is what the golden-winged would display; a golden head (both, sort of), substantial gray across the nape and back (golden-winged), but two yellowish wing bars (blue-winged only). It didn't make sense.

Then, Don got it: "That's a Brewster's" he said, and he was right. Brewster's is a hybrid of the two warblers, though as a species it would be noted as a golden-winged (come on now, try to keep up). Don and Donna had long wanted to see one—up to that point, it was one of the few birds I'd seen that they had not—so they were ecstatic.

With just enough information, and hours of book work and iPod study, we'd actually become pretty good. Throw in all this time, time, time, and we'd begun to feel pretty confident about what we were doing. Don and Donna devoted every vacation to birds; having children made it harder for me to do the same, but still, Michigan was my third major trip in just over a year. And our conversation about Arizona had brought up other places we wanted to see together, including Texas; somewhere in the center of America; California down the line; Wisconsin in deepest winter; and even the upper peninsula of this state, Michigan. Don and I also wanted to take a pelagic trip to get all those seabirds that never fly near land. Donna, owing to a lifelong susceptibility to seasickness, was pretty sure she was going to leave us to that one, meaning we'd probably have to take a likeness of her with us on the boat so that she could pretend she'd seen the dovekies, Atlantic puffins, and other birds that pretty much never come by Prospect Park in Brooklyn.

Without even actively meaning to, this growing obsession with birds didn't just make us birders; the three of us had made a commitment to a different kind of life too. I knew for myself that I almost didn't recognize the person I'd been just a few years previously. Gone was the idea that I had a favorite TV show; gone was any real interest in advancement and status; gone was not caring about how we all treated the planet. I winced at waste; I put a sticker on my car that read, BIRDERSAGAINSTBUSH.COM and made sure that the car itself was as fuel-efficient as I could manage. Above all else, though, there was this "time" thing. Pretty much every weekend found Don and Donna in a park somewhere, walking and looking. When I had a free Saturday or Sunday, I did the same; and as my daughters got older, I was able to gently nudge them into joining me now and then on a Saturday afternoon at Jamaica Bay in Queens. On one such day, a fellow birder stopped me and paid me the most extraordinary compliment; I blush when I think of her soft words, which were along the lines of me being a good parent to have thought to have brought two eight-year-old girls with binoculars to a national park (I'm sure that she was actually just reacting to how darned cute they are). I beamed ridiculously all day long that another naturalist had noticed what I was trying to impart; the girls, for their part, saw nothing notable at all in spinning a focus wheel and saying, "Dad, what's that one again?"

"That, Amelia, is a double-crested cormorant. See how it's holding out its wings to dry them? Can you remember why it does that?"

"They're not waterproof, right, Daddy?" interjects Lily.

As we wandered back to the car, past the sign for the jail, I thought about what the intersection of birds and fathering had brought me. I tried to explain it to Donna as we walked but I couldn't get it quite right. In retrospect, it could be best summed up in a gag: "Every potential felon should have daughters like mine." A three-day trip to Michigan, a six-day trip to Arizona, a week in Florida—being away that long is hard enough, especially with reprobates like the Graffitis. I'd no more commit a serious crime, and risk being away from my girls forever, than jump over the moon.

There, I solved the law-and-order issue in one fell swoop: Give everyone an Amelia, give everyone a Lily.

No need to thank me.

Hillsdale is a nondescript town in southern Michigan, about twenty miles north of the Ohio border. To some travelers, I guess, it's a stop on the way from Cleveland to Kalamazoo. For us, and for many other birders, it is a nesting home to one of the rarer and more beautiful birds America can boast of in the spring: the Kentucky warbler.

The Kentucky is one of just four *Oporornis* warblers in the family, and to me, *Oporornis* warblers—*formosus* (Kentucky), *agilis* (Connecticut), *philadelphia* (mourning), and the one Don begged the stars to see at the San Pedro River, *tolmiei* (MacGillivray's)—had become a collective, feathery holy grail. In all this time birding I had seen precisely none of them. Don and Donna had seen mourning warblers in Central America, but still lacked satisfying, North American looks at the family. Don came close to a Kentucky in the Brooklyn Botanic Garden once, but the report of its presence had gone out widely to the faithful, and the second a tiny flit of movement was observed, seventy-three birders stepped forward in unison and cried, *"Kentucky!"* Needless to say, the bird was never seen again; Don claimed he'd caught a glimpse of it, but he wasn't very convincing about it.

Not only handsome, *Oporornis* warblers are understory birds, terrifically hard to find and see, and always the subject of intense interest in springtime and fall. It's hard to chase them, as they're so careful to remain undiscovered. Most sightings of *Oporornis* are therefore ad hoc and brief; the birds are also heard more often than seen. Of the four, Kentucky warblers are marginally the easiest to find, partly because they sing a distinctive song, and they sing it a lot. (One study reports that a single male sang every twelve seconds for three full hours. For god's sake think of the neighbors!) Because *A Birder's Guide to Michigan* notes that Hillsdale is a place where one or two pairs have spent the summer pretty consistently since 1996, we'd have to make a pilgrimage. Sure, they're rare, but the book gives step-by-step instructions on where to go. Honestly, it sounded as easy as pie.

To illustrate how wrong this was, a story: One summer, on the drive from the house in Pennsylvania, we'd stopped at a fast-food outlet. It was summertime; Amelia was three years old. Poor thing had scoffed a large piece of pie—specifically, Dianna's Blueberry Extravaganza—from the store next to our house, right before we'd driven south to the city, an hour and a half of bumping and churning through traffic before we got out to stretch our legs. So there we were, at the fast-food place, and here it came: big old custard, and she parked it right across my feet. I was wearing open-toed sandals. Amelia looked up at me with a mixture of relief and sorrow. I never thought I'd love anyone for puking on me, but you learn something every day when you raise a child. Her mother rushed Amelia off to the bathroom to clean her up; I stood there with Lily, pie-toed and diligently ignored by the employees of the restaurant. If I remember correctly, I had to wipe the floor with the bun of my burger; I may have also simply put said bun back on said burger, figuring I wouldn't notice the difference. Merciful time has blurred the details.

In any case, chasing the Kentucky warbler through a copse off a rural road in southern Michigan? Not easy as pie. Rather, the birding equivalent of having pie puked across your feet in a chain restaurant on the hottest day in July.

It was a handsome day otherwise: high blue, with distant, nonthreatening clouds punctuating the stratosphere. We drove out along Route 34, through Pittsford, then south towards Skuse Road, where the bird was said to breed. Here and there we'd stop to bird the odd copse of deciduous trees, juiced as they were by the St. Joseph River in an otherwise dry expanse of farmland. No one was around. We took our time over another least flycatcher, until on south we went, past the romantically named Lake No. 8 (not quite as impressive as Lake No. 5, truth be told), to the exact spot where this, the Lost Nation State Game Area, hid for sure a nesting Kentucky warbler.

We parked in a small pull-off, and headed up and over a small hill and left into the woodland, reading carefully the explicit directions in the book: "In about one-third mile, you will encounter the remains of an immense fallen tree. In the next 100 yards, listen carefully for Kentucky and hooded warblers."

I have since reread this passage about Skuse Road many times, and I have still yet to find the section detailing the intense discomfort of swarms of midges and mosquitoes feasting on human flesh; the incessant buzzing of a billion bugs bored from a lack of warm skin upon which to munch, now alive with the joy of misanthropic attack.

Oh yes, I've read this book many times; it's written by Allen T. Chartier and Jerry Ziarno. I don't believe those are their real names. Jenny, who knows them a bit, assures me they're great guys, but I think they're scared—as they goddamn should be—that idiots like me, and Don, and especially Donna, will one day find them and beat them to death with 660 pages of really useful Michigan birding information, because they didn't add a 661st page detailing the particular hell that is the Lost Nation State Game Area in mid-spring.

The early part of the hike had been peaceful and pleasant. We had followed a meandering trail as it headed through relatively open pastures with high trees all around. We had heard the odd warbler but hadn't seen much, which was fine by us. We were here for the Kentucky, and that bird would indeed be somewhere deep in the woodland. The air was clear; the heat unarguable yet bearable.

But once we entered into the deeper woods, the bugs joined us, intermittently at first, and then full-on. They'd zoom into our ears and up our noses; they'd bite—oh man, would they bite—and we spent more time swatting them than listening for the Kentucky. We walked for about twenty minutes, but it felt like hours. I swear one bug crawled into my ear canal, laid out a full place setting, and tucked in. There were bugs up my nose, under my eyelids, even in my shoes—*in my shoes?* I was wearing walking boots with pants tucked into the socks—I repeat, *in my shoes?* Donna was whimpering like a lost dog. Don's arms ballooned to three times their normal size, and he'd given himself two black eyes trying to swat stuff away (he was wearing glasses too, so god knows how he managed it). This was Golgotha and Purgatory, the Long March and Armageddon.

Five minutes more and Donna had a simple solution; she turned tail, and with barely a wave, beat a smart and jealousy-inducing retreat.

What was I to do? Don was in for the long haul. He claimed he'd distantly heard a call that he couldn't perfectly place, though he was beginning to think it was indeed the Kentucky. Was my pain enough to staunch the chance of an *Oporornis* warbler?

Don soldiered on. He truly does suffer from whatever is the opposite of Attention Deficit Disorder—Donna calls it his Attention *Surfeit* Disorder. Nothing would keep him from giving this hell every second he could bear. This situation brought to mind him standing in the middle of a road at Ding Darling in Florida and ignoring both the swarming midges, and the beeping SUVs trying to pass, as he photographed that balletic reddish egret. These bugs here in Michigan were never going to be bad enough to see him give up. If he would butch it out, then I would too. I had to be (and only you other British, book-editing, city-dwelling bird lovers will know how infrequently I have thought such a ludicrous thing) a man! So on we pushed, deeper into another ring of fire, and let me say right here, right now, that June Carter Cash was right: it burns, burns, burns. My swatting and cursing increased in regularity and creativity. Those bugs were hell's envoys, the spawn of evil's loins; each one was the embodiment of a person copulating with his female parent; given the chance, they would boil babies in bags; they wished to skewer nuns and puppies. They were not nice at all.

Then Don heard the birdsong once more.

"There! Listen. Fifty yards at least! That's it."

The bugs perked up their ears and stopped biting for a moment. Given that birds eat bugs, presumably they too wanted to know if what we all were hearing was a Kentucky warbler.

"Again! Clear as day! Hear that?" He was whispering now. "Get the iPod. Let's check it."

I pushed one bud of the iPod into my bright red, bug-munched ear, and held the other up for Don. On the machine, the voice intoned, "Kentucky warbler," and the bird trilled. We listened over and over, then put it on pause to listen to the real thing. Nothing. Again, the iPod; again, the world. Something distant, but what? And the bugs! Having lost interest in the bird, and redoubled their interest in us now that we were stationary, they had really lit into us. I didn't think I could take it anymore.

"Don . . ."

"I know," he said, "but surprisingly, I'm fine."

This wasn't fun anymore. It may have been an *Oporornis*, but I thought about those babies being boiled in bags, and suddenly I didn't give a rat's ass.

"I'm outta here," I whined, and with that I left him there with the bugs and the skewered nuns and the distant bird.

An hour later, the three of us sat in the rental car in silence. A few minutes after I'd left Don, he'd had a brainstorm: he'd record the sound of the bird on the digital camera by taking short movies. I have the two movies right here on my computer: In them, a shaky image pans left, then right, the urgent green of spring so beautiful everywhere, a fallen maple, vines and bushes and intense sunlight coming across the distant bug-free fields. It's like a sunny outtake from the *Blair Witch Project*. And every ten to fifteen seconds a bird can be heard, a strong and pretty three-parter of a song, *taweet taweet tawoota* it went, *taweet taweet tawoota*.

A hooded warbler. That's all we got there. For all that pain, for all those bug bites which took weeks to heal, what we'd heard was a bird that was, at that precise moment, delighting birders in full view in the Ramble, in the middle of New York's Central Park, a thousand miles away—the place I birded more than anywhere.

It was true that we were getting pretty darned good at this "birding by ear" thing; we had most of the warblers down, and a lot of the other songbirds. But it was also clear at this point that there was still work to be done. From about New Year's onwards Don, Donna, and I start to reduce the number of albums we listen to on our respective iPods in favor of repeated listens to birdsongs. We feel the coming spring keenly, and by this study every year we add a few new songs to the repertoire of ones we know instantly. Driving through Brooklyn we sometimes play birdsongs on the iPod speakers, Don keeping the sound down for the first few seconds so that we miss the announcement of what we're listening to. Then, we all guess. Donna has become extremely proficient at this game, which makes me think she's doing much more work on it than am I. It has certainly increased the numbers of birds we find. The results, once the singing migrants jangle through New York and New Jersey a few months later, are startling—Donna can walk through woodland and call out what she's hearing before any of us see the bird; Don is not much worse. I, too, can walk a nonbirder through Central Park and pick out the majority of the regular and migrating birds by sound. It's almost as though we're experiencing the fauna more in the way they experience each other, which delights us. All this has caused us to say that our new guidebook is the iPod, but it isn't foolproof: Just as we'd misapprehended almost every prairie warbler in Florida, so we'd spent much too much time in that hellish copse off Skuse Road in the vain hope that what we were hearing was a Kentucky.

Some people really can bird by ear almost exclusively. Jenny, for example, is good enough to pinpoint stuff at fifty or hundred yards in a heavy forest. It has been her job, after all, to conduct transacts of nesting birds (a transact is a designated walk of a certain length during which one's task is simply to listen and note down what is heard). This is a rare skill, and one she saw no reason to brag about, even though I was in awe. Had she been with us that morning, she might well have said, "Hooded," and we could have curtailed the hell.

Instead, we found ourselves sitting in an antiseptic rental car, nursing our wounds. To break the near silence of three people scratching their bites, Don said, "I quite enjoyed that. I'm thinking of giving it another go, actually."

And with that, I locked the car doors, turned the ignition, and sped down the hill to whatever was next.

To say that the cerulean warbler is a small blue bird is like saying that "Nessun dorma" lifts a bit at the end. The cerulean is a stunning little bird, shining blue above and streaked white and blue below, with a dark blue "necklace" that is key for identification. The bird likes to hang out at the upper reaches of the canopy, and one of the places it comes to breed every spring is this southern part of Michigan. Again, Chartier and Ziarno—those bastards—gave us explicit instructions as to where to find it, and late on our penultimate afternoon we found ourselves at the Waterloo Recreation Area.

In Waterloo, we found ourselves in a serenely pretty spot. A clay road, McLure, runs down a hill and into a clearing that boasts a beautiful small pond. Then the road rises back into the forest, turning this way and that until it runs out at a paved road called Loveland. The place is a quiet dream broken only by the sounds of birds, the odd car, and sadly, the yowl of the big-bellied wife-beater.

He was a Pregnant, middle aged, and wore a shirt that defied all laws of high fashion: he'd basically ripped the arms off a normal dress shirt, all to show off limbs that hadn't seen the inside of a gym, or the blaze of the sun, since the early days of the Carter administration. With him was a younger man; there seemed to be some kind of guru-student thing going on. As we stood by the beautiful small pond, beneath huge maples, and oaks, and ash, and beech, we desperately listened for ceruleans. The Pregnant opined to us that it was late in the day to be trying to see warblers—got it—and when a black-throated blue (warbler) sang from a distant tree, he was quick to blurt out the name of the bird as though all of us there were absolute beginners. Once we'd thanked him for his perspicacity, he went on to tell us that the magnification of our binoculars wasn't correct for this type of birding; that our field guide was the fourth edition, not the more current fifth; that Don's glasses were smudged; that I was bald; that Donna's shirt was too bright and might scare the birds away; and to finish, that one of the legs on the tripod which held our spotting scope had been extended, and here I quote, "probably an inch longer than the other two, meaning that even if you see a bird, which I highly doubt this time of the day, your view won't be square."

"Square, you say?" I said.

We wanted him to walk away and not come back. The Small Injustice Man section of my soul also wanted him to get run over, but I figured an ambulance would break the peace of the afternoon. Still, the place was so serene that it was easy enough to turn back to the great joy of birding. After a few minutes, the guy mercifully made for Loveland Road.

Just as we were sighing with relief, we heard it: the unmistakable trill of a cerulean warbler. It sounded close, but where was it? All around us, the deciduae loomed. They were at least seventy-five feet, and when you're trying to see a much-sought-after bird, they suddenly seem to get even taller than that. Again we heard it, and again, but try as we might, there was nothing to be seen. We were being mocked. Up and down the road we ran, Don getting increasingly agitated, Donna too; but I was the worst. I had loved this bird since the day I started to study the warblers, and desperately, desperately wanted to see it. Now, here it was. This was not a bird I could ever count on catching a glimpse of migrating through New York, though it did sometimes happen. We had a plane to be on the next afternoon, and we could hear it—a cerulean!—but we could hardly see as high as we needed to, let alone make out a bird up there. But the good news was this was its nesting ground, so we knew it wasn't migrating; it was here to stay. Surely our patience would be rewarded. Patient or no, our necks ached—indeed, everything from our lower back to the tops of our heads was once again in June Carter Cash territory.

And then, as it will, the day dimmed to the point where we couldn't really see. The bird sang on. Don said, "Tomorrow morning we have to be here before it's light."

He was right. We had one morning left. The bird was resident. If we drove directly from Waterloo to the Detroit airport for our evening flight to save a few hours, we'd have from early morning until about midday. It wasn't too late. It wasn't.

That night I lay in my motel bed filled with thoughts of a cerulean coming down to, oh, let's say twenty feet, so that I might enjoy it without too much pain. I thought wistfully of our Kirtland's warbler experience—those short jack pines and helpful guide. I thought of Jenny telling us how friendly the Kirtland's females could be.

"They come right up to you," she is saying. "They seem so curious about you, you know?"

I know, I know. And then, I'm fast asleep.

These could be the last days we ever get to see cerulean warblers. Just as the Kirtland's existence is rendered tenuous by its small numbers and its fussy nesting needs, so too the cerulean faces extraordinary stresses. This time, there's no one to blame but us.

Cerulean warblers winter in western South America, in forests on the eastern slope of the Andes, between three thousand and nine thousand feet up, and they need great unbroken swathes of trees to do so. Their "winter" range (that is, the place they go when it's winter in the northern hemisphere) stretches from Central America, northern Colombia and Venezuela, down to Peru, and even to northwestern Bolivia, an area that neatly overlaps one of South America's most important industries. If you like South American coffee, as I do, the massive decline of the cerulean warbler—the worst fall-off in terms of numbers of any warbler in North America—is pretty much your fault (and mine).

In the old days, coffee plantation owners depended on large deciduous forests with plenty of shade to grow their beans. Thanks to a combination of pesticides, advances in genetic modification processes, and new agricultural techniques, beans can now be grown in the full glare of the South American sun, taking away the urgent need to safeguard the large forests. In addition, all the usual dangers are in play: too much development, excessive logging, a massive increase in the number of farms; even some tree species, beloved of the wintering cerulean, are in decline (sycamores and oaks especially).

There's another force that's causing mayhem. According to T. Edward Nickens writing in *National Wildlife*, "No Central American country is expected to grow in population by less than 45 percent between 2003 and 2050. In South America, the total human population between 2002 and 2025 is expected to grow by 100 million."

The results are staggering. In the final three decades of the twentieth century, the cerulean warbler population declined by nearly 4 percent every single year—nearly 80 percent overall. It's surely not too much to say that should my daughters ever want to see a cerulean warbler when they're the age that I am now, there won't be any to see. As our generation is to the ivory-billed woodpecker, so theirs is to the cerulean, and possibly the Kirtland's, and many other species. The adage that you want to give your kids more than you ever had is never more apt than when thinking about wildlife. Deep inside me there's a faint dread at enjoying the cerulean if my girls won't be able to do the same.

The problems are so acute in South America that they have

produced an interesting effect on conservation here in the Northern Americas: we've begun raising money and awareness for remedial efforts in the wintering grounds, rather than concentrating, as we traditionally have, solely on the breeding habitats the birds use once they get here (no use having a nice home in the hills if there's no one coming to use it). At the forefront of these efforts is the American Bird Conservancy (ABC). In partnership with a couple of South American efforts—Fundación ProAves in Colombia, and Fundación Jocotoco in Ecuador—ABC has recently created two reserves to protect key wintering sites for ceruleans and many other migrants in the Andes. There are any number of ways that ABC raises money—perhaps my favorite is selling little bags of cerulean-warbler-friendly coffee, some of which I have in my fridge. It tastes fine, and there's even a picture of a cerulean on the bag. At best it's a start, but the efforts of such organizations mean that today, Memorial Day 2006, the start of summer, and the last day of our trip, there is at least still some hope that we'll see a blessed cerulean here in southern Michigan.

It was a warm morning even before dawn, and we sensed a hot day ready to come steaming in. We picked up non-cerulean-friendly coffees at a Dunkin' Donuts and headed out on the freeway towards our Waterloo. All the way out Don kept the iPod speakers propped up on the dashboard, playing and replaying the cerulean's song. Every time I braked or turned a curve, he'd have to thrust his hands out to catch the speakers. But the song was sticking.

At Waterloo, just as first light was rising, we parked in the same spot as the day before. We looked like undercover detectives staking out an illegal gambling den, right down to the coffees and doughnuts on the roof of our car, and the gun-holster-like man-bras which supported our binoculars.

We were listening hard. Thrushes (wood and hermit) sang in the day. Frogs barked. We heard a distant black-throated green warbler do its *zee zee zee zee ZO zee*, perhaps the easiest warbler song to learn. (But not to imitate. I tried it once in a restaurant in Florida and someone rushed over and attempted to give me the Heimlich maneuver.)

Then, we heard it again: the now unmistakable song of the cerulean warbler, a bird that a few months earlier had been many thousands of feet up the Andes. We were hearing many, in fact, and we had at least until noon to see them. In the words of Wezil Walraven, it was showtime.

Excited, we split up. Don took the northern edge of the song, Donna the middle, and I stayed nearer the car. A curious set of hand gestures from Don soon had the three of us together under a huge tree, where in the now-full light a cerulean was going at its song full tilt.

Suddenly, Donna said, "There! There!" and in a different tree, behind us, we could see the silhouette of a small prancing warbler; but the light was from behind it, so we could make out no color. We couldn't claim it for sure. Above us, much much higher, at the original tree, the song continued, and we turned our attention back to it. For an hour we listened and strained our necks, but still we caught not a glimpse. At this point, I would have taken being shat on.

After a while, the three of us realized that there was, indeed, a bird attached to the song. Way up we could see the warbler flitting bough to bough, working each leaf and cranny to find bugs to eat. We were able to follow its movement, and we knew we had a cerulean warbler in our binoculars. But it was so high! Don set up his scope but never found it. We were desperate for it to come down to a manageable height. I was even hoping that a couple of them might get into it—they're aggressive little birds when baby making is at stake—and that the ensuing fight, which generally starts with a midair collision and proceeds through avian fisticuffs to a dramatic fall to the ground, might just bring a bright male to eye level. No such luck.

Just as we were running out of hope, we saw the bird about fifty feet up, close enough to make out the diagnostic dark necklace on its white breast. But the wonderful azure, the magnificent cerulean blue? Barely, and just as we imagined it might come lower—*damn!*—it flew.

In painful resignation, I threw myself to the dirt road and lay like I'd been run over by a truck. It was wonderful, down there. Above me, the high oaks and birches swung like pretty dancers, and the azure sky lay unfathomable; a few thin clouds slipped along, perfunctorily. I listened to the natural "silence": no cars, no voices, no phones, just leaves in the wind, frogs, birds, the creak of trees rubbing together. Nothing is as alive as much as the silence of a forest. I was alive then too; I put my fingers to the dirt and listened, for those few minutes, as I've never listened before or since.

This, then, is why. This.

NOW WHAT?

❧

A friend of mine got an e-mail from a friend of hers, a guy called Ted Olinger. Ted lives in the Pacific Northwest, and has a problem with woodpeckers, specifically, northern flickers. The problem is this: they drum on the roof of his house, every day, all day long. A study in the late 1950s described the sound as akin to that of a "miniature pneumatic drill." That sound is beginning to drive Ted Olinger nuts.

The original e-mail eventually makes its way to my in-box. Now that I'm known as a birder, I get notes like this forwarded to me all the time. The subject lines of too many of my work e-mails say things like, "Prospect Park and birder harassment," or "Ivory-bill," or most regularly the simple, "Fwd: Birds." If this was England, where "birds" can be a synonym for "gentle lady folk," I might get a call from human resources. Here, I'm just thought of as mildly odd, the work colleague who has binoculars on his windowsill and a picture of an eastern meadowlark on his wall. A lot of the e-mails about birds I read and delete, given that they're actually about birds and not women; but the one from Ted I saved, given that his annoyance at the flickers was real, and gentle, and intriguing. I could tell he loved the woodpeckers, but he had a real problem too: it's hard enough to get a four-year-old boy to sleep past six A.M. as it is, but when a family of flickers are pretending to be the Warrior Drums of Burundi, well, then you have to find a solution.

Beth, his wife, is a bit more enamored of them. According to Ted's e-mail, she's been known to crouch in her son's treehouse and watch the parents and their brood of three chicks. The solution, such as it is, is that Ted has nailed a birdhouse to one of the firs in the garden, to try and get the flickers to leave the roof alone. All this seems to have done is encourage a *pileated* woodpecker, a bird many times bigger than a flicker, to drum on the fir while the flickers drum on the house.

As if all this weren't enough, there's one more elephant in the room, up there in Pierce County, Washington. For all the pounding on roofs and firs, what all the birds actually love most is to drum on something else entirely. Ted, in his e-mail, mentions that his yard boasts, in Beth's words, "the most expensive bird roost in the western hemisphere." This is now her mantra, he says.

What could it be? I e-mailed Ted directly about the flickers, and he e-mailed me back, and I e-mailed him again, subtly mentioning the "expensive bird roost," and he e-mailed me back without clarifying. Now I just had to know, and was relieved when the Olingers invited me to come see them and their raucous garden.

I couldn't wait. It had been months since Michigan, and I was itching to travel again—plus, what the heck is sitting in his backyard? The great advantage of the Northwest would be that I'd have the chance to see any number of coastal birds whose range is limited to the Pacific Ocean. I could imagine Don's excited opinion: *You'll up your life list by twenty, thirty, no problem.*

But they were not words Don Graffiti spoke out loud. He had no opinion about Seattle. While I was making my way west, he and Donna were heading south.

FIVE

Pacific Northwest:
People of the Grass Country

End of the year and here I am, in the "gateway to the Olympic Peninsula," Gig Harbor, Washington, just across Puget Sound from Tacoma, and a place that is, as you have no reason on earth to know, the sister city of Sakhalin Island, Russia.

After a summer of drought, by late November this part of America was flooded out, and the people had gone crazy. Checkout aisles became battlegrounds, and the roads were choked with rage. Folks said it was a reckoning, and muttered at the sky warily, in case God was listening. The *New York Times* reported that this November was on course to being the wettest on record in the Pacific Northwe(s)t. William Yardley, writing in the paper, likened the rain in Seattle to "bass, not lead guitar," persistent rather than loud, which was fine as far as analogies go, but didn't change the fact that people were ready to kill each other. Seattle-Tacoma International Airport, where I landed late in the afternoon of November 21, had recorded more than fourteen inches of homicidal rain for the month.

This was to be my first major birding trip without Don and Donna, who in an act of hideous selfishness had forsaken the chance to be cold and wet and had booked themselves a birding trip to tropical Costa Rica. The Olingers had an interest in birds, thank god, but it was mostly limited to their nesting woodpeckers and a set of heavily frequented feeders on their deck, so it was clear I was to be on my own vis-à-vis "mad birding."

The possibilities were mouthwatering though. Would I see hundreds of bald eagles on the Skagit River? I was a bit early, but they start to arrive late in the year. Would I see murrelets in Puget Sound? Would I score a northwestern crow, a bird restricted to the coastline up above Aberdeen? Whatever the case, I'd surely miss Don and Donna's perspicacity, their willingness to dispute identifications, their commitment to making every available hour of light count, even their obsession—well, Don's obsession—with my eating habits.

But maybe it was good they weren't on this trip; the weather would have driven Don nuts. Bad weather had that effect. A few weeks before my Seattle jaunt the three of us had driven up to the Adirondacks for a long weekend. I had e-mailed Don and Donna every day in the days before our trip regarding the weather forecast. It was pretty clear: it was going to be wet, for at least the first part of the weekend. I only track such things so that we're prepared, but for Don it's akin to one of the worst forms of betrayal: the betrayal of hope. The man who coos at snakes will not countenance what he views as pessimism, even when it's backed up by Doppler 93,000. Don refuses to give any credence to weather forecasts. "They are continually, and spectacularly, wrong," he says; Donna thoroughly agrees.

That weekend in the Adirondacks he woke me at first light in what has become his habitual manner, bursting through my door, his arms fully extended in front of him and his hands clasped together. His index fingers he thrusts forward into the classic pose of the gun-toting cop of detective movies, and he shouts, "Stay down!" or, "Let me see your hands!" or, echoing every officer on the TV show *Cops*, "Where's yer wife at?" He finds this enormously amusing, still laughing long after I've managed to peel myself off the ceiling and swallow down a beta blocker the size of a kiwi. That morning in the Adirondacks, once I'd stopped hyperventilating I noticed his jacket and hat were soaked through; I took my chance to get a point back by saying, "So the weather is exactly as I and News Channel Four predicted then?"

Don said, "Well, it is *technically* raining."

What would he have made of Gig Harbor? That first night I fell asleep under a skylight that thrummed to the sting of an icy deluge. In the morning, the rain was still falling—or more precisely, was hurling itself against the roof and windows in a soggy rage. I was lying in bed, listening to the rain and imagining the birds Don and Donna might be seeing in Costa Rica. Then my reverie was suddenly and quite rudely obliterated, not by Officer Graffiti, of course—he was too busy being warm and happy—but by two snuffling pug dogs. They had broken open the bedroom door and made a beeline for my belly, which they hurled themselves onto like Olympians performing the vault. Once they'd landed (my stomach muscles being tight enough to repel a shot bullet, you understand), they proceeded to sneeze liberally in my face, as though they'd gotten heavy colds in all this bad weather. Great globs of pug snot subsequently licked off my eyebrows, I was then completely ignored so that they could get down to some pretty graphic gay pug love. When they weren't bouncing up and down off of my abs, B——and B——would spend most of their time either humping like there was Viagra in their Alpo or licking each other's alienlike eyeballs. They were shameless, and quite gymnastic. I swear to god I caught the younger one smoking at one point. I was just glad my daughters were safely ensconced on the East Coast; how would I have explained these dogs' behavior without forever besmirching their innocence? "Sometimes, girls, when a dog loves another dog—yes, it's another boy dog, Amelia, but let's not . . . Anyway, when they love each other very much . . . What's that Lily? Well, yes, it is, really a rather excessive amount . . . well, anyway, he sometimes wants to go to that other dog and . . . well . . . Why don't we all go outside and look at some birds?"

But two outrageous pugs were not the main surprise this

house in Pierce County held that morning. Wandering down for breakfast, I blearily went to the window. It was raining and raining and raining, and there in the garden sat the elephant in the room.

An ark.

Ted Olinger had, for some of his adult life, been a kayak instructor, but by the time I stayed with him and his family in Gig Harbor, he was unable to take folks down the Skagit anymore. A serious battle with Hodgkin's in his early twenties, and the subsequent lifesaving brutalization of radiation therapy, had left Ted, by now in his early forties, with a body that simply refused to cooperate. A meal I'd shared with him a year earlier in New York City had caused him to continually excuse himself to vomit. His esophagus was shot, and an operation to close a valve had been all too successful, meaning food simply got stuck and came back up. Now, a year on, he was doing better, he said, but he quietly admitted that the operation would need to be redone in a few years, starting the painful cycle again. Such a physical burden would leave most people suicidal.

Ted Olinger is not most people.

For a start, there's the not-so-little matter of what's sitting in the rain out back. The boat building began when he and his wife, Beth, lived in the fabulously named town of Puyallup, just east of Tacoma (itself the birthplace of Bing Crosby, and early workplace of Ted Bundy). There, Ted Olinger got the notion that he could escape the world in which he found himself and sail the seven seas. Beth had seemed fine with the idea, he said, so around the turn of the century they started to put a boat together. The building went in fits and starts, and as often happens when one's mind is occupied, something else turns up, and their boy, Jack, was born in 2002. Every time Ted and Beth tried to restart the serious construction, fate intervened; before I arrived, for example, a plan to work on the hull was jettisoned when Ted had to care for his sick mother. As a consequence, the boat barely made it past looking like the carcass of a dead animal. And then needing more space (for the boy, and the boat), they decided to move.

By the time I stayed with them, the transportation of a half-built forty-foot trawler from Tacoma to Gig Harbor was merely the amusing contents of a videotape trotted out after dinner; at the time, it must have been hell on all seventy-two wheels.

The movie begins with the low-loader arriving; measurements are taken; utility lines are dismantled; Jack runs around excitedly; there's a crack and something falls; damage is assessed and deemed acceptable; and suddenly we're on the road. The Tacoma Dome, the breast-shaped arena on the eastern side of town, passes to our right; approaching cars are seen swerving when they come across a half-built boat. We cross the Tacoma Narrows Bridge, the boat perhaps yearning for the water below. Then we're in Gig Harbor, and by dint of some miracle the truck manages to make the ninety degree turn into Ted's driveway.

Here, Ted pauses the video for effect, and announces, "Only one tree was harmed in the making of this movie. It was a pine." Then the low loader is gone, and a new house has a big yard made smaller by a boat. Jack runs around excitedly.

And there it now sits on that rainy morning, soaked through and hulking. I was enormously impressed, of course. By this point in my birding mania, I felt I had a handle on male-pattern obsession. I had never thought to build a boat though. When I owned my house in Pennsylvania, I had strongly considered constructing a treehouse way up in the pines so that I could get a literal bird's-eye view of avian proceedings. I went to the local Agway, priced out the wood and everything. Then I remembered I had absolutely no woodworking experience whatsoever, not to mention a crippling fear of heights, and bought a new birdfeeder instead. Ted Olinger, on the other hand, had actually half built an ark. This meant he was one of us, only much more manly. I would never say this to him directly, of course—the most he'd get would be a grudging nod and a nonchalant question about specs, but on the inside, I was awestruck.

On the patio, birdfeeders do a lively trade: a chestnut-backed chickadee, my first life bird in this state, hangs upside down like an acrobat and feeds briefly. Beth comes to stand with me and bemoan the weather. She says, "It's the most expensive bird roost in the western hemisphere." The flickers are quiet in the torrential fall.

It was clear that any joy in birding that day would have to be chiseled out of hard stone; the rain was general all over the peninsula, and the wind didn't help by blowing it horizontally. But there was so much to see, and as ever, so little time; plus, the dogs looked like they were about to start into it again.

At least without Don and Donna I was free to scour forecasts for a possible break in the weather, and by mid-morning I'd convinced everyone (save the dogs) to accompany me to Point No Point, on the northern end of the Kitsap Peninsula. I hoped to scope some of the seabirds that would come that far inland, the Puget being saltwater. And, who wouldn't love a place called Point No Point? Every depressive should visit there at least once.

The lighthouse at Point No Point, a fairly unimpressive and surprisingly squat building, is the oldest on Puget Sound; it's been silently screaming "mind the rocks!" since 1879. A dentist from Seattle by the name of Maggs was the first lighthouse keeper. On his first day of its operation, the lens and the glass hadn't arrived, so he stuck a piece of canvas over the south window to keep the kerosene lamp from getting extinguished. Now, 127 years later, it's a regular lighthouse, housed above a little white building on top of washed-up logs and rocks. We parked in a little lot next to it as rain started to fall. Before we knew it, Jack had run off excitedly, leaving the rest of us to bundle up and look warily at the sky. The day was blowing hard, and the drizzle quickly turned into a sharp rain falling sideways, up and under the brim of my hat and into my eyes. I assembled my spotting scope and headed after Ted and Beth and Jack, but it was hard out there on the point, and they soon retreated to the warmth of the car.

Me? I was loving it, and planned to stay out there as long as I thought my hosts (Jack especially) could stand being cooped up in a coupé.

There's something besides obsessing on birds that leaves me immune to the weather: I spent the first quarter century of my life in a cold and wet country, being steadily toughened, or rather, gradually inured against complaint. England boasts a unique mixture of dampness and low temperatures. Efficient heating systems are considered "namby-pamby," as is air conditioning in the "summer." But it's the winters, which generally run from September through the following July, that really bite.

I spent much of my pimply youth playing soccer, and much of that time trying in vain to get warm. I can still vividly remember one such brutal cold-weather game for my high school team. I was twelve years old. My legs were bright crimson from the intense cold, the soccer field hidden under five inches of snow. We were using an orange ball so we could see it. Note, also, that I was wearing shorts. It was well below freezing, the field was snow-covered, I was not yet a teenager, and I was being forced to run around after an orange ball in ecru shorts. My school was named after St. Francis of Assisi, meaning all the kids, and most of the staff, were forced to wear the brown family of colors pretty much constantly. Even at home.

I spent the first hour of the match avoiding all contact with both ball and other players, fearing, not unreasonably, that my legs were so cold that any such liaison might actually snap my already twiglike limbs in half. I was being yelled at for my recalcitrance by our coach, Sister Calista, a woman who claimed she'd once been an Olympic swimmer (she still had the shoulders). In the end I couldn't take her verbal pummeling anymore, and reluctantly chased after a pass.

Bad idea—I was nowhere near quick enough to reach it, and watched in horror as the huge defender on the other team took a swing at the ball. Time lagged. I watched the orb approaching like a bullet in a slo-mo movie, and my life flashed in front of my eyes (crowning; mum's breasts; solid food; measles; first day of preschool; Cordelia Weston puking in the doorway of our classroom; *Star Wars*; pimples; dad's first heart attack). Then, *slam!* His clearance hit me just above my nearly frozen knee. Using the Wong-Baker Faces Pain Rating Scale, where 0=no hurt (big smile!), and 5=hurts worst (grimace, four tears), I scored a 37 (entire head implodes, leaving only a gaping hole). I hit the ice like I'd been shot. All around me, adults on the sidelines, as well as fellow scabby preteens from both teams, ignored my wails. Sister Calista shouted words to the effect that I was not being man enough. This, coming from a woman as untouched as the snow inside the goal nets.

All this happened in England, in June.

Of the many, many things I love about America, perhaps the most fundamental is the fact that it has a climate, rather than just weather. I like being able to organize a barbecue knowing that "next Saturday" will be dry and warm. Not that I've ever actually organized a barbecue, you understand, but I like having the option. Don's lack of trust in weather forecasts strikes me, therefore, as oddly un-American. I'm never happier than looking at a map of the country and seeing a big ol' weather system roaring in from the west, and knowing it will land at precisely two twenty-eight the next afternoon. In England, one could organize a barbecue if one so wished, but one would need to clear at least five rain dates ahead of time, and chances are one would still have the barbecue indoors, where one would not be allowed to complain about the smoke.

Here, the day before Thanksgiving on a spit of beach in Puget Sound, I was entirely unaware of cold or rain or wind. Out in the bay, I watched as a murrelet slowly floated west, and distant western grebes buffeted and bobbed in the swell—two life birds in as many minutes. Once in a while I'd pause to wipe my scope lens or dry off my binoculars, but I felt my birding brain taking over, and I could have been in sunlight or storm and it wouldn't have mattered a jot. On I walked, south towards the bluffs, just in case the beach or the sea harbored a bird worth finding. A happy hour passed; I wished only that I could stay till dark. In the distance, I could just make out Mount Rainier through the drizzle; in the foreground, a black scoter puffed up its wet wings.

It was only when I got back to the car that I realized my jeans were soaked through, my shoes the same. I wore a huge smile.

Ted said, "There's something wrong with you."

As a general statement of fact, this was absolutely correct; but Ted clearly meant "you've been out in terrible weather, my god look at you," and he was, in this case, off the mark. I'd found something essential out there. Once again, birding had loaned me a calmness that seemed to push me apart from the concerns of the world.

That murrelet, for example. I had noted the overall feel of it, then its feathers, and then the book knowledge I'd earned from hours of poring over field guides kicked in, narrowing down the possibilities. Murrelets are smallish seabirds, and that particular bird out there could have been one of six kinds, most of which have fabulous names: Xantus's, Craveri's, ancient, Kittlitz's, marbled, and long-billed. The mere fact that it was here, in Washington state, at this time of year, ruled out at least four of them. Xantus's likes warm water offshore; Craveri's is closely related to Xantus's, and it too likes the warmer waters; Kittlitz's doesn't often come down this far south; long-billed is a Siberian bird that seldom comes down here either.

So that leaves ancient and marbled as my options. Now, the wind is blowing a gale, and the bird is far out; there's rain on my scope, and I don't have a camera with me. The looks I'm getting are hardly laboratory-perfect, yet I'm feeling confident. I know, too, that I need to concentrate on the drawings in the book that show plumage in November; birds molt, and the attendant changes in their look is an important thing to take into consideration. But there's something even easier here for me—the ancient always has a pale bill, the marbled does not. Even in this atrocious weather I can see the bird's bill is dark. The overall feel of the bird is slighter too, which argues for marbled; and there's conspicuous white on the sides of the bird that isn't present in the ancient.

Thrilled, I mark down "marbled murrelet" on a scrap of paper, tagged with an *(L)* for "life bird." In all this seemingly technical effort I never once feel like a scientist, never once like a researcher or intellectual, and never like a lister. I am, instead, a witness to something elemental, which accounts for the gratitude and the awe I find pumping through my blood.

But the nascent scientist in me could also now go study this mysterious bird more deeply. For years there was a great puzzle regarding murrelets: where did these seabirds raise their young? No one had ever discovered a nest. The massive reward of one hundred dollars was offered for anyone who could solve the riddle, and somebody presumably paid their rent for a month in the early seventies when a chick was discovered far inland in a tree. It's the only alcid that nests in such a spot; the others use cliffs and the like. Sadly, logging has severely hurt their chances all around the world, and they're now "globally threatened."

Knowing all this, however, only added to what was, for me, pure feeling, or what some might call love. I resisted hard the temptation, borne of a Roman Catholic upbringing, to describe it to myself or to others as the feeling of being connected to God, and the wonders of Creation. It seemed to me truer to the experience to be simply astounded that a small bird floated out there in this century, as its forebears had done for thousands of years before either Jesus or any of the rest of us. Nature had no moral imperative: nothing helped the bird; there was no fellow love for it out there; the water didn't help it, save harboring its food source; the other birds wouldn't mourn its passing; the weather was just the weather. A man stood on the beach, watched it pass, and spoke out loud its name, in wonder and intense joy.

By mid-afternoon the rain was so torrential that I gave up and sat watching the sodden birds at the Olingers' feeders. As we dried ourselves by the wood-burning stove, Ted regaled us with tales of his days as a kayaking instructor. He'd once led a training class from Port Townsend down to Seattle. It took five days, and along the way they had actually passed Point No Point, in pretty much the same conditions as today. The learners, in their turn, had been passed by a large canoe helmed by what Ted assumed were members of the Quinault Indian Nation—these hardies "steamed by at five knots," he said, "all clad in T-shirts and jeans. They were singing. We lumbered along in fleece and Gore-Tex, and I had to make a big paella on the beach that night to get people happy again."

He went on, "One hypothermic worthy confessed to me that if I had invited her to *walk* from Port Townsend to Seattle, she would have said I was 'fucking crazy,' and she wasn't sure that wasn't true anyway. In true survivalist fashion, she then hitchhiked to a liquor store and returned with ample morale-boosting supplies for all."

I am all for such morale-boosting supplies, and to celebrate my visit Ted had extravagantly bought a bottle of Veuve Clicquot, and now he determined to show me how to use a sash sword to take the cork out of the bottle.

Ted said, "Son, go get me the sword."

Happy Jack sped off like a missile, his smile as wide as the sound. On his return, and the scabbard duly removed, I was presented the sword by Ted, who schooled his son on exactly where I should hit the bottle. The rain bounced high up off the back porch as I raised the saber, and on my first attempt the cork and a tranche of glass smacked down as champagne charged up. I have since discovered that it's a standard Southern ritual, but to this Englishman it was nearly as impressive as fireworks on the Fourth of July, and just as delightful. Flutes were filled and, Jack gloomily dispatched to bed, a night became an early morning. And somehow, another one of those things that each successive year serves to chill the blood arrived without want of further fanfare or joy.

It was my birthday.

Also, it was Thanksgiving, and the Pacific Coast beckoned me. I had spent a little time farther south in California scoping the waves, but this far up I'd have a shot at some really cool birds; plus, sea to shining sea and all that.

I set out in yet another steady rain; it seems redundant to even mention it. The roads were slick and empty, and I settled into a driving rhythm easily, set as it was by the swish of the windshield wipers and the splash of the water up off the tires. For a while the rhythm quickened, the rain in torrents at Case Inlet, and down I went through Whites and Elma and Satsop, on a four-lane highway through pines, the wetness everywhere, names of towns I'd never know slipping by. Then, Central Park, a village a few miles east of the Pacific, brought to mind the other coast and New York City, and warm spring evenings chasing birds through the Ramble. I could only dream, now, of lying back in the warm grass of the park's Great Lawn, gazing up at a blue sky, as here the rain slowed for a deceptive bit before picking up once more. Would some kind of climax be reached? As I reached Aberdeen, the gray skies parted just enough for sunlight to appear. Even though Aberdeen itself was drab and shuttered (what else would Kurt Cobain's hometown look like?), the coming break in the weather bathed the car in a glow; the wipers off, the road drying, and the prospect of the Pacific lifted something off my spirits. It did indeed feel like a birthday, and a thanksgiving.

I skirted the North Bay of Grays Harbor and reached the Pacific as the sun finally shone bright and hard. But a strong wind had picked up too, making birding impossible. Against a seawall at Point Brown (St. Francis would have been proud) I tried to scope distant sea ducks, but apart from a hundred gallons of spray, my eyes picked up little. It was a relief, though, to be otherwise dry; the few other people who were avoiding Thanksgiving football and turkey laughed at the buffeting we were all receiving.

A dog ran to the water and splashed about. Gulls were blown sideways in the joy of sun, and inland a bit, a crow landed on a streetlight. This is exactly what I'd been hoping would happen. One has to be this far north, and this far west, to be able to claim it: the northwestern crow, defined by David Allen Sibley's field guide as "not identifiable except by range." Actually, it has its own specialness: it's 10 percent smaller than a regular American crow; croaks at a lower pitch; flies with a quicker beating of the wings; and has, if you can believe such a thing has been measured, smaller feet. Sibley is right in practice, though: in the field it's identifiable only by range—you want to get close enough to measure a crow's feet? But I'd parked my sorry butt in the right place at the exact time when what to all appearances *seemed* to be a northwestern crow sat on a piece of street furniture. As victories go, it pretty much defined Pyrrhic, but I'm claiming it.

Then, drizzle. I was keen to stop at Grays Harbor National Wildlife Refuge, as I'd read it was "one of the four major staging areas for shorebirds in North America." "One of the four" sounded pretty special; unfortunately, late November was the wrong time to be there, and the rain only got heavier. There was something dreary about the place so late in the season. The air-craft hangars that line the western edge of the refuge were quiet and dark. I followed the boardwalk out into the estuary, but found little except people walking their dogs where they were expressly forbidden to do so. Small Injustice Man almost said something, but didn't, as it was his birthday, and Thanksgiving. I was only temporarily cheered back at the car by a sign for Lana's Café, which boasted the following hours:

MON–TUE	**8 AM–4 PM**
WED–SUN	**8 AM–4 PM**

All this reminded me was that it was time to give up on the Pacific and head back to the Olingers. I didn't feel I'd made the most of it at all, except for the northwestern crow.

It being Thanksgiving, there was nowhere open to eat, so in Aberdeen I stopped at a corner deli and bought stale bread and a hunk of cheese for a late-afternoon meal. As I sped back east, humming "Smells like Teen Spirit," the drizzle hardened into sleet, then a brief snow shower came, then rain once more. By the time I reached Gig Harbor and the Olingers, I was able to get my final bird of the day—a turkey was roasting in the oven—and a torrential downpour was in for the night. The gay pugs rolled around on the couch and, in full view of all of us, gave each other rollicking canine orgasms.

A female cat with a bent tail appeared. The oddly named Henry seemed entirely disgusted by the pugs' display and hid under the living room table. It felt like the last days of Weimar. I fully expected to wander into the kitchen and find Liza Minnelli swinging her fishnetted legs one over the other, lighting a ciga-rette, and singing about how life is a cabaret, old chum.

I needed a break. Upstairs in the office, I logged on to the Washington state rare-bird alert blog, and discovered that a tropical kingbird that had been seen in Seattle proper since November 16 was, as of my birthday, still hanging around. This was terrific news. Though it's a bird of southeast Arizona and the Rio Grande Valley in Texas, it is, according to the *National Geographic Field Guide to the Birds of North America*, "rare but regular during fall and winter along the west coast to British Columbia." I'd read somewhere that a "gene glitch" is thought to be behind why (mostly immature) tropical kingbirds regularly turn up along the Pacific Coast. Basically, though they should know to go south to Mexico in the winter, they turn the wrong way.

Vagrancy is one of those things that keeps birders fervent about their endeavor. Once in a while a bird will turn up in exactly the wrong place, and excitement is general and unalloyed. Recently on Long Island there was a field at the Deep Hollow Ranch in Montauk that in the space of a few short weeks boasted a scissor-tailed flycatcher (a bird usually of the south central United States and northern Mexico); an ash-throated flycatcher (a Western bird); multiple western kingbirds (ditto); and a pink-footed goose (a European bird). There was even a barnacle goose, a bird that breeds almost nowhere but Greenland; Svalbard, an island chain between Norway and the North Pole; and Novaya Zemya, an outcrop of Russia that juts into the Arctic Ocean and has been, as an aside, the site of 224 nuclear tests in its presumably extremely noisy history. Birders on Long Island couldn't believe their luck, just as many of the same birders thanked their lucky stars when a Scott's oriole, a bird of the Southwest, turned up in Union Square Park in the center of Manhattan at around the same time. It was the first such oriole visit in the history of New York state, and capped a banner month for New York bird nerds.

Birders will travel hundreds of miles to see a vagrant. Recently, a western reef heron—a bird of the coasts of tropical west Africa, the Red Sea, the Persian Gulf, and India—showed up behind a Home Depot store in southern Brooklyn. This bird has been seen in the United States on just a few occasions in recent memory, the first reported time ever was on Nantucket in 1983. This poor thing, arriving in New York, must have wondered what the hell had gone wrong. For a start, that particular corner of Brooklyn waterfront is a godforsaken strip punctuated by abandoned mattresses and shopping carts. The bird didn't seem to mind; it hung around for weeks. Hundreds upon hundreds of birders tramped from all over the eastern seaboard to see it, to the point where Home Depot kept a door in the fence of its parking lot open to make it easier for people to get to the water.

There are a number of theories about such vagrancy. In the case of something like the pink-footed goose, or the western reef heron, they probably got blown this way in a weather pattern, perhaps a lashing storm. For birds like the tropical kingbird in Seattle, the western kingbird in New York, the flycatchers (ash-throated and scissor-tailed), and the Scott's oriole, scientists think it could be a genetic quirk that makes the species more vulnerable to vagrancy—an inbuilt weakness for going off course. When birds show up in migration on the opposite coast from where they should be, we surmise that one of their usual means of migration—following the stars—has failed them. One theory has it that they forget to flip the pattern of the stars when going south, so they migrate down the wrong side of the country; but no one really knows for sure.

In fact, migration itself is such a complicated and ill-understood phenomenon that many books on the subject read like books about what we *don't* know. We know some things, of course: much migration for songbirds happens at night, when it's cooler and predators are resting up. At night, too, the air is stiller, making long journeys less arduous. Paul Kerlinger, in his book *How Birds Migrate*, cites this last factor as a crucial one, but he also says that nighttime migration may well be to do with the need to forage during the day. And what about the phenomenon that Donna, Don, and I have seen at Cape May, and which Kerlinger cites, where birds arrive from the north during the fall migration, only to turn *back* north at dawn? Probably they're off to find somewhere to feed, but who knows?

There's still so much we are yet to learn; or maybe we'll never know. Miyoko Chu, in her fascinating book *Songbird Journeys*, cites the fabulous tale of a bunch of bird researchers who found themselves on Gulf oil platforms as thousands, maybe on peak nights even millions, of birds migrate past the structures. The scientists were there to see what effect such massive edifices had on trans-Gulf migrants. Surprisingly, in bad weather some of the birds rest on a platform before continuing on, giving the lie to the assumption that such places are a complete detriment to the health of birds; during a particularly bad storm, one observer, Jon King, counted at least two thousand warblers on "his" platform. Some birds did indeed die in collisions that spring, but many more gained succor from the rest. The majority just sailed by on southerlies the researchers couldn't see, ignoring the platforms altogether in their urgent need to get to where they're going.

The total number of birds that migrate in North America alone each year is probably beyond a billion. Given that number, it's amazing that vagrancy doesn't happen more often. When it does, sadly it is often a bad thing for the birds themselves. We feared greatly for the purple gallinule that got blown to southern New Jersey one spring: they don't usually come north of South Carolina, and lord knows how it would survive being so far out of place. The ash-throated flycatcher in Brooklyn's Prospect Park at Christmas must have struggled mightily for food, and the weakness that would result could cause it to be a prime target for a predator like a hungry red-tailed hawk. We can hope this isn't the case; but hope may not, in fact, be the thing with feathers.

What all this adds up to for birders is neatly described in the adage "What's bad for birds is good for birders." In the case of Seattle's tropical kingbird, I was excited to go chase a bird that avowedly should not be where it is. It might make up for all this weather.

Back downstairs, all licking had momentarily ceased. I was grateful for this small miracle, and raised a toast to my gracious hosts, and it being Thanksgiving, to the country that had so generously hosted me this last decade or so.

I had come to the United States somewhat against my will—I never really wanted to live in America—but after much traveling in my twenties, in the last decade I had grown to adore the country more than any other I'd lived in. I now regarded my first quarter century as almost a wasted time. In America, I had found a people and a culture that let me be, but that also gave me opportunities I'd never gotten in England. My children were born here, and that thrilled me almost to distraction. Already they displayed great American attributes: they were kind, and funny, and ready to help anyone at any time. Yes, the United States' recent foreign policy sucked like a love-addled pug; yes, we were propagating a ridiculous war; yes, America gave the world both Paris Hilton *and* Dick Cheney. These things were undeniable, but they were no more true than the fact that if a tsunami wrecked a coastal town in Anycountry, the first people on the scene, and the most generous of benefactors, would have American accents. I gave genuine thanks that night to a place that had welcomed me, and which I loved back now with a quiet frenzy.

Bored by my pontificating, the dogs snuffled away from the table and got comfy in the living room. Another glass of something was poured. I was thirty-eight years old, and seven thousand miles from England. I had gotten blown here by winds I still didn't understand. I had avoided most of the predators, and had found a food source and a place out of the weather. I was a vagrant in North America; I was the first sighting of myself on these shores in the history of the country. Fortunately, no one was stalking me, no one taking digital photos through a scope; I wasn't about to show up on a blog. There was no page for me in any field guide.

That was all fine by me. What wasn't fine was this weather. I walked over to the darkened windows and looked into the gloom. Out there in the sleet, a half-built boat creaked in the storm, and chickadees huddled for the night, safe in the knowledge of chickadees. And I started to consider just why this half-built boat had so affected me. I guessed that Ted was, like so many of us, drawn to flight, drawn to escape. We humans no longer make great treks across continents like America, no longer migrate to find food and safety and land. All we're left with is a kind of terrible, perverted version of it: Bosnians fleeing to my hometown of Birmingham, England, in the 1990s (I taught them English; they taught me how to swear in Serbo-Croat); the Vietnamese boat people in 1975, sailing anywhere; the 2.5 million of Darfur; and all the refugees still to come.

But still, what Joni Mitchell called an "urge to going" persists in individuals who sense the prison bars of a sublunary life. I was halfway through a trek around America; Ted's dreams lay in the dark garden, and were no more ridiculous or unattainable than were my own. And above us all, the very last of the fall migrants would wait out this storm in the hope that tomorrow would be a good day to go.

The next morning, as we lounge around eating breakfast, Jack runs in from the yard, and excitedly shouts,

"There's a hairy female on the deck!"

Assuming he's referring to a hairy *woodpecker*, I'm both impressed at his budding knowledge of nature, and something else: why isn't the boy soaked through?

Ted sits in his usual spot, in his recliner by the stove, doing a crossword. He barely reacts to Jack's ejaculation because he's stumped by 16 across, which asks that he find a five-letter answer to a clue that consists only of the following series of letters:

A, B, C, D, E, F, G, . . . P, Q, R, S, T, U, V, W, X, Y, Z

In his lap, Ted rests a BB gun, and asks Jack to leave the deck door open so he can get a better shot at the European starlings who seem intent on stealing all the food from the feeders. Once in a while he shoots off the gun, but succeeds only in chipping away at the feeder. After a few more shots he puts down his cross-word and gun and goes back to perusing the blueprints of the boat; there's a new round of work about to start.

Perhaps yesterday, amidst all that rain, the answer to 16 across would have come easier. But the reason Jack was out in the yard, and not soaked when he came back in, is this: *Seattle is dry*.

I couldn't believe I was even thinking those words, let alone saying them out loud, as I drove across the city the first morning of my thirty-ninth year, past the University of Washington and up towards Warren G. Magnuson Park.

Thereabouts, in recent days, the tropical kingbird had been seen behind a bunch of former naval buildings on the western edge of the park, at Sand Point Way, and again up into the residential areas south and west. Such were the details one could now glean thanks to the power of the Internet. Each day someone would post the current status, often with strident headlines like "Tropical Kingbird—NO!!!", or as the most recent put it, "Tropical Kingbird—YES!!!"

This fabulously named *Tyrannus melancholicus* is a bright yellow fellow sporting a dark stripe through its eye and a squat head. But it was eastern kingbirds that were the first tyrant fly-catchers I ever got to know, up in northeast Pennsylvania. Each spring morning I'd watch as a pair twittered and flirted and caught bugs by the hundreds, the white terminal band on their tails catching the first of the sun. I often paused there, by the

Mason farm, simply to watch their theatrical displays of court-
ship and feeding, at the foot of the same hill where up above I'd
find bobolinks bobolinking in the tall grass. Later, in a field at
Higbees Beach in New Jersey, Don and Donna and I stood trans-
fixed one spring morning as perhaps more than a hundred eastern kingbirds littered almost every available stalk of long grass, a
spectacle of abundance and beauty we'd do well to ever beat. But
now, in northeast Seattle, I was after a single flycatcher only, and
a tropical one at that. The rewards would be different.

Different, not least because Don and Donna were thousands
of miles south soaking up some tropical sunshine, while I was
chasing a tropical kingbird in a brief break between Northwest
storms. I wasn't asked for my opinion on tomatoes—that was
pretty exciting. Exciting too, the prospect of a bird so far off
course. I reached the parking lot where the bird had most often
been seen, parked the car, jumped out, and waited.

It was a depressing spot, in truth. I walked up and down a
littered hedgerow that backed onto Building No. 11, bringing
back happy memories of Lakes numbers 5 and 8 in southern
Michigan. Once in a while I trained my binoculars on a flock of
sparrows, one of which I was pretty sure was a bright Lincoln's, a
favorite of mine with its subtle, almost-purple coloration; a
hummingbird came by briefly too, but I didn't see it well enough
to identify it.

I realized then that without Don and Donna, I was inclined to
be much more conservative in my identifications. They both bring
great intellect to the pursuit. Don has a rigor and a dog-with-a-bone
attitude that leaves no bird unnamed. He won't stop until he's hec-
tored us into describing over and over a bird's characteristics.
Then, the bird book comes out, and options are debated; then
more verbal sparring, and the book is once again consulted.

Donna is more conservative still. On a recent trip to Brigantine National Wildlife Refuge on the New Jersey shore, Don and
I spent half an hour identifying an American golden plover, which

was standing stock-still next to a black-bellied plover. The differences were hardly substantial: the golden plover was a smaller bird, and had a faint "golden" wash. But to my eye, there was plenty enough to signify that we were looking at two different types of plover. Donna was having none of it. I almost wished that like Kirtland's son-in-law I could shoot the birds and dissect them on the spot, maybe even do a bit of DNA testing. Instead, Don and I looked at each other behind Donna's back until she caught us and harrumphed off to the car. She checked our excesses, and we loved her for it.

Here in Seattle, I could have used their input. The hummingbird I missed completely, and though I felt more confident about the Lincoln's sparrow, I still needed their voices to chime in. There was another way of putting it: I was lonely. As I was beginning to think about giving up, a car pulled up and a woman asked me if I'd seen the bird. I told her that I'd been there half an hour and there was no sign of it. As she drove away, she told me that the bird had also been seen up the hill in the residential area.

Nothing much was doing here in this depressing parking lot, so it was worth a shot. I left the car there and walked up the hill. One block in, I found myself standing on the Burke-Gilman Trail, a storied bike and walking path named after a couple of nineteenth-century railroad pioneers. It seemed as good a spot as any to stalk the bird.

Setting off south I scanned every last tree and bush, peering over suburban fences and into peoples' gardens. I felt a bit like a pervert, but only a bit, and it was mid-morning on the day after Thanksgiving, so there weren't many people about; I guess most everyone was either back at work or shopping. The odd cyclist whizzed by, but no one stopped to ask me what I was looking at. I was grateful for that. Being accosted by "civilians" and asked what you're doing is an occupational hazard when you're dressed in camo and carrying binoculars and a field guide in a residential area. Mostly I say "I'm looking at birds," and more often than not

I'm delighted to pass my binoculars over so that nonbirders can share in what I'm seeing. Once in a while, though, I want to say, "Seriously, folks, I'm wearing khaki, I have binoculars strapped to my chest, and I am clearly unfuckable. What does it *look* like I'm doing?"

The Burke-Gilman Trail wasn't giving up much, so I headed farther into suburbia. Up and down streets I stalked, looking for all the world, I suppose, like a madman on the loose. Every once in a while I'd stop and listen. I could have sworn I heard, in the distance, the distinctive, rising, three-part trill of the bird; or was it the ghost of Burke and Gilman as they banged the rails into the hard Seattle ground? The sound was leading me back south, until I found myself on Fifty-eighth Avenue NE, where at house No. 6909, out of the cornerest corner of my eye, I thought I saw a flash of yellow high up on a tree behind the residence. As I raised my binoculars, the glint of yellow dropped down behind the house . . . and half an hour later, nothing had reappeared. The street was quiet, the morning about to end.

I turned to ask Don and Donna what they thought. But they said nothing, as I knew they would. They were busy on their own birding trip, looking at a tropical kingbird, perhaps, one that had turned the correct way when migration began.

As I drive in to Nisqually National Wildlife Refuge on my last afternoon in the Pacific Northwest, I am struck by the peace that has descended. Partly this is to do with the weather. From behind high gray clouds a water-wasted sun appears, and shines like a kind of benediction on these lands. The leaves on the trees jostle for light, and wild high clouds rush away. It's the kind of afternoon that makes you think a precipitation record won't be reached, after all.

But it wasn't always so peaceful. This land had ghosts, not all of them old.

With a name like Sluggia he should have been a clean-up hitter, or a rap artist, but since it was the middle of the nineteenth century, he could be neither. Instead, he chose to be a small-time betrayer, and the man at the center of one of the more depressing episodes of U.S.–Native American history. His name is all but forgotten now, but not so the name of the man he betrayed. That's justice of a sort.

Sluggia was born of a tribe who call themselves "People of the Grass Country, People of the River." Once a strong and peaceful band, today the Nisqually number just over five thousand, some holed up on, but most living off, a reservation on Fort Lewis military base in western Washington state. For eons, though, they had fished their namesake river and Puget Sound, mostly harvesting salmon. American settlers were said to be surprised if they heard of the Nisqually getting belligerent; they were as pink as the fish they caught; so peaceful, in fact, that they didn't actually need, let alone have, a chief. But there was land to settle. We were moving west, and the Nisqually were in the way.

In 1854, a guy called Isaac Stevens, who was then the territorial governor of Washington, appointed a couple of Nisqually—Quiemuth, and the now more famous Leschi—to be chiefs, so that he could have them sign the Medicine Creek Treaty, a document that preserved some fishing rights for the tribe but took away their prime farmland. Leschi refused to sign and took off, setting in motion what is now known as the Puget Sound War, which was basically a series of barely connected fights, including the "Battle of Seattle" (which did not, according to most historians, involve Muhammad Ali or Joe Frazier). In one such altercation, it got back to Stevens that a militiaman by the name of A. B. Moses had been killed, and that Leschi had reputedly been present. Leschi was captured in late 1856, and tried twice. First time resulted in a hung jury; second time, in February 1858, just a hanging.

The story of how he was captured is almost as upsetting as the frontier justice Leschi suffered. Leschi was a talented horseman by all accounts, and knew the Puget delta intimately, so how the hell had they found him?

Enter Sluggia, Leschi's nephew. Having stolen away one of Leschi's wives (Mary, who soon realized she'd made a mistake and returned to the chief), Sluggia decided that the posted reward of five hundred dollars was well worth risking an eternity of being likened to Judas Iscariot. He and a pal, E-li-kuk-ah, tricked Leschi into leaving the confines of the camp Leschi and a bunch of his followers had established on Puget Sound. Tying Leschi up on the back of a horse, they delivered him to his pursuers. Some accounts have Leschi surrendering to "the Bostons," as Americans there and then were known, but given his history of defiance this seems unlikely. And the five hundred dollars? Somehow it morphed into fifty lousy blankets instead, and less than a year later, another Nisqually leader called Yelm Jim tracked Sluggia down, put a cap in his ass, and rolled him off a bluff into the sea.

As I arrive at Nisqually Wildlife Refuge on Puget Sound that afternoon, the story of Sluggia and Leschi comes to me as a counterpoint to my previous night's encomium to America. And yet, pretty much nothing affects my love of the place for long.

I leave the rain gear in the car and walk. Ted and Beth and Jack will join me later, but for now, it's just me and the birds and the sky and this picturesque place. A wide expanse of grasslands stretches out to a low bluff in the west. Trails head out north toward the sound, where there's a large white barn and a viewing platform. This is the perfect habitat for the northern harrier, a bird that ranges low over such expanses, stalking small vermin in the long grass. The birds' face is disclike, owly, and there's a telltale white rump patch which makes them one of the easier raptors to pick out from a distance. This day, I'm surprised to see two very far away to the south, but if I set my scope up in time, I should get good looks . . .

They're not northern harriers! I should have known; harriers tend to hunt singularly. No, out there in the fields I've come across a bird I've been after for a couple of years. At Brigantine, in New Jersey, they are regularly spied, supposedly hunting in the wide marsh to the east of the main pond. Don and I have spent many fruitless hours waiting on them; they had become a nemesis bird, one which, though supposedly easy to find in a given geographical area, has nonetheless remained elusive. But here in Nisqually, the short-eared owl is nemesis no more. Two of them, in fact, are swirling and pouncing in the sweet light of the afternoon. Their tawny coloring seems to glow, and their wide round faces harbor such eyes. Every once in a while I catch one of the birds in my scope and swirl and pounce along with it too, until it spins out of my field of vision. Then, I go back to the binoculars, scanning the distance until I find them sitting in the deep grass, and turn the scope back to the spot, and so on.

Best of all, no blog had brought me here. This is my discovery alone.

I wonder how I filled my life before I had this. To watch two hunting short-eared owls range across an expanse of wild grass, on the southern end of Puget Sound, the day after Thanksgiving— *I'm not in a mall*, is all I keep saying to myself, *I am not in a mall*. And I think again of Leschi and his people, how such birds would have been, for them, nothing to write home about, just another part of the landscape, something else to weave or carve and venerate.

I could watch those owls until dark, but it is time to go meet the Olingers. Jack bounces out of his car seat and races off down the trail, all energy and innocent hope. The rest of us follow, enjoying the feeling that the rain is finally gone. Out on the viewing platform, we watch another short-eared owl hunting; behind us, in the barn, barn owls screech like the haunted-house birds they are. From the north comes another bird I'd hoped I might see: a white-tailed kite twirls high in the coming gloom, and is gone. As if on cue, out of the distant sound a bald eagle appears, gathering mass as it approaches, and comes to roost in its massive nest above the barn. Jack's eyes widen like an owl's. Then, he goes back to what he does best: running around excitedly.

By the time we get back to the car it is dark. It is my last night in the Northwest. Back in Gig Harbor, Ted and I stand out in the freezing clear night and look at stars. I wish I lived closer. There is a boat to finish, and I have an urge to build. Its huge empty frame seems to swell behind us, starlight picking out a mixture of promise and reproach.

On the road to the airport in the morning, I watch as Mount Rainier finally peeks fully through the weather, and slips gently by my windshield in the bright sun. As it passes, I make a private farewell to the people of the grass country, to the people of the river, to the Olingers' pugs, and to their elephant.

Then, traffic. Car rental return. Shoes off. Boarding rows ten through twenty. The airplane is fully booked, so please quickly find your seats and turn off all electronic devices and prepare for departure and cross-check and. Gone.

NOW WHAT?

❧

I was the only person there—this was not surprising. Though the forecast called for "scattered showers and the occasional thunderstorm," what we actually got was a New York morning filled with constant heavy rain. It felt like Gig Harbor, only noisier. Great puddles of April lay all along the path; a mud patch caused me to "aquaplane" and jar my sciatic back; and then one of my binocular straps snapped and swung my bins perilously close to the soaking sidewalk.

And still, I was happy as a pig in shit.

Here's what happened: Suzanne, my ex-wife, had scheduled knee surgery, and because I'm one of the only people in New York who knows she's allergic to sulfa drugs and penicillin, I'm still the next of kin, which is right and proper—you spend a decade learning this important stuff, you may as well use it. Her gimp was to be fixed by one P.M., and luckily for me, the hospital was just a few blocks from Belvedere Castle in Central Park (twenty-two blocks, to be exact, which when you're birding, equals next door). For the past few days Belvedere Castle, or at least the flowering trees around it, had boasted the appearance of an orange-crowned warbler. A bird common in the West, it's rare here and brings birders from all over. And with a name like that, it sounds like a looker, yes?

Erm, no. The key diagnostic giveaway of the orange-crowned warbler is that it has no key diagnostic giveaway; its very drabness *is* its field mark. If you're looking for wing bars, or bright undertail coverts, or chestnut sides, or a tail dipped in black ink, you'll get no such thing; instead, you'll know that this plain Jane is, in fact, one of the rarer finds in a New York spring. You'll know it because it's so dull that it can't be anything else. It's a bird of elimination. And no, you'll probably never see the orange crown—it's more often than not invisible in the field. Compare this to the worm-eating warbler, a bird that eats plenty of insects, but never worms. There are any number of confusing bird names. The ring-necked duck, for example, doesn't have a ring around its neck. The long-eared owl has long, earlike tufts, but they're not ears—they're just tufts. And don't even get me started on the blue-footed booby. Well, it does have blue feet . . .

So why go chase the orange-crowned if it was drabber than a Mormon at a gay wedding? Because it's also as *rare* as a Mormon at a gay wedding. And by spring 2007, I was only a few warblers shy of a full set, at least of ones I might reasonably see in the United States. This was an achievement, given that I had been birding for just a few years. If I found the orange-crowned, I'd have only the Swainson's warbler, some *Oporornis* warblers, and very rare birds like the golden-cheeked warbler left to see. Imagine that: of the fifty-four warbler species I could hope to find, these little five-inch sprites jumping from limb to limb for a few weeks every spring and fall, I now had nearly fifty of them.

My socks were soaking. I was birding while holding an umbrella. And this would be North American life bird No. 400.

I had about thirty-five minutes before Suzanne needed me. The rain was howling and even the birds seemed to be hiding. I found nothing; I saw no one. Up and down the walk next to Turtle Pond, there were only white-throated sparrows picking under leaves and a ruby-crowned kinglet displayed a bright red crest above me—sorry, buddy, but I'm neither a kinglet, nor a female. Happy Birding Time, even in the soaking rain, passes twice as fast as Regular Standard Time in all zones, and suddenly that time was up.

As I walked past Belvedere Castle on my way to leaving the park, another kinglet disported above me. Again there was a slight flash of color on the head as it twisted its body around a twig to look for . . . wait a minute. Since when did a kinglet not flit and flit and flit from leaf to leaf? This bird was active, yes, but it's bigger and slower than a kinglet. Other than that, though, it's a drab thing. I stopped and took a second look. There were faint lines across its sides, and a needle beak, and . . . there were really no diagnostic signs at all. Its very drabness was the identification.

Oh sweet Jesus. Bird No. 400.

A few days later, Don meets me at the Ramble at dawn, and before I've even said hello, he starts in.

"I have bad news," he says.

This scares me greatly. Did he lose another baseball cap when he was away last week? Did Derek Jeter only go two for five last night? What, Don, what is it?

"We're going to need to go to Texas at some point."

"Texas?"

"Oh yes, my friend. Amazing place to bird. You could up your life list by fifty, sixty species, no problem. For a start, there are all those Mexican rarities. How about a clay-colored robin? Or a green jay? Or even, dare we dream, a ringed kingfisher?"

"The big guy?"

"Uh-huh. Amazing bird. We only get the belted here in the Northeast, but down there they get the ringed on the Rio Grande, and the green kingfisher. Great stuff! And then there's Barbara Kennett?"

'Who?'

"You don't know who Barbara Kennett is?"

"Actually, yes I do. I just said 'who' just to piss you off. *No!* I don't know who Barbara Kennett is."

"She's a hero," Don says, ignoring me. "Has a house on South Padre Island. One of the most amazing migrant traps anywhere in the country. Apparently, there are some fabulous bird photos all over her house—people travel from all over the world to take pictures through her windows."

I am still suspicious.

"What's your plan?"

"Well," says Don, "we'd fly to Houston, do East Texas—and let me tell you, that's a fabulous place to bird. The Piney Woods, two words to stir any birder's soul. Be full of character there too; it's poor though. Then we could swing down to the border, do South Padre and Babs and Laguna Madre and High Island. Did you know that High Island is the premier Big Day place in all of America? They get hundreds of species in just a few hours when the weather cooperates. Migration should be in full swing, if we time it right—this could be the most extraordinary trip we ever take. After High Island, it's on to the Rio Grande. Then we finish with the golden-cheeked warbler; can't leave Texas without seeing that little dazzler. There are some extraordinary places to bird down there—and the birds themselves! I don't mean to go on, but plain chachalaca, groove-billed ani, even the gray-crowned yellowthroat, should we be so lucky. Candy bar."

He says this as he strides away; seems he's remembered a meeting he's late for, and suddenly I'm alone. Do I really want to go to Texas? I want to see some rarities, and a flood of migrants, and a hero or two, yes. I sure as shit don't want to leave the park. But Texas?

SIX

Texas:
No, No, It Was a *Ringed* Kingfisher

Entry:

> *The gray-crowned yellowthroat was re-found today at the west end of the Marsh Bridge.*

On the morning of Wednesday, May 16, 2007, that note appeared in the log book at Sabal Palm Audubon Center and Sanctuary in southern Texas. I know, because Donna told the ranger to write it. We had refound the bird by seeing it fleetingly, in a dark gap between two trees. Don was delighted for her, and for me.

It was the kind of day that made you yearn for shade, or simply wish for fall. Because I have a tendency to burst into flames in even the weakest sun, I was wearing my obligatory long-sleeved shirt, wide-brimmed hat, and long pants. I would have been warm enough in late winter; here, in an early Texas summer, I was boiling alive and it was barely dawn.

Sabal Palm sits at the southernmost tip of Texas, down below Brownsville on the Rio Grande. We arrived at seven, just as the day was heating up the roads. Bugs busied themselves; plain chachalacas screeched in the warm air. The ranger station was closed, but the trails were not, and after stopping to admire the buff-bellied hummingbirds at the center's feeders, off we went, hopping from shade to shade, peering up at the palms which harbored a few birds—a vireo or two, and a chestnut-sided warbler—but not a huge number. Just as in Florida, we feared we'd missed the migrants. Our original plan had been to drop ourselves into the state right in the middle of the spring. Mid-April Texas is one of the first stops for trans-Gulf and trans-Mexico migrants on their long trek north. But our jobs and lives conspired to push our visit back by a full month. At Sabal Palm, there was at least one very rare bird that we could happily chase. For a few weeks, the blogs had been noting a gray-crowned yellowthroat at Sabal. Though it is similar to the very common common yellowthroat, the gray-crowned is a truly rare bird, basically a Mexican native. It used to be fairly common up to Brownsville, but no more. To get it in the United States would be a fine achievement.

The blogs had been explicit: down along the bridge, to the end, over by those trees, right over there. As we walked along, we were grateful to have such good directions, but also a little wary that the finding would be too easy. The rise of blogging had achieved three different, even opposing, things: one, it activated birders to go chase specific birds in specific places; two, it took away a bit of the fun (a bird blogged and thereby found might not be as satisfying as a bird discovered and enjoyed); but three, it gave us confidence. Would we ever see a bird such as the gray-crowned yellowthroat and seriously tell others we'd found it, though, without already knowing crack birders had noted it in this spot?

The appearance of the Scott's oriole in Manhattan's Union Square Park, for example, was first noted on the New York Birding List in January 2008. The bird had been present since the previous mid-December, but the people who found it had thought it was an orchard oriole (much less worth screaming about) and had simply posted a few pictures of the bird at the start of the year. The reaction was instantaneous: one birder yelled back that it was a Scott's not an orchard, and all hell broke loose. By the time I showed up a few days later, about twenty birders were standing around bored—the bird was already yesterday's story.

Now, would I have ever thought to go to a bustling city square to look for birds in the first place? Probably not. Even if I had, would I have called what I found a Scott's oriole? *Very* probably not. What the blogs did, beyond alerting idiots like me, was amass different opinions and help give some semblance of form to an otherwise diverse community. The back-and-forth about the oriole's identification was enlightening and often extremely technical. Despite the deep science and the sometimes-annoying lists of what people saw on their Saturday afternoon birding walk, there wasn't an hour that went by that I didn't check one of the blogs to see what was about.

When I went to Union Square that winter, no one made explicit reference to the blogs—they'd "read somewhere that there was a Scott's oriole in the city," or said they'd "heard about the bird," and then their voices trailed off. I think this was because birders didn't want to appear bound by the somewhat artificial nature of what we were doing. None of us had actually discovered the songbird—we'd simply clicked on a Web site, rode the subway, put binoculars to eyes, and said, "Wow! A Scott's oriole! In a city park! Yay for us!" The confidence this gave us was all fine and good, but had we earned it?

As ever with matters of identification, my mind came back to the day in New Jersey several years back when the Graffitis and I had alerted some Europeans to the curlews. We retell each other the story regularly, and always in hushed tones, in case anyone hears. And once in a while, when we think to tell other birders about something we think we've found, we think at least twice more, because of the Germans.

It happened at Brigantine National Wildlife Refuge, one of our favorite birding spots of all. We had just finished attending the

World Series of Birding weekend, a time when gangs of birders traipse around New Jersey, seeing as many birds as possible in twenty-four hours, all in the service of raising money for ecological causes. Winning groups total more than two hundred birds in the allotted time, after spending months extensively scouting the state. We'd spent the entire weekend birding and scored a relatively modest but pleasing 130-odd birds. As we'd forced our friends to sponsor us in advance, Don and Donna happily sent the proceeds to American Bird Conservancy's cerulean warbler effort. Brigantine was to be our gift to ourselves, a relaxed drive to end a mammoth weekend.

Sunday afternoon, we arrived at Brigantine at around three and, as we always do, immediately headed to the log book where other birders note their finds. There, someone had written, "5 Curlew, west pond." This was extremely promising. Not being then entirely conversant with the exact range of the curlew, we knew enough to understand that they'd be well worth seeing, given that they aren't an everyday bird. When we got to the west pond, there they were in the marram grass: five long-billed curlew, chowing down in the green. Their long, curved beaks and cinnamon bodies were diagnostic. Fabulous! Rare, yes, but they do sometimes get blown east, though usually south of Virginia and usually in fall and winter. No matter; we had been told that they were there, and we saw them. We even took a bunch of pictures.

Having birded the day out, and with the last light beginning to fall, we watched some night herons as they headed out to feed. Then, the tranquility was broken by the drone of an engine, and a truck pulled up beside us. Three folks got out—one young guy, and an older man and woman. They explained that they, like us, had turned the twenty-four hours of the World Series into a full weekend; they had logged something like 178 birds, and from their slightly deranged expressions it was clear that they hungered for more. This was their last stop, and they had yet to eat, sleep, or do anything much beside find birds.

Then came the inevitable question:

"You haff ennyzink?" the young man said.

"Curlews." I said the name quietly, but proudly, as is appropriate.

"Vat? Carloos?" He couldn't believe his ears.

"Yep," I said, a bit more proudly, "five of 'em. West pond."

"Das ist not possible. Das carloos? Funf carloos? Was kind das carloos?"

"Long-billed," I said.

And then, Don clinched our place in hell:

"We have photos," he said.

Donna is a smart, smart woman. Afterwards, she told us that when she saw how serious these birders were and how incredulous they were that we had seen curlews, she knew we were in deep shit. Don proffering photos was not a good idea.

"Really, they're not good pictures. The light was poor. And anyway, we really have to get going." Donna tried, she really did.

"You're so modest, Donna!" I exclaimed (for she is). "You guys are actually getting really good at your bird photography. Stop hiding your light under a bushel! Show them the curlews!"

Many regular Germans hated the Second World War as much as the Allies did. I don't think it's fair to lump them all together as nasty, brutish Nazis. Sure, some of them were nasty, brutish Nazis; but many were normal folk, swept up against their will in tumultuous times. I imagine many of them returning to their devastated homes and thinking, "Was das fuck?"

I can even imagine them looking a bit like these Germans did, here in New Jersey, at the start of a new century, when faced with Don and Donna's excellent pictures of five regular, ordinary, decidedly unrare whimbrels. Curlews do look a bit like whimbrels, but it's not exactly rocket science to tell them apart. Whimbrels have stripy heads, just like the birds in our pictures; curlews do not. Curlew are significantly bigger too, their bills a great curving arc.

And, as noted earlier, curlews pretty much never come here.

There was a sadness in the eyes of the two older Germans as they realized that we were idiots; a slouch to their shoulders, a catch in their voices. "Das . . . ist . . . ein vimbrel. Ein vimbrel. Funf vimbrel, ja, funf!" They were resigned, it seemed, to the truth of our stupidity.

Not so the youngest one, who displayed a nasty, brutish violence across his brow. He looked us up and down and said, "Zere haffnt been enny sightings off carloos in New Jersey zince 1984."

Dismayed, the Germans piled back into their truck, and we waved them off with a "good luck" and a "fare-thee-well." As they sped away, only I had the temerity to mutter Basil Fawlty's line, "Don't mention the war," but it was when they were well out of earshot and I didn't really mean it. As the final light of Brigantine vanished, Donna was almost in tears. Don looked at the black sky, and sighed. This was the low point for us all.

We wanted to find the stupid bastards who'd mistaken the whimbrel for long-billed curlew so that we could beat them to a bloody pulp. We wanted, in short, to Dresden someone. We'd never have made such a mistake without their prompting, of course.

Of course. Don't mention the war.

The only good thing about this incident is that it led to the creation of an award, the Curlew Prize, given at the end of every birding trip for the most egregious misidentification made by one of us. The winner is handed a splendid piece of pottery, created by Donna, called the Doug Kopsco Trophy, named in honor of a friend of ours whose conservative nature when calling out bird identifications in the field makes Donna look positively reckless.

When Brazil won the soccer World Cup for the third time in 1970, they were invited to take the Jules Rimet trophy home forever. And here I must tell the truth: I have won the Curlew

Prize so regularly since its inception that I'm close to keeping the Doug Kopsco Trophy for myself.

Once we hadn't mentioned the war, we stashed this painful memory and brought our minds back to the task at hand, here in our Texas morning. Splitting up, we staked out the corner of the trail where the yellowthroat was reputed to be. By now, the heat was heavy; a broken-down bench afforded some rest, but only half of it was in shade. Something was flitting way back in the canopy, and we came together to focus on it. Whatever it was, it didn't much want to be seen.

And then it happened. Don had stepped to one side for a moment, thinking there was something moving around in a different area of the deep foliage. Donna and I focused on the original spot between two trees where all three of us had noted movement most regularly. For a second only, a bird with a broken-white eye ring and a pale gray top to its head paused in the gap, then flitted away. Donna hissed, "There," and Don turned, a second too late. He looked again—we all looked again—but it was futile. Donna and I had seen a gray-crowned yellowthroat, and Don Graffiti had seen nothing at all.

So he didn't see a bird. What's the big deal? Only this: the gray-crowned yellowthroat is extremely rare in the United States; this is its only-known nesting ground outside Mexico and points south; the day was hot and sticky; and we'd wasted a morning on a stakeout of a single bird.

Maybe none of this matters. Maybe. But we all felt a little sick. Fortunately, it had been at best a flit, a pause, and then the bird was gone. It's not the most handsome bird either, being a slightly larger version of our common yellowthroat; the real reason to be excited was because it has such a tiny, North American range.

None of this really made me feel any better. In fact, I felt something close to shame. These days, I felt this more often than I'd like.

A few days before the Texas trip, I'd been crossing the street in New York with my daughters when Amelia and I got to talking about me not living with them anymore. I said, "Are you doing OK with that?" and held my breath. She was not yet eight years old, and for the last two of them her father had lived apart from her, and her sister, and her beloved mom. What was she supposed to say?

She said this:

"I'm OK. But every time I see you drive away in your little red car, I think, 'He must be lonely.'"

The street swam. Above me, I heard as though for the first time the rustle of leaves in high trees. I could not speak; I could barely think; my breathing got faster, and then stopped altogether. We stood, the three of us, on the side of the road, as though we all knew some kind of invisible line had been crossed.

Then she said, "You know, you should get a goldfish. They're great companions."

Don has a thing about what he calls the "United States of Generica," and I don't really blame him. When the original old Second Avenue Deli in Manhattan's East Village, with its Yiddish Walk of Fame stars outside on the sidewalk, is closed in favor of yet another Chase Bank—and everyone's delighted because at least it's not another Starbucks—well, you can understand Don's point of view. As a consequence, when it came to planning our trip through east and southeast Texas, he did his best to avoid Holiday Inns and Motel 6s.

"We need some places with charm, and local color. Character!" he said.

I was oblivious, honestly; I was just grateful he'd taken the time to plan the trip in such detail. We were going for a week, and his itinerary ran to thirty-nine pages. He had names of motel owners, driving directions, birding spots, places to eat, blog printouts, tide charts, seating assignments on planes, a photocopy of the Declaration of Independence, the complete works of Algernon Charles Swinburne, a full Spanish-English dictionary, inside leg measurements, you name it. We could have handily invaded Mexico with this stuff. Best of all, he had indeed managed to avoid any hint of "Generica" throughout the trip. We really would be seeing rural Texas in all its glory.

Oops.

We landed in Houston on a Sunday evening, and having procured a rental car, we wasted no time in racing east to our first port of call, the town of Silsbee, conveniently located close to the Piney Woods and Big Thicket National Preserve. The area boasts deep thickets and swamp, all designed for birding and little else.

On the way to Silsbee we stopped at Crazy Jose's, a Mexican theme restaurant outside Beaumont. Painted entirely in primary colors, the place seemed designed for small children, though even we ostensible grown-ups were enticed by the mantra printed on every menu:

BIG TASTE. LITTLE PRICES. A BIT LOCO.

We had been served by a waitress wearing a T-shirt that read *DANGER: NEXT MOOD SWING IN 5 MINUTES*, and who had seemed fascinated by my British accent, commenting that "we get excited when we see people from different cities." As dinner wound down, she brought the check and chatted with us some more, until we popped down the cash and I said, "We're done," signaling to her that we didn't need any change.

Big fat mistake. Seems something essential was lost in the translation. Once friendly, the waitress now bore out the slogan on her T-shirt. Donna proffered the idea that my comment had been taken to mean "we don't want to talk with you anymore." I had meant no such thing. It didn't matter—the waitress now sulked by the manager's station. He, in turn, looked like he was going to draw a weapon and put another hole in my southern reaches. On my way out I tried to say thank you and good night, but the girl was having none of it.

"You have clearly broken her heart," Donna said, once we were back in the car.

"Well, at least it now matches her teeth," I replied, attempting to lighten the mood. But Don and Donna were extremely annoyed, and remonstrated with me that I had to take more care with how I spoke. First, I'd offered to trash an old lady's motel in Florida, and now this.

Seems all I did these days was brush up against people and bruise their feelings, then I was gone, like an emotional pickpocket. It wasn't that I was homeless. I just had nowhere that felt like home.

Don was excited about his first motel choice. The place had looked like a find on its Web site. I suppose the photo of the sign that read

CORPORATE

AND

BUDGET

might, for lesser minds, have set off an alarm bell or two, but not for Don.

"Gonna be full of character, I guarantee you," he said. "And listen, it's *not* a bed-and-breakfast, so there'll be no need to socialize in the mornings with strangers. And, it's not a depressing Motel 6 or some such. Best of all, we're close to the Piney Woods; going to be dripping with birds."

It took an hour to find the place, which meant that at least we got a grand tour of Silsbee.

Silsbee is, you'll be fascinated to learn, the home of the WWE superstar Mark Henry, and of the late pornographic actress Chloe Jones, known locally as Melinda Dee Taylor; the *New York Daily News* once called her "bleached and enhanced," which is all you really need to know. Don had booked the motel months in advance, and after a grueling drive around the town we finally found the place.

The owner of it greeted us with prehistoric grunts and teeth so huge and white I presume they can be seen from the moon. After four attempts he finally found our room keys and waved in the vague direction of the motel parking lot—we figured he was showing us where to go, but the teeth were so blinding it was hard to be sure. Undeterred, Don led the way to his and Donna's room while I unpacked the car.

From the start they could tell that the room was laden—no, *sodden*—with local color. The smell alone was enough to make a horse gag, and Donna had decided to throw back the bedcover in the hopes that doing so would waft away the stench of the previous occupants. It was then that Don's wail of distress came through the door, letting me know, even from the parking lot, that something was wrong.

"What the fuck?" Don grated. "I mean, really. What the fuck?" I hustled over to their open door to see what was up.

"The sheets. Oh my god, the sheets," said Donna, a look of utter dismay in her eyes.

Entering their room I expected to find some kind of housekeeping horror, akin to what happened to a friend of mine who'd once stayed in a motel like this one, only to turn over in the night and roll onto a half-eaten cheeseburger. Instead, there on the sheets was stenciled the letters "KKK."

Why were we surprised? Don had been explaining to us all the way from the restaurant that this part of East Texas has been a center for Klan activity for more than a century. We were just a few miles north of Vidor, which remains a sundown town, and just fifty miles south of the town of Jasper, sadly now infamous for the dragging death of James Byrd.

Byrd was an African American guy who accepted a ride home from a party from three white guys in a pickup truck; Byrd was disabled, a bit of a drinker, a trumpet player and a singer. He could also play the piano; his assailants couldn't play anything, except, eventually, the roles of national pariahs. The nominal leader of the sorry gang was John William "Bill" King, who now refers to himself as a "political prisoner." He became infamous once arrested not only for the awfulness of what he'd done, but also for his tattoos, many of which were Nazi- and race-hate re-lated. Fewer people mentioned that he had a tattoo of Tinkerbell on his presumably tiny penis, though if I'm lucky enough to get to meet him before his appeals run out, it's going to be the first thing I mention. The Three White Men picked up Byrd on, ironically enough, Martin Luther King Boulevard, ostensibly to offer him a ride home, but having beaten the crap out of him behind a convenience store for no apparent reason, they pro-ceeded instead to chain him to the back of their pickup truck and drag him three miles along a country road. Byrd was probably alive for most of it. Only when his head hit a culvert did decapita-tion end James Byrd's unimaginable agony.

And now, here we were looking for birds of our own, but instead had found sheets stenciled with the brand of the Ku Klux Klan. Don said, "Luke, get in your room right now and check yours."

Sure enough, I had letters on mine too. But in my room,

thank god, the sheets read "MMM", not "KKK"—meaning, I guess, that it was simply the motel's odd way of assigning linens to each room. Given the nature of the area, it did seem a tad ill-considered. Mollified a bit by my *M*s, Don then turned his attention to the state of their bathroom floor; suffice to say, whomever had enjoyed the room before him hadn't had his enjoyment expunged quite as well as one might hope. Through the paper walls I heard Don yelling.

"Donna! Do not, under pain of death, go into that bathroom. If you must do so, keep your shoes on and your laces tied tightly."

For my part, I lay awake all night listening to the five guys outside my room as they lounged around the back of an open pickup, drinking forties and blasting Tex-Mex music out of their trucks' open doors. I've stayed in hotels in New Jersey actually owned by the state's infamous Devil; in joints in Florida where an alligator would ask for a room change; and one in Cleveland, Ohio, whose owner actually argued with me when I didn't want to pay by the hour. This, though, was the worst place I'd ever stayed. Tomorrow would be better, I told myself.

At last it was dawn. The pickup truck had finally left. I was able to let go of my wallet, cell phone, car keys, binoculars, shoes, pictures of my children, hat, passport, toothbrush, camera, spotting scope, tripod—oh, and my entire genitalian outcropping—all of which I'd clutched tightly through my dark night at the hellhole. I hopped into the shower and turned the faucet, eager to start the day fresh. Out of the nozzle came a slow trickle of brown water that looked like it had been pumped directly from a sewage treatment plant.

Not even Don could put on a brave face when we met outside. As we walked to give back the keys, he said, "Well. Extraordinary. Quite, quite nasty. The bathroom floor . . ." His voice trailed off as we entered the office. There, the man with the extraordinary teeth grinned, blinding us, and asked us how we liked the motel.

"First class, thank you," said Don, blinking furiously. We both had one thought in mind: let's get the heck out of here.

As we drove away, I noticed that the motel sign that on the Web site had promised

CORPORATE

AND

BUDGET

that morning read

HIRIN G

HOUSEKEEPER

We've become proficient enough now that we can pretty quickly sniff out a birdy day or a non-birdy day, and this was the latter. Though the Piney Woods and Big Thicket were impressive in a physical sense—a winding trail through high thickets and past dank eerie swamps—we also remembered that we're not big fans of trails through woods and forests; the denseness makes seeing birds that much harder. Not that there was anything to see. The place was dead.

Lunch, on the other hand, was something special. A kind ranger at the Big Thicket visitor center told us to head to a barbecue place called the Bar-B-Q Pitt, and we were grateful for her advice. The place served the best barbecue I've ever had—the ribs had been cooked until the bones melted, and even the coleslaw tasted like each carrot had been hand-grown in angel-tear-watered loam—and boasted, in addition, a fabulous collection of memorabilia on the walls: Patsy Cline concert posters butted up against pictures of Elvis next to ads for state fairs under bits of farm machinery. After heaping plates of Texas barbecue we sat in the car like three fat happy people and drove south, past a sign for a First Baptist Church whose pastor clearly had a keen sense of humor:

THE GOOD LORD DIDN'T
CREATE ANYTHING WITHOUT
A PURPOSE, BUT MOSQUITOES
COME CLOSE.

We were on our way to High Island, but we sidetracked ourselves on a back road to Taylor Bayou, a place we'd read about in various blogs, in order to chase prothonotary and Swainson's warblers.

Prothonotaries are many people's favorite warblers. Bright motes of godlight, they glide through swamps and marshy woodland, where they breed. Swainson's, on the other hand, are both more drab and terrifically hard to see, and as none of us had ever even come close, it was well worth the detour.

In any case, this was our favorite kind of birding: turning off a main road, pulling the car to the side, and seeing what we find. We knew there must be nesting prothonotaries here: it was the perfect spot. We were in the middle of a cypress swamp where wood ducks nested, and on both sides of the road a stagnant pool harbored egrets and anhingas. After a half an hour in which Don managed to get bitten by a crayfish in the middle of the road—he put his finger down to attract its attention, and attract it he did—there they came a prothonotary warbler pair darting through the trees of the swamp and out across the road to the pond on the other side. They buzzed past us, back and forth, until one landed on a stump not twenty feet away. At one point I scoped one on a post by a nearby brown-water roiled river, a rare moment of a prothonotary way out in the open.

Besides being lovely, prothonotaries also played a bit part in American history. As it turns out, Alger Hiss, amongst many other things, was a birder. Whittaker Chambers, his accuser and adversary at the House Committee on Un-American Activities hearings in 1948, had privately told investigators that Hiss had been excited to see a prothonotary on the banks of the Potomac. Hiss independently corroborated the bird to the investigators, as any good birder would: *Yes, it was definitely a prothonotary. Unmistakable.* This corroboration led the committee, which included a young man by the name of Richard Nixon, to claim it proved the two men were acquainted with each other—how else could Chambers know such a detail about Hiss? Much of the case rested on whether or not the two men knew one another. The rest is spy versus spy.

We could have stayed there forever and birded the rest of the spring at Taylor Bayou, but High Island itself was beckoning.

High Island is another much-beloved spot in the birder's catalog, famous for spring "fallouts," when bad weather drives desperate trans-Gulf migrants to land at the first available spot: the low trees and shrubs of one of the Houston Audubon Society's High Island Sanctuaries, such as the Boy Scout Woods, a series of short trails and bird blinds in town. We arrived there late in the afternoon to find the place deserted, proof again that we were here too late in the season. In peak migration this place must be hard to beat, given that the trees are indeed low and there's dense brush in which birds can rest up before the next step in their travels. That said, when we saw the main photograph blind—a wooden shack with peepholes so that the birds aren't freaked by all the telephoto lenses—and signs stating that one must book ahead and not go beyond one's allotted time, it struck us that we might not have entirely loved this place after all. Nothing turns us off more than crowds of birders when we're trying to bird. Though we're terrifically witty and warmhearted and always delighted to make the acquaintance of other birders, the pursuit remains for us a private one, albeit shared by three people, rather than a team sport for hundreds.

In a recent edition of *Winging It*, the newsletter of the

American Birding Association, a self-proclaimed "fanatical lister" called Iain Campbell describes the situation in High Island, and the fact that "7,000 to 10,000" people come through the place every year from March to May. This swells the town by up to a cool 2,000 percent. Incidentally, it also provides a stunning rebuke to the law of supply and demand; as Campbell notes, "Birders . . . have to leave High Island to find a good meal." We were torn. We hated development, given what it was doing to rural America, but wouldn't it make sense for one of these empty buildings in High Island to turn itself into a birder's rest stop? We didn't need a guitar-shaped swimming pool and a Jacuzzi in every room; just a bed and a warm meal. What the people of the town most seem to care about, according to Campbell, is the traffic problems thousands of migrating birders create. I don't blame them—no one wants their little town ruined by the cars of tourists—but it still seemed a bit rich, this being oil country. There used to be two hundred oil wells working this "salt dome," the geophysical feature that gives High Island its name. It is, in fact, the highest spot on the Gulf of Mexico between Mobile, Alabama, and the Yucatán Peninsula (don't get too excited; it's only thirty-eight feet above sea level).

To mitigate all the cars in spring, the town is talking about using golf carts to get everyone around, which is a great idea. Let's hope the "somewhat depressed local economy," as Campbell kindly calls it, takes note and ups its golf cart production by, oh, I don't know, how about 2,000 percent?

As it was, at the Boy Scout Woods that evening we got great looks at a pair of black-bellied whistling ducks, a lifer for me, as well as eastern kingbirds and the night herons. We also spent some time on a troublesome woodpecker, a bird we later agreed to have been a golden-naped, a target bird for this trip. Our real hope, though, was for a successful early-morning trip back to the Boy Scout Woods to see if any late migrants might be moving through. Before then, however, we had to find our next motel.

"East Texas is not exactly sublime, is it?" Don said, as we drove away from High Island towards the town of Winnie, where he'd secured us two rooms. "I'm a little bit nervous about the place I picked, I'll be honest with you. I'm not sure that this part of the world quite understands the needs of the sophisticated traveler."

This new place was in many ways entirely different from the previous night's habitation, in that it was close to a million times worse. Silsbee's pickup truck full of lurking Son Norteños fans had, for instance, been replaced with upstairs neighbors who were, for want of a kinder phrase, crack whores. At least they were (a) friendly, and (b) not brightly lit. Out of Don and Donna's bathroom window, the forecourt lights of an Exxon station shone like a rock concert, illuminating the dirty walls of their room.

My room was something else again. How to describe it? Let's begin with the hole in the wall, covered with a piece of cardboard held up by silver electrical tape. Next to this there was some kind of anteroom, the entry to which was barred by a woven rug featuring a herd of deer by a mountain lake. I daren't go in it. Over the—get this—*flat-screen* TV, there hung a picture of Sikh deities and what I took to be a swami of some kind, though he looked for all the world like Regis Philbin in an up-do.

But we were hungry, and it was late, and there was no time to ponder the mysteries of transcendent talk-show hosts. Or to find another hotel. So we set out to find something to eat, Don certain we'd find a cozy bistro where slowly roasted chickens would be served on beds of wilted greens, something indescribably delicious drizzled across their succulent rumps; the waiters pressed but unhurried; the wines from ancient vineyards in countries one would struggle to locate in a good atlas; dessert an acre of chocolate something-or-other topped with so much cream that a starving cat would struggle to finish it all.

Slowly roasted chickens. The mere phrase put a catch in our voices as we declined the offer to Super Size our meals. For some reason, the kind lady behind the counter told us that she'd made some sort of obscure cash-register mistake, and the meals were free. We were grateful, but this didn't make them delicious. On the wall behind me, an "art installation," consisting of one red and two gray squares, separated by a representation of what appeared to be the lower section of a blocked human colon, hung as if to mock us.

As we left, Don commented, "I'm not being superior. But these people are backward."

On the way to the motel we passed our best hope for coffee next morning, though the "US" of the friendly yellow sign being comically unlit cheered us hardly at all. We pulled into the parking lot of

WAFFLE HO E

and cased the joint. When we'd plucked up the courage to enter to ask if they would be open at six the next morning, the waitresses had looked at us, not for the first time in East Texas, like we had two heads each, or six total. Upstairs back at the motel the hoes waffled, all right; they also whooped and hollered. I was too tired to care.

The following morning brought no new migrants, except we three blasted birders, slogging towards our date with the Galveston ferry. We headed west along the Bolivar Peninsula, stopping just off the busy road to scope sleeping common nighthawks and a distant white-tailed kite, one of which I had seen a few months earlier all the way up in Washington state. The common nighthawks were especially a treat. By day they sleep on fence posts, looking like bulky things that were dolloped onto their perch; at dusk and dawn they rouse themselves to hunt and are transformed into angular acrobats. It's almost as though they are a different species when they rest during the day.

Time was short, as it always was when we birded. On the

ferry across Galveston Bay we sailed, watching a distant and high magnificent frigatebird swoop in lessening rain. We made it to Houston airport with literally no time to spare. An officious little man was reading our names over the loudspeaker as we stood in front of him, waving our boarding passes. Finally, he put down his telephone and looked at us. It was another disaster for Donna and me, for Don another vindication. What could be better than arriving at the plane as your names are being read?

The little man continued to stare at us. We looked right back at him. Out on the sticky tarmac, a small plane waited to take us south to Harlingen, and the second leg of our Texas trip. In my heart I bade East Texas a weary farewell, promising to return, just not anytime soon. Something beeped—it might have been the little man himself—we were admitted to the plane, it took off, and we were gone.

We had birded in salt marshes, and in old growth forests. We liked grasslands, and pine forests, and being on the tops of mountains. Birds had come to us across lakes, over seas, and in city parks.

But it's never good to be told that the birds one seeks are behind a convention center. So it was on South Padre, a thin barrier island that separates the Gulf of Mexico from Laguna Madre on the eastern tip of southern Texas. We arrived that afternoon in Harlingen and sped east in yet another rental car. Given our troubles in Silsbee, though, this time I'd paid extra to get an OnStar navigation system, and we amused ourselves by fooling with "Barbara." That's the name we gave to the weird electronic voice who found herself saying things like "make the next available legal U-turn" more often than she ever had before, as we kept changing the destination just to see what she'd say.

As we crossed the causeway into town we were thankful that it was the off-season; South Padre Island is a big spring break destination, and in the summer it is packed with second-homers. Now, the place was fairly deserted, and it was pretty too. We weren't in East Texas anymore.

The Laguna Madre Nature Trail was said to be a great spot for shorebirds, and for migrants on South Padre. It does indeed snake round the back of the South Padre Island Convention Center, a 45,000-square-foot yellow box built on the edge of the Laguna Madre itself. The nature trail had been developed as a sop to those Texans who might argue that a massive convention center in such an important spot for migrants might not be the best use of the land. Whatever its origins, the trail is said to be one of the best places in America to see all the regularly recurring rails, a family of skittish marsh birds that one hears more often than sees. A raised wooden walkway leads out to Laguna Madre, where one of Don's favorite birds, the black skimmer, dropped its lower mandible and scooped up a meal. The sun dripped into the bay.

And get this: that night we too had a fabulous meal in a restaurant on the water (there was drizzling! oh yes, something had been drizzled on my succulent meats!), and slept at the Brown Pelican Inn, a fabulous bed-and-breakfast run by a Frenchman and an Englishwoman, Yves and Chris de Diesbach. Yves, the Frenchman, was a bit put out that we arrived late, since he was hoping to accompany Chris to a talk that evening in town. We missed exactly what the subject of the talk would be; Yves's sturdy Gallic accent delivered only the words "Tatture Kernference." His indecipherable accent brought to mind the British guy in Arizona, and his "laffly banal." Yves was extremely gracious though, and the rooms to which he showed us were positively palatial. I almost cried when I saw the fancy soaps. I don't remember much else; I was fast asleep in seconds, sinking in downiness and clean.

Next morning, we went back to the convention center and, right next to it, in a little stand of trees, witnessed something of a fallout of birds. This wonderful treat included Baltimore orioles; American redstarts, magnolia, and black-throated green warblers; and yet more buff-bellied hummingbirds, this time whizzing to and from a feeder. Out along the boardwalk we also saw a life bird for me, the least bittern, which was so tame I took a bunch of half-decent photos of it as it gently swung in the swaying reeds. Then we raced back to the B&B, where we were served a delicious and delicate breakfast by Chris, who regaled us with the truth of the "Tatture Kernference." Though I'd assumed the good folks of South Padre were given pause by waterboarding and other Guantánamo treats, in fact they were discussing animals with hard green shells. Shame Yves had to miss an entire evening devoted to turtles. Somehow the conversation morphed into families. I told her about my girls, back in New York, and how much I missed them. I was glad she quickly changed the subject to tell us about her beloved nephew, whom she described as being in kindergarten, and, with a happy laugh, "satanic."

"We call him Diablo!" she said, laughing, love in her eyes. Despite her English accent, I liked her, and we were sorry to leave such a beautiful place. Before we left, she kindly pointed us towards our next stop, a suburban house on South Padre Island, and the hero Don had told me about.

Barbara Kennett was once, of all things, a police officer in Los Angeles. By the time we met her that spring, she was an eighty-four-year-old facing the encroachment of development into her backyard sanctuary. In between, what a life.

In 1973, Barbara had retired from her position on the West Coast and moved to South Padre, where her backyard on Ling Street at the time boasted the usual green manicure of suburbia. One day, she happened to notice a set of beautiful birds on the lawn. Turns out they were a painted bunting, a dickcissel, and an American redstart, a pretty impressive collection for any backyard in America. She didn't know that then, though; like many of us, she fell in love with the birds before she knew their names. Like some of us, she got a birding guide and looked them up.

Something about what Barbara Kennett saw that day changed her. She bartered away her lawn to a local nursery, getting a bunch of native bushes and trees in return. Then, she waited.

Now, Barbara Kennett's Ling Street lot is a known stop on any thorough Texas birding trip. That morning she welcomed us wonderfully, her dachshunds yapping at our feet. With great pride she showed us the walls of her house, festooned with extraordinary bird photos. Here, then, are birds of every kind: tanagers, rare sparrows, warblers, you name it—a treasure trove amassed across the more than thirty years she's welcomed birders to her home.

One photo in particular elicited a story from Barbara that showed the true scale of birding obsession. Some years ago, a Townsend's solitaire, a bird primarily of the western mountains, showed up in Barbara's garden. She called a friend in Ames, Iowa, who'd never seen one. The guy hung up the phone and immediately drove thirteen hundred miles, almost directly due south, to Ling Street and to Barbara.

He arrived two hours too late.

But it's getting late early for Barbara Kennett's haven. All along Ling Street, lots are being bought up, and she doesn't know how long she can hold out. Already the construction has turned the street into a noisy spot for migrating birds, but still they come. They have just crossed six hundred miles of gulf, and are on their last wing beats—what other choice do they have?

Bidding dear Barbara farewell—and jotting down in our minds the phrase "Barbara Kennett (L)"—we found ourselves back in the street and watched as trucks sporting the names of construction firms spilled men and machinery onto the sidewalks. Lots like the ones maintained by Barbara suddenly looked like anachronisms. As we started up our car and as OnStar Barbara called out directions for the next stop, we wondered if this was the real Barbara's last bird-filled spring.

We'd seen what development could do in Florida, in New Jersey, and elsewhere. Did we stop long enough to think to ask what we as a culture were playing at? In South Padre, the building is fueled by the needs of spring break kids and rich Texans with an urge for a seaside home. I imagine those kids now, arriving in March and April, descending on this street and others, ready to party. In their bleary mornings we might imagine them peeking out into the light and seeing a bird over the fence in Barbara Kennett's garden: Its bright blue head, and scarlet chest and neck, shine below a chartreuse back. It has a sturdy beak, and around a large black eye a thin ring of orange glints. What price some kid wondering out loud what this extraordinary songbird is called?

It's a painted bunting. Look it up. Or else, do what we did and knock on Barbara Kennett's door. Don't mind the dogs. She'll happily tell you what you've been missing, assuming her garden hasn't been paved over. Heck, she once had a guy drive all the way from Ames, Iowa. He was two hours late, but what's the betting the trip was worth it anyway?

On the western edge of Laguna Madre lies the largest protected area of natural habitat left in the Lower Rio Grande Valley, Laguna Atascosa National Wildlife Refuge. This was an important destination for us, and we had a long afternoon ahead of us to enjoy it. But before we'd had the chance to check it out, we felt the need to have a run-in with a bunch of guys in a pickup truck.

Having driven away from San Padre, we left the town of Buena Vista and headed north towards Atascosa. Dialing in the coordinates, electric Barbara smoothly intoned each turn in a voice that made me think she and I might one day have a future together. How sexily she told me to "turn right in 1.2 miles"; how she soothed my worried gas-pedal foot with her sultry tones. Best of all, she was smart; she'd cleverly managed to get us safely to a long, straight back road in the middle of nowhere.

I was beginning to like her quite a lot. I felt that she could appreciate me. My ex-wife, after all, was always impressed by what she called the "metal plate" in my head, by which I displayed an almost perfect sense of direction. Don, unfortunately, believes me deficient in this area. It's true that there have been times when I turned right instead of left, gone north instead of south, but it was only under great Graffiti-inspired pressure, and was often at the end of long trips that had heavily featured birding over sleep. In Barbara, though, I'd found a soulmate. For a start, she was on my side against Don; she would take none of his blather about which way to turn. Further, she negated the need to do the one thing all men hate, which is to stop a car and ask for directions. Mostly, though, I just liked her voice. I was particularly pleased by the fact that once in a while she ended her instructions—I felt sure—with the words "big boy," "sailor," or "oh, handsome one." Some might say she sounded a bit computerized, but to me her voice was the music of the spheres.

I was beginning to find it tough to get out of the car, truth be told; it was so hot out there, and Barbara so delightfully cool. But outside Buena Vista she delivered us to yet another fantastic spot, and we happily pulled over, got the scopes out of the trunk, and went about some serious birding. A crested caracara, so briefly caught in Florida, this time hung around so that we could thoroughly enjoy its fabulousness. What a wild bird, in every sense. It has been described as a mixture of an eagle and a vulture, and given its scavenging tendencies, people do still sadly take a potshot at one now and then. Humans generally distrust scavengers. The crested caracara eats its carrion in an unusually fastidious way: it strips the meat, leaves it in a pile by the carcass, then once it's done carving, flies to a tree to eat it all in one go. Less fastidiously, it will eat pretty much everything: young alligators, skunks, birds, insects, and amphibians of every kind, fish, eggs, and once, a nine-banded armadillo. They sometimes hunt in pairs, and one such duo was even accused of going after lambs.

Given all that, you'd think we'd steer a bit clear of the bird, but we can't actually get close enough. It's completely crazy looking: this male has a big red face and a silver, vulture-sharp beak; a bad, bad hairdo (short at the front, longer at the back, basically a flat, black mullet); a big black and white body; and long, orange legs leading to huge, nasty-ass looking talons. It's not often one gets to say this, but, poor baby alligator.

The caracara wasn't the only treat we found on that back road. Lark sparrows and dickcissels perched on wires long enough for us to sketch them. We even scored a mighty find, a white-tailed hawk, a life bird for all of us, and a bird whose range in the United States is restricted to the Texas coastal savanna, where it often hovers above its prey before falling to the kill. Seldom a car came by, though we had noticed in the distance some kind of razor-wire-surrounded building, which we had promptly ignored.

As we scoped yet another common nighthawk and discussed how many birds we were seeing—by this, the middle of the trip, we'd already scored more than 150 species—a pickup truck filled with rippling guys in wife-beater shirts passed us. Don and Donna were oblivious, but my hackles raised immediately. About fifty feet after it passed us, the truck stopped; and then it slowly backed up.

"Can I ask what you're doing?" said the driver, a mustachioed, tattooed tough guy who looked like he'd know his way around a bar fight.

"We're looking at birds," I said, as Don and Donna looked on.

"Birds?"

"Yup."

The driver and the four other guys in the truck turned to look in the direction of my scope.

"Where?"

"On the post," I said.

Again they turned; blank.

"I don't see nothing."

"It's a common nighthawk," Donna said, as though they were retards.

"Want to see our photos?" said Don, dangerously echoing the curlew incident with the Germans.

The driver, like the women at the Waffle Hoe before him, looked at Don as though he had two heads.

"No," he smirked, rolling his eyes.

I couldn't work out if we were about to get robbed, beaten to death, or simply laughed at some more. I would take anything, as long as it was quick and they didn't hurt OnStar Barbara.

"Do you know what you're looking at?" the driver said.

"Nighthawks. My wife just told you," said Don, a trifle shortly.

"No, I don't mean the birds." More smirking. "I mean over there, on the horizon."

"No idea," I lied.

"It's a federal detention center. So, you looking at it, with telescopes, well—"

"Well what?" said Don, rising now to the challenge. He was dressed in knee-length shorts and had binoculars around his neck. Even I found it hard to take him seriously. Not that I could say anything—I was again sporting a khaki shirt, beige pants, and a huge-brimmed hat. At best I looked simple.

"We're law enforcement," the driver said.

"Ah," I said. So we're probably not going to get robbed, but still could be beaten to death and most likely would be laughed at. Good to know.

"We're just checking things out." The driver was friendly, all of a sudden, figuring, I guess, that we were completely harmless, or at least a danger only to ourselves. "Have a good day," he said, and with that, they were gone.

"I didn't even notice the truck pass us," said Don redundantly, as it disappeared into the vanishing point.

"You didn't . . . oh, brother. I noticed them straight away."

"They had fishing poles," said Donna. "I thought they were out fishing. Nice disguise. I'd make a terrible illegal migrant."

"Yes, you would," said Don, romantically.

"I'm going to talk to Barbara," I said.

At Atascosa, we spent quality time with a bird we'd heard all about but had never seen, the fabulously colorful green jay. And it's not just green either: a cousin of the blue jay, the green jay is a spectacular lime-and-yellow bird with a black breast and a cerulean top to its head, and azure on the sides of its face. Its range in the United States is restricted to south Texas, so we were ridiculously excited to see it. A whole slew of them, in fact. The refuge had set up a feeding and watering station, and we spent a happy hour taking photos of lots of green jays swooping around and generally being flashily colorful. We even saw the aberrant "blue" morph green jay that Barbara Kennett had told us to look out for. A morph is a bird that is not a separate species but has different colorations or markings than expected—this one has blue where there should be yellow. We took more movies and photos of all the birds—buff-bellied hummingbirds, and Couch's kingbirds; plain chachalacas and Altamira orioles. We watched as green jays bathed, and as the aberrant blue morph comically argued with perfectly regular red-winged blackbirds. There was a great kiskadee on a rock above a water snake.

As the high heat of the afternoon set in, we decamped back to the air-conditioned car to drive the refuge roads, hoping against hope that we might see one of the most endangered birds in America, the aplomado falcon. Sadly, it was nowhere to be found; but we did watch a comical road runner take a dust bath in some short grass, and a bone-thin coyote jog away from us hungrily as a northern mockingbird harassed it.

I could have been on a different planet. We saw no one in the refuge that day; and the calmness and joy that invaded us as we took in all that nature made us quiet. There were no people save us. We even turned off Barbara as we drove.

There were no people. Except Donna; except Don.

"So, I have a question to ask you," he said, as the hot light poured through the car windows.

"Tomatoes, right?"

"Here's the thing. No tomatoes, right?"

"No, Don, he likes tomato soup. Right Luke?"

"Very interesting," said Don, once again. "What about tomato on a sandwich?"

"You *know* he doesn't," said Donna, almost impatiently.

"Well, I *think* I know it, but I need to check. So Luke, tomato on a sandwich. What's your final position?"

I can't believe this, I really can't.

"No, Don. How many times?"

"Fascinating! What is it that you don't like? It can't be the flavor. You like other tomatoey things."

"I have no idea, Don."

"Nuts. That's what I'll be needing to know next. Where are you on pistachios? Do you like a nice bag of pistachios with a cold beer?"

With that, we all dreamed of cold beer. I also dreamed of a

world with almost no people, but certainly no spring breakers, no law enforcement, no Pregnants. Where Barbara Kennett was more famous than Britney Spears. A place where birding was thought of as normal. Here in this car was what I dreamed of.

Birds, generally speaking, love borders. (One learns always to bird the parking lot.) Hungry birds come to edges of habitats, be it a forest or a stretch of parkland or a beach, because there's food there, and they can easily rush back into hiding at the merest hint of danger. They like and need water too: oceans, seas, lakes, rivers, streams, marshland, even puddles in fields.

Birders, too, like borders. In Texas, just as we'd done in Arizona, we were birding the border; the Rio Grande was never far away. But with borders come stresses; someone's always trying to keep someone out, or someone in. We'd already come across five law-enforcement types in a pickup truck, and everywhere we drove we saw Homeland Security plastered on the sides of cars and trucks. Mexico was just a strong swim, or a fast boat ride, away.

The talk all that year had been of the fence. Already, 1.2 billion bucks had been appropriated to ruin 370 miles of the U.S.-Mexico border. The effect on wildlife would be catastrophic. Family ties across the border, pervasive and age-old, would be ruined too. It was interesting that people thought a fence would stop anything; already, part of it in San Diego was being handily scaled, albeit with extremely sophisticated equipment. (Ladders.) Here, in the place where the central and Mississippi flyways meet, where the northernmost range for many bird species ends, here they build a fence.

At Anzalduas County Park we looked across the Rio Grande to Mexico. The three of us had all lived through 9/11 in New York City, but still we thought border fences completely lunatic. Even before 9/11 I had been a rabid patriot—as I'd said in Gig Harbor on Thanksgiving, I loved this country passionately for what it had given me. But I found it hard to believe that hordes of terrorists were really pouring over this porous border. For a start, after scrambling along the cliffs, we found ourselves five hundred feet from the Anzalduas Dam. As usual, we were carrying our spotting scopes, which are coincidentally the approximate size and shape of shoulder-mounted rocket launchers, and we carried them on our, erm, shoulders. So much for "homeland security."

Back in the park proper we staked out the nest of another bird whose U.S. range is limited to here and a few spots farther west, including the spot above the Patons' house in southeast Arizona: the gray hawk. Thanks to a tip from Keith Hackland, the guy who runs the wonderful, birder-friendly Alamo Inn, where we'd stayed the previous night, we easily found the tree in which the nest rested. After a half-hour wait we heard the high call of a returning parent, which quickly entered its lair and sat there, regal and serene, while we three birders went mad with excitement a hundred feet away.

As ever, Don wasn't done—one good bird always leads to another. Thank god Donna spotted a black phoebe on a wire as we were about to leave the park; we'd seen the bird in Arizona, and Hackland had told us it was here too, even though that meant it was farther east than its usual range. Don snapped a picture, and away we went. We should have been happy.

But Anzalduas County Park had been kinda depressing. It was partly the aesthetics, but there was something else too. The place catered to a recreational, picnicking crowd most of the time, and to be a birder there on a Friday morning in overcast weather left us feeling low on energy and joy.

The next park we hit, however, was something else again, though our visit didn't begin auspiciously.

Bentsen–Rio Grande State Park is a 760-acre facility outside the town of Mission. It also happens to harbor about three hundred species of bird, making it one of the most productive birding spots in all North America. Since the park is closed to traffic, a little bus wanders around the place, picking you up and dropping you off.

Only we didn't see a bus, nor a bird, for the first hour of our visit; the place seemed deserted. We'd been traveling for a week and were tired, coming on close to dejected. There was a long list of birds we'd hoped to see, led by the clay-colored robin, the northern beardless tyrannulet, and the ferruginous pygmy owl. The first is a Mexican "trash" bird—go three hundred miles south and it's as common as our American robin in spring—but here in Texas it's a big rarity. The second is a small flycatcher, the last a tiny owl; both are resident in south Texas only, as well as points south, and in beloved southern Arizona. But our hour's walk around the place had yielded little. We needed a visit from the birding gods.

Enter Jim Booker. Jim is an official park naturalist, but unofficially that day he came close to being some kind of deity. As we grumpily arrived back at the visitor center, where some consolation had been afforded by a small flock of barn swallows and an Altamira oriole on a wire, Don and I watched as Donna got collared by a ranger, and our hearts sank.

"Oh no, officialdom. What did we do?" said Don, the recent victim of four burly, officious Brooklyn police officers who almost arrested him for carrying a tripod in Prospect Park.

"Clearly we don't have the correct credentials," I said, hurrying to go save Donna.

We needn't have worried. Booker was only asking Donna what she'd found.

As we caught up with them, we heard Booker's throaty laugh.

"No owls? And the clay-colored? Hold on right there, let me get the van," he said.

In no time at all a park vehicle was procured, and we were

embarking on our own special private tour, and with a gifted birder at that.

"There, in the road. See?" Jim had pulled the truck to the curb, and there, in the gravel, lay nesting lesser nighthawks, the exact color of the stones. "They flush before I run them over," Jim said, as Don and I took pictures.

There was more to come. Booker is a terrific mimic, and we stood spellbound as he hooted and pished and generally turned himself into Dr. Dolittle. For the owl, he cupped his hands around his mouth and made a repeating single note, breathy and insistent—it reminded me of Laurie Anderson's song "O Superman." In a faint distance the ferruginous pygmy owl called right back. Then it was on to another part of the park and it was the simplest of tasks to pick up our binoculars and focus on the clay-colored robin he found for us. In the distance, a family of Javelina edged by like a gang of motorcycle toughs.

We then spent twenty minutes watching Booker try to call in a tyrannulet. Nothing. He wasn't happy, but watching his efforts I certainly was. The tyrannulet, Booker explained, was the only tyrant flycatcher that don't have "rictal bristles." Even Don stifled a laugh.

"Don't have *what*?" I couldn't resist. Could this be where the jiz was most concentrated?

"Rictal bristles. At the base of the beak, where it meets the face. Why?"

A calling alder flycatcher—his first in the park—distracted Jim from our juvenility and seemed to cheer him a bit. But still he seemed to think he'd let us down.

He had not—we were only sad when we piled into the van for the last time and headed back to the visitor center. There, we drank coffee and Booker filled us in on his life and work. In his spare time he birds for fun. He was planning a big trip to eastern Venezuela to fill in some of the holes in his massive life list.

The rest of the time he sees his son, who lives with Jim's ex-wife out West. Unlike me, Jim couldn't bear the twice-a-week-and-every-other-weekend thing, so he moved away entirely and lives for the extended visits he gets in summer and during school holidays.

It is a club, then: lonely dads, looking at birds. Later, I found myself wishing for a friend like Jim with whom I could commiserate—and bird—though all I felt right then was crestfallen and a little angry at myself. We had left, after all, both of us fathers. In other time zones our children walked streets we couldn't name. They saw fathers and mothers on their TVs, and they probably wondered what it is they'd done wrong.

Nothing. Absolutely nothing.

Barbara, my OnStar lover, had no idea how to get us to Chapéno. "I don't seem to recognize the coordinates," she said. "Try again." And, to me: "Will you ever forgive me, darling?" Of course, my sweet. But not easily: Chapéno was the town Booker had said was a great place to find a whole host of Mexican rarities, including the ringed kingfisher.

The ringed kingfisher was one of only two target birds now left on the trip. A bird solely of the Rio Grande area in the United States, the ringed is larger than our regular belted kingfisher, and its raucous rattle and swooping dive would make it a fabulous find; not to mention that if we got it, we'd have the full set of North American kingfishers, having lucked upon the limited-ranged green at Santa Ana a couple of days earlier. Again, it came down to borders; not only did we hope to see it, but we also hoped to see it on the U.S. side of the Rio Grande. We'd be thrilled to get it on the Mexican side, of course, but to count for our North American list, it would have to alight in the United States or at least cross an imaginary center line in the river—that is, it would need to immigrate illegally, at least for a second or two.

But we never found Chapéno. Barbara's sorrow eventually

turned into blind anger, and even though we turned her on and off repeatedly, she insisted we make legal U-turn after legal U-turn until Donna almost threw up and Don fell asleep. I figured that all new relationships have a honeymoon period, and that this was just one of those early fights that in future years we'd laugh about. "No harm done, darling," I said. "We'll get through this. Just you wait and see." At this, Don woke up and looked strangely at me.

"Where *are* we?" he moaned. "Who were you just talking to?"

"Me? No one," I lied.

With his eyes narrowing he said, "Do you think Barbara will ever bring us to Chapéno?"

"I don't know, honestly," I replied, quietly enough so that Barbara wouldn't hear. "Why don't we just pull over and bird, like we normally do?"

So we did, and were having a super time—seeing a painted bunting, and a vermilion flycatcher on a cemetery cross—until a nervous couple in a farmhouse came out and told us the road was private. It clearly was no such thing, but rather than risk yet another confrontation, we gave up and made our way to the river at the nearby town of Salinéno. Little did we know what we were getting ourselves into.

To call us uneducated about that area of Texas is like calling Pluto "a bit far away." This stretch of the Rio Grande, from Brownsville to points northwest, is a porous border, smuggling country. Sorry to admit it, but Washington at least has that right. To patrol this entire stretch of river would be an impossible task; though putting a fence through it would be as futile as it would be stupid, too.

Salinéno itself, falling down a steep hill to the Rio Grande, is a tiny and poor town—not even three square miles, and with 40 percent of its folks well below the poverty line. According to census figures, the median income around here is about thirteen thousand dollars a year, and the population is 99.34 percent Hispanic/Latino, which for a total of 304 people means there's just over 2 people who are not Hispanic/Latino. I can't decide who I'd be more interested in meeting: the 2 people who *don't* claim Latino heritage, or the .064 of a person left over. What is that, an eyelash?

That Saturday, as we drove down to the water, we found three or four young men fishing, knee-deep in the brown river. There was also a trio of what Don described as "earthy lesbians" from San Antonio, finishing up a day's canoeing. Soon enough, though, the women left in their SUVs, the fishing boys put away their rods and trudged back up the hill, and we were alone.

Into this new peace came a pickup truck, racing down to the water's edge. The guy in the passenger seat, seeing us by the river, waved a friendly hello. I waved right back. It seemed a sweet place; the setting was spectacular; and as the truck roared back up the hill, we walked about a hundred feet west into the falling light. Right on cue a ringed kingfisher swooped into view, first in Mexico, then, bless its heart, crossing the river to the U.S. side and giving us all gratifying looks at a bird we'd probably see nowhere else in North America.

Farther west, the river opened out at a curve, and we fancied that as a great spot to look across the river for an Audubon's oriole. Setting off, we walked another three or four hundred feet and set up our scopes. This is what it's all about: no one here but us birders, and the chance of a lifer or two.

Then, from the distant curve we heard the thrum of an outboard engine, until we could finally make out the speed of it. It was a cigarette boat, roaring in from the west. There were five men in it: two up front, three in the back.

As they passed, Don waved. A couple of hands sheepishly waved back.

"Fishermen," Don said. "Friendly. Nice boat too! Those things can really shift."

In the noise of the wash we didn't notice that the pickup truck from a few minutes earlier had returned. The boat came into the Salinéno slip, and its engine idled. I don't know why, but something about this scene didn't spell "fishermen," so I quietly turned from Don and Donna and made to head back to the car. Before I'd gotten ten feet though, I found myself face-to-face with the driver of the pickup—he seemed to appear from behind a tree. The first thing I noticed about him was his glassy eyes, followed by his copious tattoos; then I saw his ostentatious hickeys, wounds so profoundly crimson that it appeared he was in the latter stages of bubonic plague.

Then he started talking.

"What you doin'?" he asked, sounding not entirely unfriendly.

"Birds. We're looking at birds," I said.

"Oh yeah?" He was fidgety, tweaking; he quickly looked back at the boat. "What kind of birds?"

"Belted kingfisher," I said, a bit nervously.

"No, no, it was a *ringed* kingfisher," called Don from behind me.

"OK, Don," I said, shooting Don a "for-hell's-sake" glance over my shoulder, and turning back to the guy to change my story. But he had turned too, and was walking away towards our car.

Something about how he'd asked the question and not waited for the answer struck me as significant. The rental car was filled with our stuff, and next to it now sat a battered pickup truck and a recently arrived go-fast boat.

As I trailed the guy, the three men who had been in the back of the boat jumped out and ran to the pickup truck. Then I watched them peel away at high speed up the hill. Now, all that was left was me, the truck's driver (now without a ride), and two guys who'd helmed a smuggler's boat fast along the Rio Grande. Even I could work this one out.

The driver went over to talk to the boaters. I nonchalantly

set up my scope next to our car, and with my back to the river made as if to scan the trees on the U.S. side. I heard the boat's engine change pitch, and turned to watch it speed off back to Mexico.

Now there was just the two of us, and in the distance Don obliviously birding. Donna had come a bit closer, to about five hundred feet away, but at least she was watching what happened.

Hickeyman came up real, real close.

"What's that?" he said.

"It's a scope. For the birds."

"No," he said, barely listening to my answer, "that thing attached to it."

"That's a camera."

Bad answer.

"Don't like cameras."

Silence. He came even closer.

"I said I don't like cameras."

"OK, well, it's for the birds. That's all."

"Don't like cameras," he repeated, slowly slipping his hand into his jeans pocket.

So this is how it's going to end. That was my exact thought. Once that thought had nestled safely into my quickly softening lower colon, a more extended thought came to mind: *I'm going to get my face blown off on the Texan border because I witnessed . . . I have no idea what. A bunch of guys in a boat, and now in a pickup truck somewhere? I have no idea what's in their backpacks. I'm an immigrant too. It seems a bit unfair, the whole face-blown-off thing.*

As my mind unraveled, he brought his hand out of his pocket.

My last thought was, *I wonder if it will hurt.*

There, in his hand, lay a crumpled roll of what looked like fifties.

"Here, for the camera. I don't like cameras."

I don't know why, but his gesture did two things: one, made me realize he wasn't going to hurt me; and two, really pissed me off. I mean, I'd seen what I'd seen, whatever it was, but hadn't he noticed that my traveling companions had been more bothered with the correct nomenclature for a recently apperceived life bird than with whatever he might have been doing? Hadn't they noticed Don wave? Hadn't this ass seen me try to be friendly when he needlessly came over to me and nosily asked me what I was up to? What, does he own the fucking place? Hadn't he at least seen the look of terror on my lily-white face? Couldn't he tell I already suffered from a bowel whose functions I could barely control at the best of times, let alone in a stressful situation such as this? Didn't he know I had children to feed?

Mother. Fucker.

"I don't want your money. Just go. I didn't see shit. Just go."

I was surprised at my tone; this guy was clearly on some kind of narcotic, and had just facilitated either people and/or drugs being smuggled into an utterly remote part of south Texas. And the Brit—all five feet nine and 140 pounds—had stared him down, and told him to leave. It could still go either way.

"I don't like cameras," he said, a little less forcefully.

"Fine, I heard you," I said. "But it's for the birds. Just go."

And then I said something which I now realize was odd.

"I'm on your side," I said, and with that, the air between us cooled, and he turned and walked up the hill out of sight.

I stood there shaking, not knowing what the hell I'd meant. On whose side? On the side of some addict who'd probably just helped smuggle a bunch of drugs into the United States? Or on the side of a guy who'd helped illegals gain a foothold on the other side of the border? Was I thinking, then, of the skinny female coyote we'd seen the day before at the Atascosa refuge, harassed as she had been by a northern mockingbird? Wasn't I just what I'd always been, an illegal immigrant myself, made good in the eyes of American bureaucracy by ten years of now-failed marriage? Was I, too, simply high on something—in my case, birds?

Into this feverish reverie strode Don Graffiti.

"He was a friendly chap!" Don said. "But I can't believe you said 'belted kingfisher!' My man! That was a huge life bird for us, and you blew it! Oh, that's funny. Just like Brigantine and the Germans. A curlew moment! You are hereby awarded the Doug Kopsco Trophy in perpetuity. You are officially the 1970 Brazil soccer team! Jules Rimet, eat your heart out!

"Belted kingfisher!" With that exclamation he took off his baseball cap and sighed at the evening.

"Don?" I said, looking up the hill. And then I changed my mind.

"Get," I whispered, "in-the-fucking-car."

Almost exactly one year earlier, near this very spot, U.S. Customs and Border protection agents had seized more than 1,350 pounds of marijuana, worth a cool million bucks. Someone had called to say they'd seen a blue and yellow Chevrolet Suburban pick up several large bundles of something near the river, in the exact spot where, that late afternoon, I turned our car around and headed up the hill. The driver of the Suburban had made a run for it. Well, at least I knew how that felt.

In the article I read later there was no description of the runner though, nothing about hickeys, or glassy eyes. Nor had authorities yet gotten names of the five immigrants found dead in the river here five months after the drug bust. The four men and one woman carried no identification. They washed up nameless.

All that came later. For now, we had a drive ahead of us through the black Texas evening.

After the upset, Barbara had recovered her cool and now calmly called out the directions to San Antonio, where we'd spend our last night in Texas. As we drove the three hours north, Donna and I filled Don in on the strange tale of the hickeyed smuggler, and after a while he seemed to realize that correcting my misspeak was a tiny bit beside the point.

"Funny. How oblivious I can be. I really thought he was interested in the birds. That said, IQ isn't a constant. Sometimes, one is perfectly intelligent. But just as quickly, one can be a cretin."

"You're not a cretin. It's your Attention Surfeit Disorder flaring up again," said Donna. "I knew straightaway the guy was trouble."

"Why didn't you say so, sweetie?" said Don, a bit aggrieved, seemingly, to have missed the action.

"I knew Small Injustice Man could handle it," said Donna.

The improbability of this statement made us all pause and look out our respective windows. Even Barbara snorted. The merest light danced on the otherwise black horizon; ahead of me, a straight Texas freeway, ours the only car. On the stereo, Antony, of the band Antony and the Johnsons, was singing, "My Lady Story," the second song off his amazing record called, appropriately enough, *I Am a Bird Now*. We'd been listening to the CD all week, and as we reached the outskirts of San Antonio, Don finally worked out Antony's warbled, strange lyrics.

"Is he saying, 'My lady story is one of breast amputation'?" Don whispered, Donna asleep in the back.

"Yes, Don, did you only just notice?" I said, perhaps a bit too tartly.

I'm sorry to report that there's a Yellow List, and there's a Red List. And though it's not good to be on either, finding yourself on the latter is a sure sign that your time on earth is perilously close to an end. Our final target bird on the Texas trip was decidedly on the World Conservation Union Red List of Threatened Species, putting us once again in Kirtland's warbler territory; this time, however, there was no government guide to show us where to find one. We were on our own.

First, it was incumbent on us to have a plane to catch to add to the tension. It was a Sunday morning, and it seemed to me that Barbara had decided yesterday's fight was a sign of something deeply wrong in our relationship. That day, she couldn't have found her way out of a paper bag, which is where we were tempted to put her, given the continual confusing of east and west, north and south. We had driven out of San Antonio heading towards Austin, where the bird we wanted to see was known to breed: specifically, in a big state park called Pedernales Falls, between RV parking lots 19 and 21, down the hill, along the trail, stop, just over there.

But we had to find the g-d park. We spent the first hours of the morning at Warbler Woods, a private, 126-acre garden in Cibolo, generously opened to the public by its owners, Susan and Don Schaezler and Margie Bonnes. All you have to do is call ahead, and promise to tell them what you see when you're there. The list of birds seen on the property is astonishing, names to thrill any birder's soul: common paraque, buff-bellied humming-bird, black-capped and yellow-green vireo, zone-tailed hawk, and dozens of others. The chief draw for us was the warblers promised by its name: it boasts thirty-six species. Unfortunately for us, despite the warm welcome we had received from Don Schaezler, all his wonderful place had offered that Sunday morning late in the season was an infestation of chiggers in my ankles so bad that I would spend the following weekend sick in bed with weeping, pus-addled legs and a killer fever. (If you don't know how chiggers do what they do then you might want to look away from the next paragraph.)

Here goes: Chiggers are the larvae of mites which attach to your skin, and during feeding inject a kind of fluid that actually dissolves the tissue of your freaking body. Then, get this: they eat the goddamn liquefied tissue! Not only are they horribly painful, but it's all for naught: they get so little susten-ance from the leg goo (something to do with the human im-mune system shutting off the carbs) that they die before they get to dessert.

Don Schaezler had told us ahead of time that Warbler Woods had chiggers, and had even shown us where he kept his sulfur for dusting (that's supposed to stop them attaching). But attach they did, and not just to my legs. Suffice to say that a few days later, when spraying the top of my inner thigh with anti-itching lotion, I managed to freeze one of my testicles so thoroughly that I could have taken a sharp kick to it and not fainted.

For now, though, Warbler Woods had been a bust and we were lost in the Hill Country south of Austin. Barbara was posi-tively screeching at us, and it was then I realized: she didn't want us driving the car back to a faceless airport where, in all likeli-hood, she and I would never meet again. Poor dear. I did the only thing I could—I turned her off for good, like so many other women I'd known.

Don was peering out the windshield as though there would be a sign on this back road that would be in some way useful; Donna was boning up on the specifics of the bird we'd see, if we ever found the park, and trying to ignore two grown men argu-ing about which way was east.

And then by complete happenstance we found it. Pulling in, we were surprised to find that the Pedernales Falls State Park is sponsored, in part, by Toyota. The back of the map the kind ranger handed to us boasted a huge and apparently not ironic ad for the Tundra Double Cab.

The park itself sits atop high hills west of Austin like a double cab above a set of monster tires, and is pretty much given over to RVs and camping and riding the Pedernales Falls in a tube. We wondered out loud how many folks here knew that the park has nesting in it our target bird, the golden-cheeked warbler. The golden-cheeked resembles the black-throated green warbler, except that instead of olive green it has a black crown and back. Of all the warblers, the black-throated green is one of the greatest delights, buzzing around a forest, alert and startlingly colorful. Its song *is* the spring; I never tire of it. Its close cousin the golden-cheeked would have many of these charming attributes, but in addition it could also boast extreme rarity, which was the real reason to chase it. The golden-cheeked warbler is the only bird that nests solely in Texas and nowhere else in the world, but its preferred habitat of ashe juniper and oak woodlands in the Edwards Plateau of central Texas is fast disappearing.

In the World Conservation Union's 2007 assessment (coauthored, incidentally, by someone called J. Bird), habitat loss of one quarter in the twenty years since 1961 is the main culprit for the bird being designated endangered. Texans even purposely destroyed some of their habitats right before the listing took effect so as to avoid the strictures the new law would force upon them.

There were thought to be fifteen thousand to seventeen thousand golden-cheeks in 1974; less than two decades later, that number had dropped to under five thousand. No one has any real idea how many are left—one estimate in 1990 came up with the hilariously literal number of 4,822 to 16,016 pairs (it was calculated from averaging out birds found, multiplied by habitat mapped); another now says "9,600 to 32,000." The Audubon Society Web site comments that a new population survey is "vitally needed." Well, yes. With such guesswork abounding, we have no idea how much longer we'll be able to see the bird. On that day in Texas, we'd given ourselves just about an hour to do so; our plane was ready and waiting to take us back to New York.

The path that began between RV parks 19 and 21 left the

hubbub of the people and cars and sloped steeply down the hillside through high cedar oaks (the colloquial name for ashe junipers). In the distance we could hear the rush of the Pedernales River; up here, all we cared to hear was the buzzing song of the golden-cheeked. A light rain had begun to fall, and we huddled under some low-hanging branches to wait it out. But time was charging ahead, so we stepped back on to the path. As we'd done in Arizona to chase the elegant trogon, we split up, Don and Donna back towards the parking lot, me farther on, each of us silent, straining to hear the *zee-ZO, zee-zee ZO zi* of the call. I wandered away farther still, until I could no longer see Don and Donna.

There I was, lost in the Texas Hill Country, bone-tired from a week's birding. But I could bear not to see the golden-cheeked; after all, I'd seen a gray-crowned yellowthroat, and a lesser nighthawk, and the gray hawk, and green jays, and . . . the list went on and on. I was content, then, to savor what I'd gotten, and not get greedy.

Then Donna came running, urging me back towards she and Don with a grabbing motion, almost falling on the slippery path.

"Come on," she whispered. "Come on, we got it!"

I ran back with her to where Don was standing. He was sad. "It flew."

"But you got it?" I said.

"Oh yes, for sure. Pretty, pretty bird. We were hearing the song forever, and then it briefly alighted on that branch, right there. Great looks. Then it was gone."

It didn't matter. In a way, it made up for the gray-crowned yellowthroat that Don had missed at Sabal Palm. Donna and I wandered back away from Don, back to where she'd found me daydreaming. I wasn't sad; it had been an amazing trip. That night I'd get to see my kids.

A little bird with golden cheeks came by right then, and alighted on a low branch. Donna looked at me; I looked at her; we both looked at the bird. Was it one of 9,600, or one of 32,000? One of 4,822, or one of 16,016? I focused my binoculars perfectly, and stared hard at it through them, just in case it was the very last one of all.

NOW WHAT?

⤙⤚

On an uptown number 6 train heading to Seventy-seventh Street in New York City, I listen to birdsongs on my iPod and freak out the guy next to me, who's clearly unaware that I'm the source of the sounds rattling around in his brain. "I hear chestnut-sided warblers, Doc, and sometimes northern parulas. I can't get them out of my head! You gotta help me!"

Today Donna and I find fourteen species of warbler in Central Park, including amazing, *National Geographic*–movie looks at one of the prettiest of all, the Cape May. Don't let looks deceive you—even though they sport a translucent reddish-orange patch on a sparkling yellow face, Cape Mays are aggressive little birds, often chasing away other warblers from trees. Also, here's a great secret about them: they have tubular tongues, the only warbler to have such a thing; it helps them collect nectar in the winter, though their main food is spruce budworms. I think of them as the Roman Catholics of warblers, given that they have the biggest families of all the *Dendroicas*, probably to make the most of when there's a budworm eruption. There has been talk of such an explosion this year, given that Cape Mays have been regular visitors to city parks all spring. This day, Don is away on business; I wonder out loud if Donna won't tell him about the Cape May, given that he's missed it every day it's been noted. Donna plaintively answers, "But he'll be happy for me." And anyway we have our Colorado trip coming up.

That fall we finally found Don a Cape May in, appropriately enough, Cape May, New Jersey. Warblers are duller in the fall than in the spring because they're not trying to make babies; sometimes they change their colors completely from bright to drab and confusing. Still, Don was excited, but then, he always is.

Donna leaves, and I walk to Hallett Nature Sanctuary, where an active Canada warbler makes an inactive black-crowned night heron seem sulky; along the walk, a solitary sandpiper teeters on the edge of the lake; but in the Ramble, the reported mourning warbler is nowhere to be found. A teenager, two big dogs, and a younger brother in tow, rush up to me—"you seen the mourning, heh?" the teen chimed. He has writing all over his ripped jeans, long lists of numbers separated by commas, and words I don't recognize. We bird together for a while, and it is clear he is both brilliant at it, and a little lost somewhere deep inside his own head. I leave him and his brother there, and head out, reminding myself that humanity can make a recluse of the best of us, whatever our age.

A female mallard tucks her beak into her feathers, just a few feet away in the lake. Grackles fly across the water, still busy. A common yellowthroat reminds me of the pink house, briefly finds me interesting, then leaves. I can sense the summer approaching—a time of few songbirds, at least in late June and July. It feels elegiac, somehow, the way the end of summer used to when I was a kid. Across the next weeks the blogs will call in mourning warblers and a cerulean—a cerulean!—at Prospect Park, but here in Manhattan, the European starlings and house sparrows are reclaiming this land as theirs and theirs alone.

I walk over to the Maintenance Field, a little place that's often hailed as a great migrant trap. There, under a tree, a man is lying on a russet blanket. He's naked, except for an exceptionally tight pair of turquoise Speedos. It's hard not to stare. The man is displaying a significant, ballet-dancer bulge, the kind that ballerinas use for a step up. He does calisthenics as he lies there, bending his legs back over his head, or thrusting them up into the air. I can't look for birds in the tree above him because I can't point my binoculars his way—I don't want him to think his package is small. That would be a travesty. The thing is like a Coney Island hot dog.

Beyond, under another tree I'd also like to survey but can't, stands a young man dressed entirely in black, sporting a ponytail down to his butt. He passes a glass ball around his fingers, over the backs of his hands, up his arms.

New York City. Oh, the things you'll see.

As for me, I'm strapped into my man-bra, which dangles my binoculars at my belly. I'm pishing—*pish pish pish*, I whisper—at a newly hatched American robin feeding on the ground. The bird comes closer and closer, inspecting me and the odd noise I'm emitting. Me, the "normal one" of the three in this city park.

The bird assesses the birder with a blank eye, cocks its head, and flies away.

SEVEN

Colorado:
On the Trail of the White-tailed
P-TAR-me-jen

So for a while it was the book I read aloud to them. At bedtime we'd huddle around each other and I'd begin: "Turnagain ptarmigan! Where did you go?" From there, we'd rhyme our way through James Guenther's endearing picture book and witness the different molts of the willow ptarmigan, Alaska's state bird. In the brief summer it showed rufous; in winter, full white; whatever it takes to avoid predation. The girls didn't care about predators though. For them, it was simply a pretty bird, able to shape-shift on blooming tundra and snowfields.

Today, I'm crouched on Medicine Bow Curve, high above the Poudre River Trail, watching a family of gray-speckled *white-tailed* ptarmigan edge across the tundra fifty feet below. Don is running with both scopes; behind him, Donna jogs too, desperate to see. And in my head I gently sing to them, *turnagain ptarmigan, please don't you go.*

We had birded the edges—East Coast, Michigan, Pacific Northwest, southeast Arizona, Texas, Florida—and now it was time to make a bull's-eye. The interior of this great country is as rich in birds as anywhere, and we had been remiss not to venture deep into it. So now we'd go smack into the middle, spending a glorious long weekend in the Rockies and the Pawnee Grasslands to the east. That is, as long as the altitude didn't kill me.

It was a real concern; I'd been here before. A few years earlier I'd come to Colorado on business—flown to Denver, then driven the Independence Pass to Aspen. There, I'd worked with a man named Aron Ralston on the book he wrote, detailing his six days trapped by a rock fall at the bottom of a Utah canyon. From early afternoon Saturday till the following Thursday morning, Aron had riddled the problem of how to free himself from the vise-grip of an eight-hundred-pound boulder. By that last morning, delirious from lack of sleep and a near week of unthinkable agony, he had been brought to a literal place of no return. Bending his arm to make the most of the fulcrum effect, he'd snapped his bones, hacked at the flesh, and freed himself. The subsequent hike, rappel, airlift, life-threatening infections, operations . . . well, the least of his challenges was to learn to write left-handed, though he did that too. In my calendar I still note his "real" birthday, and the day he was reborn. And on Halloween, I chuckle at the image of him running into a couple of guys who attend Aspen's parade as "Aron Ralston," replete with pirate hooks. The real Aron Ralston thoroughly enjoyed their discomfort.

So there I was, giving him a hand, to steal a gag from his book on a final edit of his manuscript, but I was not feeling good at all. To this point in my life I had spent exactly no time at altitude. I wasn't a mountaineer—I wasn't even a skier—and my adult years had been marked by an increasing problem with heights. In corporate offices in New York I'd have to position myself with my back to the window; a trip up to the Rainbow Room at the top of Rockefeller Center had sent me into paroxysms of nausea—I made it two steps out of the elevator before I turned tail and heaved the sixty-five floors back to terra firma.

So the Colorado altitude was not being gentle with me. My head slowed into nothing; my stomach churned. And there I was with a man who'd survived the worst extremes this planet could throw at him. Aron had lived through that hideous accident, for starters, but he was also an extreme mountaineer, on course to complete climbs of every fourteen-thousand-foot mountain in the country, solo, and in winter. (He finished the circuit a couple of years ago, the first man to do so. And yes, the last few climbs were *post*-accident.) I, by contrast, was "feeling weird," because "the air was thin." I could barely read the words on his page. I hid it as best I could for two remarkably embarrassing days before I bade him farewell and headed back towards Denver. On the way there, I paused in Leadville, elevation 10,152 feet, to ask a woman in a store if I should be worried about how terrible I was feeling. There, in the highest city in the United States, her answer was as follows:

"Well, your blood's too thick. If your lips turn blu*er*, call an ambulance. EMS will apply leeches."

I laughed. She didn't. Leeches were no laughing matter in these parts, not that they really are anywhere, come to think of it. As I drove away from her store, I pondered the Leadville 100, a nearly quadruple marathon staged in the town every year since 1983. "Bunch of wankers," I thought. "Why can't they just take a short jog around the block like the rest of us?"

Now, a couple of years later, I was back, and if possible in even worse shape than before. We were driving away from the Denver airport towards Grand Lake, a tiny town of about five hundred where Don had rented us an apartment for a couple of nights. Grand Lake rests serenely at about eight and a half thousand feet, and is the western gateway to Rocky Mountain National Park. Though I'd felt a bit "bronchial" at the airport, I figured since I'd been through this once, I'd be fine heading up through the montane and towards the alpine. I mean, come on, you're a grown man, the father of two, a responsible professional—not to mention that you've been drinking so much water this last week (Donna told you it was supposed to help) that your ankles have swollen like a pregnant woman's. You're not a water drinker at all—friends know that at restaurants there will always be a spare glass of water on the table because you never touch the stuff—you're a beertotaller. So for you to be downing pints of the stuff is notable; Donna can't believe that you keep begging for more bottles of water from the back seat.

As you turn off Highway 70 and head north on Route 40, you note, privately and nervously, that each little town is proud of its elevation. First it's six thousand feet, then just under seven, and soon . . . well, this is not good.

"Guys, I hate to say this—"

"What is it? Problem with the car? What?" Don sounds like he's revving up for a rant against Hertz.

"No, nothing like that. It's just—"

"Are we lost? As usual?" asks Donna.

"No, Jesus, no. It's just that I'm beginning to feel like crap."

"What?" says Don.

"It's the altitude. I'm feeling weird."

"God almighty, man, we're barely above sea level." Don can hardly keep the frustration out of his voice.

"Don, did you see the last sign?"

"I did not."

"Why not?"

"I was reading about ptarmigans." He pronounces it, P-TAR-me-jens.

"Reading about what?"

"White-tailed P-TAR-me-jens."

"That's how it's pronounced?" says Donna, quietly from the back.

"Well, how else?"

The answer never came. Instead, Don filled us in on the struggle to be a ptarmigan. Poor things—given the warmer winters, they're hatching much sooner than before, and they face a lack of food by being born too early. One pressure group, the National Resources Defense Council, predicts that if the winters keep getting warmer, white-tailed ptarmigan could be gone from this park by midcentury.

Which would be way too bad, given that these birds fight an intense battle with extreme weather conditions as it is. For a start, aside from their continually molting plumage, they also have feathered toes—wouldn't we all love that in January? In the lowest temperatures the bird will roost in a snowbank before it will even consider something as basic as flight. When temperatures go above about seventy degrees, on the other hand, white-tailed ptarmigans will bathe in snow to cool down; in winter they are said to defecate "on an average of forty-nine times overnight." That's all that Don would say on the matter—in my head I was literally screaming at him, "Tell me more!" But there *was* no more (except that the mean length of each poop is about an inch); I had no choice but to let it lie.

By now, my intense feelings of altitude sickness are receding as I think about defecation, and back to all the times I'd read *Turnagain Ptarmigan* to my daughters. Had I screwed up the pronunciation every single time? Don continued to call them "P-TAR-me-jens." Was I—again—a complete idiot?

"Well, whatever they're called, we might see them. But we'll have to go high," continues Don.

"How high?" I'm not ashamed of the fear in my voice.

"Oh, you know. Higher than you've ever been. No worries. The views will be splendid. More water?"

That night, I barely slept. How was I going to stand being higher than Grand Lake—all 8,347 feet of it—if I already felt like hell? I wasn't cut out for an intrepid life. I had a large stripe of fear running up my soul. I wasn't ever going to be Aron Ralston, a man who'd been stalked by a bear in the Grand Tetons for an entire day. Here, in the deep night of Colorado, I could barely summon the resolve to run out to our unlocked rental car and close it up. Don had been unable to work the key fob, and with Arizona in mind, had resisted the temptation, thank god. Gathering up my courage, and taking the deepest breath available at this ridiculous altitude—I swear, Laika the Space Dog must have had an easier time breathing than this—I levered myself out of the apartment.

Heroically, I managed to get the car snugged up singlehandedly, before the night chill and fear of death by excessive starlight hit me, and I fled back inside, where the oxygen was pooled. Unbeknownst to me, I had just passed by a predator: not a black bear, but Don Graffiti, camera pressed to the window. He had snapped a picture as I ran back to the apartment, bare-chested and without shoes or socks.

Ah, the English male sans shirt. When I was young, I looked not unlike a victim of famine; when I attended swimming lessons in grade school rumor had it that Save the Children was contacted by the lifeguard when he saw my protruding rib cage. But eventually I grew into my body, as it were, and the extra pounds (six) that I managed to pack on between the ages of fourteen and twenty-three at least made shirtless summer days on freezing beaches a tad less embarrassing. But I'd never be mistaken for a Chippendale, unless you mean the old furniture. Curiously, too, I've always had a couple of red rings around my skin, at lower chest level, as though that's where you turn me to get me in perfect focus. I have no idea why they're there, and legions of doctors have scratched their heads and prescribed me pretty much one of everything, from Cipro to those pills they give alcoholics to make them feel like they're dying if they have a drink. But nothing has taken away the lines; nor has anything helped the paleness. My skin is not exactly white, more an off-gray color, like a once vivid photograph that's been left too long in the sunlight. Women with whom I have hoped to be intimate have tended to gasp when I've taken off my shirt. More often than not I've tried to parse the gasping as desire, when, if I'm honest, I know it's actually the gag reflex turned up beyond its usual physiological limit. Now that I'm nearly forty, the faint whiff of weight is appearing in my belly region too; though if you were really looking on the bright side, you could say that it's not entirely a bad thing that I'm beginning to grow my own breasts, the breasts of others being so far from available.

In the photo Don took that night I show all these attributes, as well as looking for all the world like a tweaking crack addict, or the proverbial *Cops* delinquent being asked where his wife's at. Well, my ex-wife was at that moment snug asleep in Astoria, Queens, elevation fifty feet, if that, our children in the next room dreaming of ptarmigans molting.

I was two full days away from an elevation I could bear. Bare-chested, I slunk back to bed to the sound of Don showing Donna the picture of me half-naked. From the next room, I heard her retching. Poor thing—she must have been terribly dehydrated.

The makeup of the human body is seven tenths water to three tenths everything else—just like the planet upon which all the bodies spin—but by that first full morning in Colorado, I'm pretty certain I'd upped the ratio by at least two tenths. By dawn, after sipping and napping, napping and sipping, I was bone-tired, and there was an uncomfortable sloshing in my belly. My ankles were still huge, my pee clear as an alpine stream. But at least the restless night had given way to a startlingly clear and sun-filled day, and the view that awaited us was worth every last milliliter of Poland Spring. There, rising more than twelve thousand feet into the morning, lay Ptarmigan Mountain—as auspicious, given that the ptarmigan was one of our ptarget birds, as it was beautiful. However, not only had the day ushered in bright weather; it also seemed to have ushered in late fall.

What the hell? Could our eyes be lying? It was mid-August, but there, all over the mountainsides surrounding the town, lay evidence of autumn: dark trees and russet tones where there should have been evergreen. As we set up our scopes and got our first life bird of the trip—stunning violet-green swallows hanging around on a low roof in the center of town—I theorized that maybe fall comes early to these higher climes. It didn't feel right, but it was the best I could come up with.

I was being what Don would call a cretin. It wasn't fall—it was *Dendroctonus ponderosae*, the mountain pine beetle, and it was ravaging the West like never before. The little bastards burrow into trees, lay their nasty little eggs all the way up the center of the tree, then the eggs morph into larvae that eat the tree from the inside out. Old trees are most susceptible, but the beetle's done so well for itself that every tree is in danger. From a distance it looks like fall; close up, it looks like disaster.

It's not just an issue here in the Rockies. It's a widespread epidemic, stretching from Canada down through Washington, Oregon, Montana, and Idaho, and then to points south all the way to New Mexico, and even on into Mexico proper. Ponderosa, lodgepole, Scotch, and limber pines are all at risk, and as we drove that morning up Route 34 and into Rocky Mountain National Park, the damage was everywhere. The oldest dead trees were gray; others showed a pale yellow, sometimes orange. We were horrified to learn that even seemingly healthy trees can sometimes take nine months to show their infestation, which meant that no one could predict just how much of this habitat was about to disappear.

Let's get this straight: we're in the midst of a national disaster of some magnitude. That said, Canada got there first, and owing mainly to a four degree rise in average winter temperatures there, the beetle hasn't been as susceptible to getting frozen to death, the only real way to stem the tide. The result has been true devastation: the beetle is said to have infested more than twenty million acres and slaughtered more than four hundred million cubic feet of trees in Canada. Extrapolate this over the next several years, and experts say that 80 percent of the pines in the central British Columbia forest will be dead. And all it takes is a short leap eastward and the entire northern boreal forest, one of nature's last true wildernesses, would be faced with the same scenario.

How alarming is this? For a start, the northern boreal forest boasts about 40 percent of the entire planet's carbon stocks, and 80 percent of the earth's unfrozen freshwater. The former is central to the planet's fight against global warming (I know, I know, there's no such thing); the latter is crucial because you never know when I might need to drink more to combat altitude sickness. If you can bear two more statistics, read on: the boreal forest represents a quarter of the world's remaining ancient woodland, and about five billion birds migrate north to use it as a place to nest and raise young. Five billion. We have to stop this.

But we can't, not really. Here in the Rockies, there are extensive efforts under way to spray the healthy trees and fell the dead ones, but something on the order of a billion dollars would be needed to eradicate the problem. A few days before we arrived in Colorado, Democratic governor Bill Ritter had signed into law a bill that threw one million dollars at the problem—a well-intended 1 percent of what's needed.

According to the *Denver Post*, in the last decade we have lost nearly 7.5 million trees; 1.5 million out of 14.5 million acres of national forest in the state—more than 10 percent—is already gone. In addition, there's the problem of what these areas will look like once the trees are felled. Locals are shocked at the moonscapes created by logging. What was once sublime is becoming bare.

As lovers of nature we are shocked; it truly does resemble fall. We pull off the main road at the Bowen-Baker trailhead and take a walk. The air is crisp and new; our lungs are finally getting used to it, perhaps. I'm still swigging from a (refilled!) water bottle, and the extra hydration is starting to help. We walk by the Colorado River and let our eyes play up along the red and green foothills until Bowen Mountain juts into the blue sky. The air tastes different here. Can something taste *thinner*?

The bird we see on the walk brings to mind one of my best ever birding moments, which occurred on my previous trip to Colorado, the one in which I proved myself physically incapable of dealing with reduced oxygen. The truth is that once I'd left Leadville and slunk down the mountain, I'd started to feel a bit better, and eventually felt well enough to pull off the road at a small parking area. The views across the valley were literally breathtaking; but even those views couldn't hold a candle to a pair of mountain bluebirds perched on a wire. Back then, I was new to birding, and the shock of their azure feathers left me speechless. They were two of the most beautiful birds I'd ever seen.

Here in the valley near Bowen Mountain, another mountain bluebird perches a few feet away from us. And though I'd seen the elegant trogon in Arizona, and painted buntings in Florida, and in Texas too, and a bright Cape May warbler in Central Park, New York, and so many other fine and pretty birds . . . well, the mountain bluebird holds a special place for me.

This is one of the greatest joys of birding: many birds are rare enough, either intrinsically, or through the fact that I don't live where they live, that seeing them across a span of years keeps them fresh and vigorous to me. Plus, they are neutral—they exist not for me, and my crazy little ego, and most especially not for my list. They exist because this is how the universe wills it. And I'm better for it, marginally, and that's the best I can hope for.

And then we're back in the car, and as we're all a little nuts at this altitude, and because the road is busy, Don has time to clarify a few things.

"So, I have a question to ask you," says Don, as we approach Medicine Bow Curve on the Trail Ridge Road.

"Tomatoes."

"Here's the thing. Nothing?"

"No, pizza and soup. Right, Luke?" says Donna, as though we had talked about this once a long time ago and she was being clever in remembering.

"What about tomato-based sauces on pasta?" Don continues. "Bolognese?"

"That's been added to the list. I think we covered that in Arizona, and elsewhere," I reply.

"Very interesting," says Don. "Let me ask you this: Tomato, sliced thinly on a sandwich?"

"You know," says Donna.

"Well, I *think* I know it, but I need to check. So Luke, tomato on a sandwich. What's your final, final position?"

At Medicine Bow Curve we parked our car and set out for a hike. By this point, I still felt light-lunged, but there was a bird to find, so I was going to have to suck it up, so to speak. Don had researched the best place to see a white-tailed ptarmigan. According to his reading, if we walked a ways northeast up the trail, we might luck upon one. And if we found it, then we could happily fight over the pronunciation.

The path leading away from Trail Ridge Road is a little dirt ribbon, winding northeast up and over the alpine tundra. Here, where once the Ute moved from their summer to winter land, restrictions are now in place forbidding hikers from traipsing across the delicate flowers of the tundra. Alas, on that day, a blithe couple had decamped halfway up the tundra and were scarfing down a picnic. Small Injustice Man's yelling at them was lost in the strong winds that whipped across the mountains. The alpine tundra is extremely susceptible to damage—as William Bowman, director of the University of Colorado's Mountain Research Station, put it in the *Rocky Mountain News* when discussing the difficulty of mapping out a pristine place to do his job, "A severe problem is finding a summit of a mountain in Colorado that isn't trampled to death." These alpine flowers and weak grasses take hundreds of years to grow because the season in which they thrive is so short. Between them, those two superstars halfway up the hill probably ruined a couple of hundred years of life. Oh, to be armed.

Then, after we walked another third of a mile, the power of the landscape reasserted itself, and I was alone on the hill. Don had gone ahead out of sight, and Donna had lagged behind to take some photos. After a few minutes, I found Don and he was as excited as I'd ever seen him.

"I have it!"

"Don, if this is about tomatoes—"

"P-TAR-me-jen!"

"What?"

"P-TAR-me-jen!"

"Are you sure you—"

"Positive! They're just over that rise."

"No, I meant the pronunciation."

"Candy bar!" Don said. Clearly we weren't going to discuss this any longer. "I'm going to go back and get a scope."

"Really?" I said. "It's a long way, and the air is so thin—"

"Not a problem! Gotta get some photos. Go and watch, over that rise, see if they stay." With that, he was gone, striding a tad too fast, given the thin air, away back to the car.

The rise to which he had pointed was about five hundred feet away, and in between a thin stream trickled into a tiny pond. I could easily get much closer, but that would mean walking across the tundra—not an option. Then, as I turned my glasses westward, there! A white-tailed ptarmigan, in summer plumage, hobbled over the tundra and towards me. My breath caught, but not from the altitude. I could pretty much guarantee that this would be the only such bird I'd see without a trip to Alaska, and I was excited beyond reason. Even better, it brought with it some young, three or four much smaller birds, all hobbling over the knobbly ground, sticking close to the watercourse.

I was determined to drink them in. Now and then I'd lose them in the higher plants and flowers, but they didn't seem to be going anywhere soon; this was good news, as Donna hadn't seen them yet, and the moment would be ruined if she missed them. After about ten minutes I could see Don and Donna in the distance, and I urgently beckoned to them. What were they waiting for? All this way to find a bird, and the two of them were dawdling along the trail, as if they could rewind the ptarmigan reel when they managed to get themselves up to the top. I took a good half-lungful of air and got ready to let them know that they were about to miss the bird, hence screwing things up for themselves, hence screwing things up for me. And then I realized they couldn't go any faster because Don was carrying my scope as well as his own.

This, then, was the full measure of my friend. For all his quirks, what he brings most to the world is generosity, and I knew then, on that mountain, that I had lucked out so completely to have found him and Donna that it seemed almost wasted on me. I had lost count of the times Don had fought with me over some restaurant bill, but it wasn't that. His generosity ran long: if he had a rare bird in his scope, it was his urgent desire that all three of us see it. If I needed to vent about my life, he was all ears, even when he was bored (he must be—*I* was bored, and it was my life). When my marriage broke up, Donna quietly gave me a huge amount of her handmade pottery to stock my empty cabinets. Together, they put up with my ridiculous Small Injustice Man ranting and love of the odd scatological joke. They said they were grateful when I drove them around to see birds, but the joy was all mine.

As he arrived, he turned to Donna and said, "Coolio and the Gang! P-TAR-me-jen!"

I never once thought of throwing him off the mountain. I loved him. We could make his *p* silent another day. I watched him watching, and his commitment to the bird, to its beauty and to its struggle, was incontrovertible. For Don, looking was not a passive event; he looked and looked and cooed and sang praises and looked some more, well beyond the concentration of the rest, and he did so because in his looking he loved this bird and its chicks as fervently as he did birds of every kind (including even rock pigeons and English sparrows). And when he loved *people*, it was rare enough that you treasured it.

He was also a total pain in the derriere—so with a hearty, deeply hydrated belch, I turned my back on the ptarmigan (pronounced, Don-ye-effin'-eejit, TAR-mi-gun) and strode back to the car.

He'd be forever up there; there was probably enough time for a nap.

I awoke half an hour later when Don and Donna returned. I pulled the car back onto Trail Ridge Road, only to find that it had filled to the crawling point with cars; it didn't help that the road was also under construction. All the stops and starts gave us a chance to see the other treasures of the high peaks: martin, pika, mountain cottontails, a white-tailed jackrabbit, white-tailed deer, and elk—we ticked each off with glee. The pika, a hamsterlike animal, was especially a treat, even when we read about their alimentary habits in our mammals guide. With further apologies to Don and his delicate sensibilities, this one's a keeper. The pika eats a meal, craps it out, and eats it again, "to further extract nutrients." Please take a moment to consider that, as we did, up there in the high Rockies. We went silent for some minutes.

Astonishingly, it was Don who broke the silence, and with a singularly out-of-character comment:

"You ever eat a meal you enjoyed so much you crapped it out and ate it again?"

We were hugging an S-curve at twelve thousand feet when he piped up, and in my surprise I thought I did well to execute a controlled skid and only partially leave the road. I had not, in fact, ever enjoyed anything so much that I'd wanted to defecate it out onto a plate and re-eat it. To be honest, the thought of any kind of warmed-over food evokes for me a residual childhood qualm. I grew up with a dear mother for whom the temperature of a meal was indexed to its enjoyment; that is, she strongly believed the hotter the food, the better. I lost count of how many times in each individual meal she whisked our plates away and back to the kitchen, where, by an alchemy I'm yet to fully understand, she was able to increase the temperature of the "food" beyond that which it was edible in any given calendar year. I blew on food so much growing up that it's still surprising to me that I never made a living playing trombone. My brother can swallow fire.

Don, for his part, had turned his entire body to gaze out his window at Stones Peak—a full seventy-eight feet below thirteen thousand—and I do believe he was laughing at his own joke, though all I could actually hear was him saying, "Oh dear, oh dear" as his shoulders jerked up and down. Donna was so surprised by Don's comment that she wrote it down. One for the Life List.

We were now as high as I'd ever been, but at times we'd dip down below the tree line, where Clark's nutcrackers would walk on the stone walls and beg for food. This part of Trail Ridge Road—Colorado River Trailhead to Many Parks Curve—was the highest continuous road in the United States, and open for just three and a half months each year. Leaving the highest spots, we descended to a couple of trailheads in the east, Mill Creek Basin and Cub Lake, where the relative lowness of the land made our afternoon hikes thoroughly enjoyable, even easy.

We were rewarded in late afternoon with two wonderful additions to our trip: a Townsend's solitaire, the bird Barbara Kennett's friend from Ames, Iowa, missed that time in southern Texas; and a true target bird of the Rockies, blue grouse, plodding away from us up a hillside. This was quite a find. Blue grouse are careful birds, and the hillside on which we saw them was dense and leaf- and log-littered. Except in mating season, when the males display a red bull's-eye pattern, the birds are also leaf- and log-litter-colored, and they crept by like teenagers sneaking in after a night on the town.

All too soon it was time to retrace our drive. Don had booked us into a motel on the shores of Lake Granby, all the way back beyond the southwest corner of Rocky Mountain National Park. No matter; even though we had to return through the 12,183-foot spot just before the Alpine Visitor Center, by now I was used to it, and cogent enough to appreciate the peach light on distant cumuli.

The motel on Lake Granby was, no surprise, completely bizarre. Don and Donna's room featured plastic halves of mallards stuck to the ceiling, as though the ceiling were the surface of a lake—perfect for birders! Mine had one of everything stuck to the walls and the ceiling: a partial inventory might list a guitar, a tractor seat, a set of playing cards, numerous (presumably unloaded) guns, and the bust of some cowboy or other. The entire place was nerve-racking, as was the sign on the refrigerator that in part said,

BE QUIET AS A CHURCHMOUSE BETWEEN 10 AT NIGHT AND SUNRISE,
'cuz we're 'bout outta places to bury any more
LOWDOWN, NASTY SCOUNDRELS WHO KEEP OTHER FOLKS FROM GETTING THEIR SHUTEYE.

The capitalization alone kept me sitting up half the night. Though quietly, as there were a number of other threats taped to the refrigerator too, so heinous that my already thickened blood ran cold. I can say no more. I'm just glad we got out of there alive.

Next day, we took a long ride to nowhere. Nowhere and heaven; perhaps the most heavenly place we'd visited in all our trips.

Before the Pawnee Grasslands, however, we had our last morning in Rocky Mountain National Park. After breakfast in Grand Lake we once again drove up along Trail Ridge Road, but this time we allowed ourselves only one stop: at the wonderfully named Endovalley to see if we could get ourselves an American dipper, the only American songbird that swims. Dippers love fast-moving water; they dive for their food, and even walk along the bottom of streams, all in order to catch passing scraps of sustenance. Like ducks, they molt all their feathers at once, and for anywhere between four days and two weeks they're actually flightless—and thus very, very secretive. Probably unfindable.

This happens in August. Which we didn't know. It was now August.

We searched for it anyway.

Endovalley sits at the start of Old Fall River Road, the one-way, summer-only road that leads back to Fall River Pass on Trail Ridge. All was peaceful that day—except for the hordes of day-trippers—but a quarter century earlier this had been the site of a terrible disaster.

At about five thirty A.M., on Thursday, July 15, 1982, Lawn Lake Dam, a structure built by a bunch of farmers in the first years of the last century and about four miles north of Endovalley, finally succumbed to years of neglect and thoroughly, and copiously, failed. From eleven thousand feet the 220 million gallons came: eyewitnesses said a wall of water up to thirty feet high slammed down the mountainside along Roaring River at a staggering eighteen thousand cubic feet per second.

Nothing stops that much water. It's amazing that only three people died: one poor soul who was camping by Roaring River that night, and two down at Aspenglen Campground, a couple of miles east, who reportedly returned to the already evacuated campground to get their camping gear. (No, not smart.) On the torrent went, flooding out the nearby town of Estes Park and causing more than thirty million dollars' worth of damage. It was eventually halted by Olympus Dam on the eastern end of the town, although in halting the flow the water level of the dam itself rose by a full two feet.

The evidence is still here at Alluvial Fan, a few hundred yards east of the valley. Huge rocks line the roads, and there remains an impressive gouge in the side of the hill. The day we went there the place was crawling with people, most of whom seemed happy to screech and scream and generally turn a naturally beautiful place into the Mall of America. We scanned the fast waters for dippers, but there was no way a bird would put up with all this hullabaloo; in any case, it was probably off hiding somewhere, figuring that no one wants to see a naked dipper. So we gave it up, and drove down towards Estes Park.

On we went, heading for Weld County. The county's biggest town, Greeley, boasts about eighty thousand people, around half the county's entire population. As you trundle east of the town, it dawns on you that the farther you go, the fewer people there are. Once, there were no white people at all. Legend has it that the first white person (a girl) born in Colorado came into the world at the Overland Trail station of Latham, just east of what is now the city of Greeley. The area had been settled in 1869 by a man named Nathan C. Meeker, a reporter from New York on assignment from the editor Horace Greeley (he of "Go west, young man" fame), the eventual namesake of the town. Meeker called his first settlement Union Colony, and proclaimed it a community of "high moral standards." This presumably held a certain irony for the local Ute Indians, who after the white man showed up would have their moral standards raised by means of being converted from "savages" to Christians, and having their horse racetrack torn up. This last act led to their rebellion and the now-infamous "Meeker Massacre," in which Meeker, by then the Indian agent on the White River reservation, and ten of his employees perished at the hands of the insulted Native Americans.

Ghosts, everywhere. And, as we found on the Pawnee Grasslands, just as many birds.

Weld County is said to be the most productive agricultural county in the country east of the Rocky Mountains. This is impressive enough, and then you realize that no one really lives here, and you wonder how the hell they get the work done.

The Pawnee Grasslands take up nearly two hundred thousand acres in the northeast corner of Weld, up towards Wyoming. It was originally settled by Germans and Russian Germans, who farmed it extensively, until the Dust Bowl put an end to that as the government bought up the land for grazing rather than cultivation. James Michener's novel *Centennial* was written about the place and was a huge bestseller in, you guessed it, 1976. And, more interesting for our immediate purposes, more than three hundred different species of birds have been noted here.

But none of these facts account for the special nature of this extraordinary corner of Colorado. As soon as we left Greeley behind, the world seemed to expand. It may well have been our lungs calming and our blood running thin once again, but there was more: the sky appeared to swell and spread, the clouds seemed higher, as though the deep vaults of the sky had receded a few billion light-years. We were in the middle of a swirl of vanishing points; the road curved off the planet up aways; we couldn't be sure there would even be a road past where our eyes could see.

Don was uncharacteristically quiet, until he wasn't.

"Well, myohmy," he trilled. "I had no idea. Just look at this. Funk the monkey! Have you ever seen anything quite so—"

"Sublime?" I asked. One of his favorite things is to discuss whether or not a place is "sublime." I don't think he means in the moral sense. I don't think that by witnessing this beauty we're thereby supposed to be better people. Instead, I think he means "inspiring awe through beauty"—yes, I think that's what he means. East Texas, to Don's eye, was not sublime, though it was fascinating. Southeast Arizona most surely was both. Here, though, it was clear to me that we'd brought Don to the ne plus ultra of sublime.

It was dusk by the time we reached the West Pawnee Ranch Bed and Breakfast. We didn't know what to expect. As said before, Don has an aversion to bed-and-breakfasts because they involve spending time with other people, when all he really wants to do in the morning is scarf down a bagel and a black coffee and get out looking for birds. Also, he hadn't exactly excelled in his choices of places to stay. But here in Weld County, the options were not just limited; other than the West Pawnee Ranch, they were nonexistent.

Merely finding the place had been hard enough. The Pawnee Grasslands are pretty much empty, and the road system is, shall we say, idiosyncratic. The bed-and-breakfast's Web site does its best, but here's its description verbatim:

> From Highway 85, on Road 122, travel east 14 miles to Road 55. Turn left and drive 1 mile to Road 124, turn right and drive 1 mile to Road 57. Turn left and drive 3 miles to Road 130. The Ranch is 2 miles east on your left.

Unless you've lived here all your life, that doesn't help much. The roads are ill-labeled at best, and follow no real logical organization. We found ourselves calling the bed-and-breakfast once every hour we were lost to beg for help. Fortunately, Louanne and Paul Timm, the owners of the ranch, have lived in the area most of their lives, and were able to explain to us that Road 130, on which the ranch sits, has any number of branches, some north, some south, some going right across the grasslands, some just a mile or two long, but all called Road 130. It wasn't surprising that we'd driven down every one of them except the one on which their home was situated. We finally pulled up as the last light fell, late as all hell for dinner—and when there's thirty-odd miles of prairie between you and the nearest store, you better hope your hosts are still willing to cook you that steak you ordered three months previously when you booked your rooms.

Not only did they cook it; they remembered how we wanted it. They remembered that Don needed chicken; heck, they remembered our middle names. We were invited to a table where another family was already on dessert; no matter, our steaks would be done any minute. I found myself yet again wondering how I got here: an Englishman eating a fabulous steak cooked by a real-life cowboy and his wife in the middle of Absolutely Nowhere, Colorado. I hadn't had a drink in days, and yet felt an unmistakable glow.

And then we were outside under a blanket of stars, drunk on something else entirely. We'd read that this year's Perseid meteor shower would be one of the best in recent memory, and here we were at a spot as far from light pollution as it would be possible to find, at precisely the right time.

There is nothing like the silence of nowhere; the buffalo grass, and the saltbush, and the blue grama were in abeyance. Nothing stirred. Up in the dark heavens, the eons-old dust jangled at the edge of space, ready to put on a show. I imagined the coyotes peering up at the meteors: all nature, pure nature in full. It seemed apt to leave them to it. We'd retire early and bring our minds to bear on the spectacle come Sunday, when the peak of the shower was due. For now, we would merely wrap ourselves in cowboy blankets and listen to something howling, out there in the brightly pointed darkness, in the middle of a continent so dazzling we would never find the words.

Iron-colored and majestic, high in the full blue air of morning, the ferruginous hawk swirled above us and was gone. This, the biggest buteo of all, and a bird I'd longed to see (mostly because of its fabulous name), heralded a day of first-class birding. *Ferruginous* means "ironlike," and here, as it soared and sank out of sight, I couldn't imagine a more apt name. Its long and pointed wings with their white patches pushed stiffly against the sky. The pure white underneath and reddish back against the blue of the day was an image I'd never forget; for a start, I saw how it came by its name, the metallic ochre of its feathers sure and strong in the clear sky. Already that morning we'd found a plethora of Pawnee birds: lark buntings by the gazillion, set on barbed-wire fences like musical notes on a staff; killdeer and mountain plover and solitary sandpipers next to little pools of leftover rain by the sides of roads; a kestrel on a telephone wire pumping its tail in anticipation. A loggerhead shrike sat obligingly still on a fence post as I took a movie.

Shrikes, northern and loggerhead, are the militant wing of the vireo family. Once they catch something tasty, they utilize the business end of barbed wire to skewer the unsuspecting prey into the most heinous of deaths; it's their way of killing things that are probably bigger than they should really manage. There's also evidence that loggerheads use stuff stuck on spines and spikes to attract mates: one study found twenty-three round-tailed horned lizards and various bits of birds impaled, serial-killer style, on a bunch of Torrey's yuccas. That's a bird that's determined to get laid, let me tell you. Twenty-three lizards isn't exactly dinner and a movie.

This was our perfect storm: no people, birds everywhere,

time to enjoy it, nothing except the imperative to look. On one back road we pulled over to scope across a wide expanse towards the Chalk Bluffs, a pretty rise of cliffs at the northern end of the grasslands. I had another loggerhead shrike in my scope, but Don was looking farther afield.

"Do you see that ruined building? Very scenic. There's a hawk on a beautiful dead tree to the right of it. It's out-of-control classic."

He could barely contain himself; but I think we all struggled to express how much we loved it here. We drove a dead-end, overgrown road out towards the bluffs, where we were admonished by a sign that read,

NO HUNTING

NO TRESPASSING

NO NOTHING

NO FOOLING

We parked the car next to another abandoned farmstead and found western kingbirds and yet more lark sparrows and lark buntings, a Bullock's oriole and a western meadowlark. There was a solitary yellow warbler in a bare tree on a hill. Even though we were ticking off names regularly, each new find led us to want more, and none more than one of the longspurs, either McCown's or chestnut-collared—these grasslands are prime habitat for longspurs. At one point I feared Don wouldn't leave here without getting one, so I was relieved when we pulled over to scope a flock of birds in a field and found a McCown's, plain as day, walking around in the dust. It was a first-year female, meaning it couldn't have been more drab, but it was a life bird for all of us, and sometimes them's the breaks. Too bad we hadn't been here a bit earlier in the year—the male McCown's aerial display, in which it flutters high, showing off white wing linings and a splayed tail, then floats all the way down, singing as it falls, sounds like an eye- and ear-dazzling spectacle.

In the early afternoon, we headed for a prairie dog town, hoping to see if reports of burrowing owls using the holes for nests would prove true. It did, but something else proved true too: Americans like to shoot things. Around each bend we'd hear the crackle of gunfire and watch as a bunch of folks took aim at distant targets—sometimes paper ones, sometimes a stack of tin cans, and at the prairie dog town, at the prairie dogs and the owls themselves. Everyone and his brother/stepfather was out shooting that day.

At breakfast we'd discussed the prairie dogs with Louanne, who'd shown complete revulsion at the thought that we might bring a prairie dog back with us. (Erm, no plans to do so, Louanne.) Her fear was palpable. Prairie dogs and their towns are the scourge of landowners in the grasslands, so to find a father and his son taking potshots at them in federally controlled lands was no surprise. We did see burrowing owls, and we did see prairie dogs, but neither experience was a particularly happy one—the crack of gunfire made us feel sick and impotent. It was not our place to remonstrate; this was their way of life.

Fortunately, we had something else to look forward to that afternoon: a trip to the famous Pawnee Buttes. The buttes (pronounced "beauts," you ruffian) are remnants of a prairie that has been eroded some three hundred feet since the last geologic age. For some reason the buttes didn't get the memo, and having neglected to take a knee, now tower over the valley floor like huge upside-down Jell-O molds. We set out after a delicious lunch packed by Louanne and Paul. Along the drive we came across a herd of bison, lounging by the side of the road, left there, presumably, by representatives from the Colorado Board of Clichés. On we went, the dust from our tires obscuring the afternoon, on and on and on, and then some, deep into the Pawnee lands, on and on, and on and on, and Jesus wept, where are these things? Don and I wagered a dozen times that they were "just around the next hill," and each time neither of us won the bet. Just when we were about to give up, we turned a corner, and hey, presto, there they were not either. I found myself secretly praying to the heavens that this car wouldn't let us down. We'd driven for what felt like hours, and had seen not a soul, let alone a butte; we were a flat tire away from reenacting the opening scene of *Paris, Texas*.

When we figured we'd driven to the somewhere like Kansas-Missouri border, there they were, solid and strange in the valley. It had taken us so long to reach them that the evening light was already lending them an eerie glow. The shorter one, to the left, glowed first, then the southerly one picked up its lead and shone strong. Farther north, a huge thunderhead distracted us. It was a vast system, and somewhere up there a tremendous power was being unleashed. Down here, prairie falcons and American kestrels turned in the valley. All sorts of raptors nest here, but with their nesting done they now ranged about, scaring the wits out of small rodents all along the valley floor.

We were sitting on the edge of the cliff, looking out over the prairie to the buttes, soaking in the extraordinary power of the place, and it was then that Don decided to become a dentist. For reasons known only to him, in recent weeks he'd perfected a startling impersonation of dental work. One finger, jammed into the side of his mouth, worked the suction; another finger, from a different hand, was the drill. Somehow, and I hope I never find out how, he managed to use his vocal cords and a mouth full of spittle to effect the sound of both suction and drilling. It was uncanny, and quite upsetting. Throwing his head back he proceeded to extract two teeth and fill three others, all as the sun finally dropped behind the clouds and the Pawnee Buttes went to gray. Donna and I were dumbfounded, and appalled. Don wiped his fingers on his shorts, took another swig of his beer, and dangled his legs raffishly over the edge.

In the distance, I watched the spokes of a wind farm, wheeling and wheeling. In just such a fashion my girls, thinking I couldn't see them out of the corner of my eye, would twirl their pretty index fingers next to their heads, signaling after some bad joke or other that they thought Daddy, or in this case, dear Uncle Don, was nuts.

On the drive back from the buttes we did our bit for the persecuted by narrowly avoiding plowing into a burrowing owl warming itself on the tarmac of the road. Slowing, we'd wound down the windows and let the night gently in.

We made it back to the ranch for the prime of the Perseids, but Don was underwhelmed—perhaps because every time Donna and I oohed and aahed at a meteor, he was looking in a different direction. Besides, they seemed like nothing compared with the birds and the buttes, and as we sat there near midnight on lawn chairs, none of us could really raise the enthusiasm to stay up all night for shatterings of dust. The next day would be our last in Colorado, and there were still so many birds to chase. We gave it up, Don muttering about missing meteors, and woke before dawn to get back out on the road.

We were heading once again to the abandoned farm buildings over by the Chalk Bluffs. Don could not get enough. He began to talk about buying land, and building an eco-appropriate place filled with windows and light where he and Donna could escape and enjoy these amazing grasslands.

"We could do it," Don said. "I really think we could do it. A little house, here, what do you think?"

I watched Donna range her eye across the grasslands.

"It's an idea," she said, the slightest of smiles passing across her eyes like high clouds.

"I could come here anytime," Don said. "Luke, how about you?"

I wanted so to shout out, "Yes, yes." I loved it here too. But I had something that kept me in New York, and would for another decade at least. I couldn't bear to be so stultifyingly practical though, not at such a moment. So I lied to them, there in that pure place.

"I have a lot of fantasies of escape. Give it all up, get rid of the apartment and the job and the commute and the E train and smell of the city in high summer. I could live here, no problem. Maybe we should drive up to Cheyenne, or stop in at Greeley on the way to the airport, see what real estate goes for around here."

But they had stopped listening; another western kingbird was being delightful, darting off the barbed wire like it was auditioning for Cirque du Soleil. And with that, the reality of what I'd been saying hit me; I felt like an ass when I reminded Don that, for starters, he'd probably have to learn how to drive to make the most of the place.

The story of Don's one and only driving test is well known amongst his friends. When the fateful day arrived, instead of his regular instructor and his regular car, a complete stranger with two other testees (no giggling, please) along for the ride arrived at Don's door. They were driving a 1972 Cadillac, a car Don had never seen before and which he claims to this day "handled like a boat." Given the gale-force winds and whipping rain, a car that handled like a boat might have been an advantage, but as Don drove to the test site, the Rastafarian who had helmed the Cadillac to Don's house tutted at Don's skills and said, "Who taught you that, mon? You got it arl wrong."

Once they'd arrived, the inspector took one look at the Caddie and deemed it "dangerously unroadworthy," leaving the Rastafarian no choice but to go up and down the rain-lashed line, begging to borrow a car for the three tests his "company" had organized. A car somehow procured, the inspector and Don got in, but Don had no idea how to shut off the squealing alarm; an inauspicious beginning. Eventually, they started out, but within a minute or two Don had driven into oncoming traffic; within ten minutes, he had committed, in his words, "nearly every possible driving infraction." Only through the grace of some higher power had no one been hurt.

Since that time he hadn't tried to drive, though I regularly offered to teach him, much to Donna's horror. I couldn't bear to squash his dreams of a place here in the grasslands. Think of the freedom, I said, if I taught you to drive. You could bird in so many new places, and you wouldn't have to wait for me to be free to ferry you around. All this "we're basically Amish" could be a thing of the—"

"There! Quick! See them! On the post! Huge, dark birds!"

I hit the brakes, and looked. But before I could focus my early-morning mind, they were up on the wind: a pair of golden eagles, whumping into the sky, all power and glory and majesty. Jumping out of the car, we set up scopes and followed their looping flight, back and forth, until they gracefully left us behind.

Epilogue:
What Now?

According to the Audubon Society, in the last forty years, the birds most in danger in North America have experienced a population decline of an average of 68 percent, a staggering number. The very worst off now have only 20 percent of the numbers they had in 1967.

But these are not just statistics: they are actual animals and their actual decline, bird by single bird. The northern bobwhite, for example, which I've seen once and once only in New Jersey, has fallen from thirty-one million to just over five million. There's more: despite their name, meadowlarks no longer have enough meadows. Each spring and fall that we travel to Cape May, another pristine grassland has been replaced by great, ugly, mostly empty boxes where middle-aged men drive around on ear-splitting tractors, tending lawns that no bird would go anywhere near.

"There used to be bobolink in that field, right there."

That's what Don says every year we drive down New England Road to Higbees Beach in Cape May, and every year I slow my car just in case, even though all three of us know the bobolinks have long since given up.

Because of logging, mining, drilling, and global warming, the boreal chickadee, a tiny, acrobatic bird of the northern forest, has faced a falloff of nearly three quarters of its numbers since the late 1960s. The loggerhead shrike? Down more than

70 percent in the same period, because of development in the Northeast and overuse of farmland in the Southeast and West. The landscape of the Northeast is probably already too altered for the loggerhead to ever return.

In the Dakotas, a beautiful duck called the northern pintail is being decimated as natural grasslands, similar to the Pawnees, are broken up and used for crops. Pintails rely on prairie potholes for nesting. Seed the land early, or till it too much, and the pintails have nowhere to raise young. This bird has declined from sixteen million to less than a quarter of that in the forty years of the study.

As the *New York Times* put it in an editorial on the loss of birds, "The trouble with humans is that even the smallest changes in our behavior require an epiphany." One more mea culpa: one Pennsylvania morning a few years ago I had exactly that—an epiphany. And I am grateful for it.

In the few years that I've seriously birded, a partial list of notable birds I've encountered might include the following: football-shaped least grebes, and their polar opposites, the American white pelican; magnificent frigatebirds high on thermals, and northern gannets falling fast into the ocean; an American bittern in silhouette, and a roseate spoonbill out of the corner of my eye. I once made Don come all the way to Jamaica Bay to see a common eider, but forgot to tell him it was a drab female, so I drive him and Donna to Montauk on Long Island every winter to make up for it. Spring has brought us white-tailed, Mississippi, and swallow-tailed kites, white- and red-tailed hawks; and summer the ferruginous; eagles, be they bald or golden, be it winter or be it not; two separate crested caracara in two different states; so many peregrines, two even (hopefully still) nesting above a twenty-four-hour Apple store in New York City.

The plain chachalaca is hardly plain at all, raucously chattering in Texas; and a single silent northern bobwhite ran across a New Jersey road once, my kids in the back of the car making all the noise. We've thrilled at a blue grouse, and my heart has swelled to see the white-tailed ptarmigan. A purple gallinule in New Jersey, far north from home, was exactly where the World Series birders said it would be: in a parking lot. We've had Wilson's plovers, but never the long-billed curlew. The bird whose name I love more than any other, the Hudsonian godwit, was a treat; as was a single ruff by the Cape May hawk watch—like me, far from its Eurasian home. I have seen a parasitic jaeger hassle other, more boring, gulls for food, right across the beach from where the ruff no longer is, and a flock of hundreds of black skimmers made Don exclaim on a Jersey beach one mile southeast of there. Puget Sound brought me the magical marbled murrelet; we've seen roadrunners, a groove-billed ani, and two cuckoos, but the third, the mangrove, I've seen only in Puerto Rico, which almost counts, but does not if you're a lister.

That's why I'm not a lister.

When I began to bird, I desperately wanted to see one owl—just one, please god. Of the nineteen owl species regularly seen or heard in North America, I've now seen or heard all except five (OK, I'm a bit of a lister: I still need the great gray, the northern hawk, the spotted, the northern pygmy, and the flammulated). I've heard the whip-poor-will and seen two kinds of nighthawk: common in the air, lesser on the ground. A number of the smallest of all birds, the hummers, have buzzed past me too, but in the East we only get the ruby-throated, so let's give it praise—it beats its wings even faster than the violet-crowned—fifty-three times a second. The elegant trogon came, as did the ringed and green kingfishers.

All the eastern *Empidonax* flycatchers have confused me; there was a vagrant ash-throated flycatcher in Brooklyn's Prospect Park one Christmas, though I've seen them closer to their western homes too. I can tell you that green jays can be blue, but the northwestern crow can only be northwestern—you can tell by the size of the feet. I have seen all the bluebirds there are. I got poor looks at a Townsend's solitaire in the western mountains where it lives, and great looks on Long Island where it doesn't. (I have never been to Iowa.)

The clay-colored robin was as clay-colored as the name suggests; the common myna might one day be so, much to the horror of mankind.

When I pick up *The Sibley Guide to Birds*, it falls open to the wood warblers, the family of colorful small songbirds unique to North America in spring. Sibley lists fifty-four; I've seen forty-eight, including all the *Oporornis* save MacGillivray's, as well as Kirtland's, golden-cheeked, and cerulean, each of whom may yet go the way of the Bachman's, a bird that is probably now extinct because of—you guessed it—habitat destruction. Oh, and the gray-crowned yellowthroat. (Don't tell Don.) A lazuli bunting flitted away before Donna could see it, the painted of the same stayed a while. I won't mention sparrows, as they're incredibly tough to identify correctly. Meadowlarks, western and eastern, thrill me every time they sing; the bobolink is my secret favorite bird. (Don't tell *anyone*.) There be nine in the family Icteridae, genus *Icterus*; I'm still missing a third of them: streak-backed, spot-breasted, and Audubon's (orioles). I don't love freezing temperatures enough to have ventured north to see rosy-finches, pine and evening grosbeaks, redpolls, nor the crazy crossbills.

Who am I kidding? This is America. I barely feel the cold anymore. In fact, I saw a hoary redpoll just yesterday. It was snowing.

The list of North American birds I have seen is shorter than the list I haven't seen; it's not even half. That's not the reason why I bird though. The reason is this: given this great gift of nearly 450 birds in a few years, I am now charged, as we all are, with witnessing them all over again, while we can; and all the others too, while they still exist. Yes, we must get involved in conservation efforts—the Audubon Society, in its heartbreaking report, didn't just depress us, it also gave us myriad ways to get involved in making things change—and we must educate those around us, like dunce families in Florida (please choose a better way of doing it than I did). But to my mind, the effort begins with a simple act of looking.

I thought again of the law enforcement guys in southeast Texas who, even when it was pointed out to them, couldn't see a bird ten feet away on a fence post. One of my happiest moments birding came in New York City a few winters ago. A headline from the *New York Daily News* said it all:

BIG HOWL FOR RARE OWL

A few days earlier, during the Christmas Bird Count (a day set aside for birders across the country to help ornithologists chart how many of which birds are where), a smart New York birder called Jim Demes found a saw-whet owl in a high pine right next to the Tavern on the Green. Only, he hadn't found a saw-whet owl at all. What he'd misidentified as a saw-whet was actually a boreal owl, a very rare bird so far south—it seldom strays from distant northern Canadian forests. What it was doing in Central Park God alone knows (assuming He can bear to look at what goes on in Central Park). For days a small band of birders, including Don, Donna, and me, camped out in a children's playground next to the pine, and pointed expensive scopes and binoculars at the poor thing; it mostly slept through its visit.

One freezing day that winter I was walking away from the boreal owl site in Central Park when a bunch of New York City firefighters called me over to ask me what was going on. I explained to them that these odd-looking people were not kid-fiddlers; they were, instead, using the playground as the best spot to look at an extremely rare bird. Proudly I told them it was the first live one ever reported in New York City (there was one found dead in Queens in the 1940s), and that all us bird nerds had dropped everything to come look at it. My excitement at the visit of the boreal owl could not be contained.

When I'd finished my breathless explanation, one of them piped up to his friend, "I guess we should go take a look, right, Danny? I mean, it's a rare owl. The gentleman here tells us so."

And with that, a smokiness of burly New York firefighters shrugged as one, jumped off their idling truck, and entered a children's playground in the middle of a freezing December day in New York City to look at a bird. Just about every firefighter cooed and oohed and generally acted like a kid on Christmas morning. The birders couldn't wait to show off their knowledge.

"It's clearly not a saw-whet owl—the two birds are very similar of course," said Lloyd Spitalnik.

"Of course," said Danny the firefighter, without irony.

"But the boreal shows a full disc of color around the face," said Jim Demes.

"Yes, I see that. Easy mistake to make, though, huh, fellas?" Danny spoke, but never looked up from his borrowed spotting scope.

His pals all nodded as one, and waited for their turn to look. All it took was showing them; they couldn't help but be moved by what they'd seen. I solemnly believe that if a truck full of New York City firefighters can be brought to care about a rare bird, then surely the rest of us . . .

Who was I kidding? Back in that Colorado morning, a distant golden eagle had beat out the drum of its future extinction on thermals we couldn't see, let alone harness to fly. And maybe this was the ultimate lesson: We envied them their freedom, and when *Homo sapiens* envy, the results are never good.

"What a happy little ditty," interjected Don, looking longingly across the Pawnee Grasslands.

Seems I'd been saying a bunch of this out loud. Oops; maybe that was a supremely bad idea.

"Ah, I was just thinking of something else," I said, trying not to spoil a perfect Colorado day.

Donna said, "Your girls. I get it. You must be missing them."

Yes. Very much. How could you tell?

New York City, January 2008

Acknowledgments

I'm grateful to all the birders who so generously gave us tips on where to find birds on our travels. We seldom learned their names, such is their selfless love of sharing the joy of a discovered bird. There is a great army of amateur ornithologists out there who quietly document and appreciate the wonder of the avian world. We should be thankful they care. I am especially grateful for the generous help afforded us by Lloyd Spitalnik, Jim Demes, Tom Fiore, Rob Jett, Doug Gotchfeld, and Doug Kopsco in New York; Wezil Walraven and Marion Paton in Arizona; Haley Breniser in Michigan; Robin Diaz in Florida; and Barbara Kennett, Keith Hackland, Susan and Don Schaezler, Margie Bonnes, and Jim Booker in Texas.

In addition, there are wonderful people all over this country who give sparkling accommodations to weird travelers like us: the staff of the Ramsey Canyon Inn, Arizona; Yves and Chris de Diesbach, Charles and Lena Vieh, and Keith Hackland again, all in Texas; and Louanne and Paul Timm in Colorado.

A shout out to the wonderful Cornell Lab of Ornithology and their Birds of North America Online. I could have spent years, rather than just the months I did, reading that Web site. It's jam-packed with stuff about how birds live and breathe and eat and fly and mate. I loved every minute I spent on it, and recommend it to all, not just birders.

Thank you to Nick Trautwein, my wonderful editor—any

man who can invent the compound "ass-scissoring" to describe the hell that is the month of January gets my vote. Also to Maureen Klier, and to Annik LaFarge, Peter Miller, Carrie Majer, Kristina Jutzi, and Liz Peters at Bloomsbury, who supported the book throughout; to Kris Dahl, my literary agent, and to Laura Neely, Montana Wojczuk, and Liz Farrell at ICM.

Ted, Beth, and Jack Olinger opened their Gig Harbor home to me and were extremely kind, not to mention a laugh-riot. I miss their dirty dogs. Henry, the female cat, is sadly no longer with us.

I'm grateful to David Hirshey, Gillian Mackenzie, Russ Galen, Toby Cox, Mary Choteborsky, Nevada Breniser, Chris Santella, Michael Bartsch, and Josh and Iva Benson for their friendship and support of this project. A shout-out, on the one, to the Railbangers: John Hughes, Paolo Pepe, and Neil Pepe.

My brother, Simon Dempsey, has been kind and generous in equal measure; I have almost forgiven him for being the true writer in the family.

Both Christine Aronson and Elizabeth Keenan have been the greatest friends anyone could wish for.

Suzanne Donahue was always willing to help me have time away from New York City in order to take the trips described in this book. She is, without question, the very best mother our children could have wished for. They are lucky to have her; I am lucky to know her.

Those children, Lily Adele Solskjaer and Amelia Margaret Cantona, have put up with my absences with extraordinary grace. They are the loveliest people I've ever had the good fortune to meet. But it's not just me: everyone says how cool and funny and just plain great they are. I did not exaggerate when I said that the world would be a better place if everyone had a Lily and an Amelia in their lives.

The characters of Don and Donna Graffiti are, in fact, mostly a product of my fevered imagination. In real life they run an animal-testing laboratory; Don eats steak almost exclusively; Donna is a Wiccan. I was fortunate, however, that they did introduce me to David Drake (another bird name!) and Deborah Jaffe, who, when the need arises, do periodically allow Don and Donna to steal their identities. In all our travels, the two Ds have been generous and kind and always, always, utterly hilarious. In addition, their close reading of an early draft of this book saved me from absolutely making a fool of myself—the errors of fact and taste that remain are entirely my own.

Elizabeth Stein did an early edit of this book that should be placed in the Editing Hall of Fame. Fortunately, it was, simply put, quite, if not very very, utterly superb; indeed, actually, she eventually fixed me up—of course! She is my favorite nonbirder of all, not to mention the funniest; more, she reminds me of my father.

And it's with that thought I'll stop rattling on, pick up my binoculars, and head out. Wanna come with? You never know, you just might like it.